Praise for *The Best Part of Prison*

"What if the worst thing you've ever done didn't define the rest of your life, but taught you how to live it? Jesse Crosson's *The Best Part of Prison* is more than a memoir. It's a reckoning, a blueprint, and a prayer for anyone who's ever wondered whether broken people can build something beautiful. Crosson doesn't just take us inside the prison system. He takes us inside himself. The violence, the shame, the silence. And then—almost impossibly—the spark of accountability, service, and hope. I've spent years fighting for second chances. Jesse's story reminds me why."

—**Louis L. Reed, author, activist, and film producer**

"With raw honesty and unflinching detail, Crosson brings readers into the darkest corners of addiction, violence, and incarceration, and then shows us what it takes to claw your way toward redemption.

Too often, stories of prison life get flattened into clichés of either horror or redemption. Crosson resists both. He does not shy away from the pain he caused others or the depths he sank to himself, but he also makes space for humanity and for the people who offered him kindness, for the small acts of dignity that sustained him, and for the difficult, uneven road of accountability.

For me, what makes this book stand out is its refusal to offer easy answers. Crosson names the destruction he left behind, but he also shows how people can change when given the chance. In doing so, he forces readers to confront uncomfortable truths about our justice system and about ourselves: Who do we write off as irredeemable, and what possibilities do we lose when we do?

As someone who has spent years inside prisons, talking with both incarcerated people and those tasked with guarding them, I can tell you this book rings true. It is messy, painful, and beautiful in the way only real life can be. Crosson doesn't just tell us the 'best part of prison,' he makes us see how even the worst places can produce transformation when people are willing to do the hard work of facing themselves.

This is a book I would hand to anyone who believes in redemption—or anyone who doubts whether it's possible."
—**Glenn E. Martin, formerly incarcerated entrepreneur and activist**

"Few books capture both the pain of incarceration and the hope of transformation like this one. Jesse shows us why second chances matter—not just for individuals, but for families and communities."
—**Jessica Jackson, CEO of REFORM Alliance**

"*The Best Part of Prison* is a rare and radical story of transformation. With honesty, grit, and grace, Jesse Crosson turns the darkest chapters of his life into a blueprint for redemption. This isn't just a story about surviving prison—it's about the power of self-reflection, accountability, and community to make us fully human. Jesse shows that change is possible not because the system works, but because the human spirit refuses to give up. His writing is raw, wise, and deeply moving—a testament to what can happen when we stop throwing people away and start believing in their capacity to change."
—**Lara Love Hardin, *New York Times* bestselling and Christopher Award–winning author of *The Many Lives of Mama Love***

"A painful and powerful story that demonstrates hope and resilience after incarceration."
—**Michael Kostis, coordinator for Florida Coalition Higher Education in Prison**

"*The Best Part of Prison* isn't just a memoir; it's a revelation. Jesse Crosson takes readers deep inside the walls of himself, and deeper still into the human spirit's capacity for both damage and repair. From trauma and addiction to remorse and healing, his story moves beyond punishment into transformation, showing how accountability and hope can grow even in the darkest places, and how you can heal if you choose to.

Told with vulnerability and hard-won grace, this is a book about what happens when a man stops running from the ghosts of his past and starts rebuilding his life, brick by brick. It's about the power of seeing worth in those written off as irredeemable, and the power of second chances to heal not just one life, but the world around it.

Jesse Crosson is a brave and courageous hero of his own story. You will cheer for his victory, and you will cry for his loss. *The Best Part of Prison* reminds us that no one is beyond redemption, and that the hardest walls to break are the ones we build within ourselves."

—Chandra Devam, NASA Award–winning CEO and cofounder of Aris MD

"*The Best Part of Prison* is stripped to the bone. It's not polished or performative; it's a naked, honest truth about what it means to fall apart and find your way back. Jesse Crosson doesn't hide behind excuses or pretty words; he faces himself and invites you to do the same.

What makes this book unforgettable isn't just where he's been, it's how brutally honest he is about what it takes to change. The shame, the silence, the accountability, the pain, it's all there. Nothing softened, nothing spared.

This isn't a story that flatters the reader or its author; it's one that humbles you. *The Best Part of Prison* doesn't ask for sympathy; it demands reflection and a conversation."

—Scott Edgar, NASA Award–winning chief technology officer and cofounder of Aris MD

"Jesse is such a phenomenal character. Meeting him and speaking to him I wonder how I would have coped with being imprisoned for most of my adult life and then released with barely any notice. He is such a down-to-earth, caring guy that you can't help but like him. How many other people in his situation would have done what he has done, spent so much of his time and energy working to help other previously incarcerated people? Read this book to understand his journey and the impact he has made since leaving prison. Jesse is one in a million and I admire him greatly."

—**Sue Black, OBE, professor of computer science at Durham University**

"Jesse Crosson's *The Best Part of Prison* is more than a memoir—it's a raw, unflinching account of how a life shattered by addiction, violence, and despair can be remade through reflection, accountability, and transformation. Crosson takes the reader from the chaos of his teenage descent into drugs and crime, through the crushing realities of prison life, to the moments of clarity, mentorship, and self-discovery that opened the door to healing."

—**Rev. George T. Chochos, cofounder of Listen Out Loud Media, national public speaker, prison reform advocate, and public theologian**

The Best Part of Prison

The Best Part of Prison

The Power of Second Chances and
Reclaiming Life Out of Darkness

Jesse Crosson

BenBella Books, Inc.
Dallas, TX

The Best Part of Prison copyright © 2026 by Jesse Crosson

All rights reserved. Except in the case of brief quotations embodied in critical articles or reviews, no part of this book may be reproduced, stored, transmitted, or used in any manner whatsoever, including for training artificial intelligence (AI) technologies or for automated text and data mining, without prior written permission from the publisher.

BenBella Books, Inc.
8080 N. Central Expressway
Suite 1700
Dallas, TX 75206
benbellabooks.com
Send feedback to feedback@benbellabooks.com

BenBella is a federally registered trademark.

Printed in the United States of America
10 9 8 7 6 5 4 3 2 1

Library of Congress Control Number: 2025042185
ISBN 9781637748015 (trade paperback)
ISBN 9781637748022 (electronic)

Editing by Rick Chillot
Copyediting by Kaya Skovdatter
Proofreading by Becky Maines and Martha Gallant
Text design and composition by Aaron Edmiston
Cover design by Sarah Avinger
Cover image © Adobe Stock / Edifi 4 (fence) and SusaZoom (cloud)
Printed by Lake Book Manufacturing

**Special discounts for bulk sales are available.
Please contact bulkorders@benbellabooks.com.**

To the younger part of myself that I did not yet
know how to protect, and to all the people I harmed
and wronged until I learned how to do so.

Contents

Prologue   1

Before

1	What I Did	5
2	Stewing in Jail	17
3	Trapped and Deceived	27
4	Isolation Was the Best Thing	33
5	The Sentence	39
6	What Is Wrong with Me?	45

My New Life

7	Entering the System	53
8	Getting into the Routine	67
9	No One Is Just One Thing	73
10	Unexpected Teachers	77
11	Seeing Things as They Are	83
12	What Violence Taught Me	93
13	Making Lemonade	101
14	Ignorant to Education	107
15	Selfish to Service	117
16	Hurt to Healing	127
17	Excuses to Accountability	133
18	Closed-Off to Connected	139

Future in Question

19	The Tipping Point	153
20	Old Law, New Law	155
21	Prison Highs and Lows	163
22	The Power of Adaptation	171
23	Sudden Release	183

Reentry

24	Outside	191
25	Early Days	197
26	Reckoning with the Past	203
27	Work and Navigating Insanity	207
28	A Million Second Chances	213
29	Second Chancer Foundation and PrisonTok	219
30	The Fairy Tale	225

Challenges Outside

31	Existential Crisis	233
32	Seeking Home	239
33	The World Gets a Lot Bigger	243
34	Slow Down	249
35	Full Circle	253

Epilogue — 259
Acknowledgments — 263
About the Author — 265

Prologue

"I'll shoot you dead boy!"

He pointed the assault rifle directly at my chest. The barrel seemed to grow and grow until it filled up my entire field of vision. I glanced up and saw the SWAT officer's eyes behind his goggles. The shocked silence shattered. I heard his yelling, and his words finally processed in my brain.

It was the end. December 11, 2002. The day the madness I had been living was done and the end of my slow, passive suicide. The rifle I was staring down, the officer yelling that he would kill me—these were the only things that finally stopped me.

I put my hands above my head. They were throbbing, my heart was pounding, every beat coursing through my body over seconds.

"Walk backward down the steps!"

I looked over my shoulder at the ice-covered stairs and back at the officer. He was all goggles and helmet and black tactical vest. I briefly thought how nice it would be if he pulled the trigger, or if I slipped and broke my neck on the steps. I didn't want to keep feeling my pain. I didn't want to keep running from the monster that I could never quite identify. I didn't want to face the consequences.

I took one step backward and nearly slipped. I waved my arms awkwardly and caught myself. I took a few more steps and lost my footing again. Then I was at the bottom, and a swarm of officers grabbed me, pulled my arms behind my back, and put me in handcuffs. They asked if I had any weapons on me. I nodded to the knife on my belt. They took it—and the belt. They ran through my pockets and examined the still-damp cocaine in a baggie, the wallet with bills and the pack of cigarettes I had just opened, with only one missing. They missed the cigarette pack full of .22 bullets that had fallen through a hole in my jacket pocket. They jingled quietly inside the lining as the officers walked me to the car. It was almost like the beat of a song, like the soundtrack of a movie as the credits began to roll.

Before

Chapter 1

What I Did

I had just turned eighteen, just graduated high school. I said I was taking a year off before college. I said that I was exploring, and I would find myself. This wasn't true. I was stuck.

Three months before, as the leaves were changing, I had run into a steady cocaine connection. I quickly shape-shifted from a wide-eyed kid, hungry and curious about the world, into a feral animal, willing to do anything for a fix, anything to keep from drowning.

The first time I did cocaine, it was the answer. I felt smart enough, strong enough, confident enough. I felt fully "enough." For the first time in my life.

Someone cut me out a small line at a party. It was short-lived, and I immediately wanted more. However, no one in my high school crowd regularly used anything harder than weed or hallucinogens, and I didn't know the guy from the party or where to get more.

Then, I was searched in school. They found a pipe and a scale, though they didn't find the weed I had concealed in my bag. They made me a deal: They would let me graduate but I had to complete all of my course work from home, and I wasn't allowed on school grounds. Essentially, I was out of school, and so, at seventeen, I started working construction. The guy who drove me to work sold coke on the side. He gave me some for free, then started selling me small amounts. Before I knew it, in moments of insecurity I relied on cocaine being just an expensive phone call away.

Buying from him and selling or sharing with friends led me to meeting a girl. At a party, we flirted back and forth. We walked away from everyone, went into another room, and shut the door. Almost like in a comedy, we pulled coke out of our pockets at the same time and asked if the other wanted some. We laughed, did a line, and talked about where we had gotten it. Her connection was much better than mine. Soon, she introduced us and the fact that he liked me and that I spoke fluent Spanish unleashed a perfect storm of nearly unlimited access. I was able to get it for less than most dealers I knew. Like any other backwards entrepreneur, I started selling to support my own habit. It felt like a zero-cost arrangement, though it was anything but.

At first, it was girls and music and fun. I did a line first thing every morning and kept going throughout the day. Then, when I couldn't sleep at night, I drank and ate sleeping pills—way too many sleeping pills. If I woke up to use the bathroom I was like a zombie, moaning and stumbling into the wall on the way to the toilet.

Each morning was like plugging directly into an electrical current. Each night was putting myself into a stupor: stumbling, slurring, falling into half-sleep.

Ernie, a former high school classmate who was also taking a year off before college, was the only one up for my craziness. He drove his rusty old Volvo out to pick me up and we rode around all night getting into trouble. Somehow, he still managed to go to work the next morning. He waited tables and was known for his charm. His big tips subsidized some of our adventures.

The supplier I had been introduced to was a stereotypical gangster kid. He was sixteen but had an ID from the DMV saying he was twenty-one. He drove a brand-new SUV and was covered in bling. He always had Marco and Francis around him. They were bodyguards and friends.

Francis was a former airplane mechanic from El Salvador, skinny and manic, prone to violence. Marco was his calm counterpart. He was from Mexico and had mainly worked in restaurants. He never let much emotion show. They were a team, and I felt at home with them. They didn't question my past, only whether we would have each other's backs and be dedicated to living a fast, fun life.

The young dealer they guarded was undocumented, so when he got pulled over and booked for possession of a firearm, he used his fake ID. That meant his fingerprints were added into the system, and he had to get out of town. With that dealer gone, Marco and Francis had no obligations. They invited me to move into the same disreputable hotel they had been staying in. We were paranoid and felt more secure being around each other.

The young dealer's father was the real source. He received regular, sizable shipments, and he became my connection. He was the opposite of his son. Rather than bling and flash, he worked six days a week and lived in a humble trailer. He was probably putting away $20,000 or more a week but you would never know it. He told me once that his plan was to save a few million then take his family back home to Mexico to buy a farm so they could live out the rest of their lives in luxury. I really liked him as a person. He wasn't like drug dealers I had seen in movies. He was just a guy trying to build a dream for his family.

Back at the hotel where we were living, we avoided sleep and unnecessary interaction with outsiders. For some reason we watched *Cops* on TV at all hours of the day and night. Exhausted and paranoid, we peeped out windows, expecting to see something but not sure what. We sold coke to bouncers so that Ernie and I, who were both underage, could get into bars. But we never stayed out for long, always rushing back to the feeling of safety being locked in those hotel rooms, often hanging out together before going back to our individual rooms to sleep, if we slept. Basically, we built our own prison and called it life.

Every time I did coke, I was chasing that first high. I wanted to re-create that feeling—strong and perfect—but I never did. The first line of the day made my teeth go numb and felt amazing. Every line after that one was just pushing the darkness back one more inch, knowing that in just a few minutes, it would come crashing in even harder. If insanity is doing the same thing and expecting a different result, we were the living mascots.

I saw threats at every turn. When a buddy offered to sell me a gun, I jumped at the opportunity. A gun seemed like safety and strength. It made me feel invincible against any enemy, real or imagined. People around me were falling prey to addiction, to violence, and some to the law. I wasn't going to let it happen to me.

The girl I had shared cocaine with became a regular in my life. We did everything together. She shared the hotel room with me, sometimes passing out before and sometimes after me. One night she stayed up, snorting line after line, waking me up repeatedly as she tried to reach under the mattress to pull the gun out. Then she went to the front desk of the hotel saying someone was trying to break in through the window. I'm surprised the hotel clerk didn't call the cops. I'm surprised we both made it out alive.

It didn't take long for things to go from bad to worse. The cocaine and money ran out because we were doing it all before we could sell it. Our cravings were running full bore. We could no longer afford the hotel so we all packed into Ernie's apartment along with his brother, who wasn't using drugs and had a concerned look on his face every time he stepped out of his bedroom. Then Marco had an idea. He sat us all down in Ernie's room, got us each a beer, and laid out his plan. He spoke in English rather than Spanish so that Ernie could understand.

He told us about a restaurant where he worked after he first arrived in central Virginia. He described the owners as greedy and abusive to their employees. He said they paid the workers almost nothing and kept the tips for themselves.

We had actually eaten—well, mostly had drinks—at that restaurant a few weeks before, and I hadn't seen any evidence of mistreatment. The owners certainly didn't seem like Cinderella's stepmother, but at that moment, I wanted to believe him. I wanted a justification to take the $50,000 he said would be somewhere in their house—the stolen tip money and unreported income. That would keep us in cocaine for weeks or even months.

We laid it out as a Robin Hood scenario. We were taking from the rich to give to the poor. We just happened to be the poor who were in need at that point. It was an utterly ridiculous justification, but in the throes of depression, anxiety, and withdrawal it made perfect sense and even fired us up. We planned to go into the home when no one was there, find the cash, and get out. It was rural but off a major highway, so easy to get in and out fast. No one would get hurt, and all our problems would be solved. My brain was cooked from cocaine in a way I can't describe. Only people who have been there know what I'm talking about. I painted myself as a good guy, just doing what I had to do, while planning to commit the most immoral and unforgivable acts.

Let's just say that the breaking and entering went off with every hitch possible. We went there together. I was on my motorcycle following Ernie, Francis, and Marco in Ernie's car. We showed up expecting an empty house, but there were cars in the driveway. In front of the house, I got off the bike and removed my helmet. Down the street, Marco stepped out of Ernie's car and waved to me. The restaurant owners saw us through the window and recognized Marco. They stepped outside, greeted him, and invited us both inside. After a brief and intensely awkward conversation (and a cup of juice), we left and Marco got on the back of my motorcycle. Panicked, we rode down the street where Marco got into Ernie's waiting car. They then followed me to a back road where we looked for a place behind the property to park. I got off my bike and they got out of the car. We collected ourselves, still shaking with nerves.

We decided to go back and wait for them to leave. Then we snuck through the woods, hunching over—as if that would help us evade notice. We thought we were performing some special operation, but we were bumbling idiots. We saw the restaurant owners at their home an hour before, yet it never crossed our minds that we would be suspects when that same house was burglarized shortly after.

I was scared. I heard a voice in my head clearly say, "Don't do it." Another taunting voice said, "You can't abandon your friends." But I kept looking for a way out. I wondered if I could thumb the button on my Nokia block phone to make it ring. I could pretend to answer, then tell my friends I had a family emergency. I didn't do any of that. I just kept sneaking toward the house with them, too cowardly to back out.

As we got closer, we saw that the cars were gone. We whispered together to make a plan: Marco and I would enter through the back door while Ernie went to the front. Francis would sit outside and signal us if anyone arrived home.

We separated according to our plan. As Marco and I slipped around the back of the house, we were worried about cameras or neighbors seeing us. I was picturing Ernie knocking on the front door. If anyone *was* home, he would pretend to be lost or find some other way to distract the person inside so the rest of us could get away unnoticed. Instead, I found out soon enough that he put on a ski mask and banged loudly on the door. A maid answered, and he stuck a gun in her face, screaming threats. He walked her back into the house and tied her up.

Downstairs, we were unaware that Ernie had gone off script. The back door was locked so we broke a window and reached through to open the latch then slid through, feet first. The rest is a blur. Running through the downstairs, emptying drawers, tearing through closets, looking for bags of money. Except, there weren't any. Not in closets, not in cabinets, not anywhere we looked. Running upstairs, I thought I caught a glimpse of Ernie pushing someone else. I'm not sure if I actually saw this or if I "remembered" it after finding out what he had done later. Growing desperate, I grabbed car keys that were in a bowl by the door, a digital camera from downstairs, and half a bottle of liquor from the kitchen. The total value of the loot was maybe $100. I invaded a home, terrorized and traumatized a family and a maid for $100. It was the most hopeless, desperate, and destructive act of my life.

I don't remember who got out first but we all rushed out of the house carrying the few things we had plundered. I bent over in the woods for a second, clutching my churning stomach, ready to vomit. I looked Ernie in the eyes and saw him stare back fiercely then drop his gaze. I recognized the same shame in him that I was feeling. We didn't talk on the way back to our vehicles. I put on my helmet, got on my motorcycle, and rode away. I started to shake. I don't know if it was fear or shame or just an adrenaline dump, but I almost wrecked the bike.

We got back to Ernie's place and pulled out our paltry loot, all suspicious that one of us was holding something back. I kept hoping someone had found a bag of money. Instead, we'd come away with a handful of costume jewelry, a bag of junk, and a fistful of one-dollar bills. We didn't talk, mired in the enormity of what we had done. Our shoulders hung, defeated. We sat there, crammed into one room of the small apartment. Our dreams of grandeur and success were reduced to sleeping on the floor and waking to stare at the walls while we tried to figure how to pay for our next meal or next fix.

Our depression lasted for days. We were nearly out of cocaine. We had pocket change that wouldn't even buy us more liquor—and we were running out. We sat around, one person playing PlayStation, the rest of us trying to gather the energy to do something, anything.

Somehow, amid a snowstorm that week, I managed to find another dealer, someone I didn't already owe money to. We met in a parking lot, and he motioned me into his Dodge Durango. He was tall and stocky and had dead eyes. He never said more than a few words, and I felt like I was being seen through when he looked at me. We drove for twenty minutes. Then thirty. Forty-five minutes after I'd gotten in his truck, I was sweating and beginning to wonder if I'd end up in a shallow grave.

Instead, we pulled up to a nice house far out in the country. There were toys in the yard outside, and I breathed a sigh of relief. This was a family home. Surely, nothing terrible would happen in a place where children slept.

Inside, we sat at the kitchen counter, where the dealer poured himself one whiskey after another. At last, he stood up and, in Spanish, said he was very angry. He paused, then said someone had broken into his family member's home. Did I know anything?

I shook my head no. It would be crazy for someone to cross him like that, I replied, also in Spanish. I waited, terrified that he'd kill me and thinking he'd be entirely justified if he did.

Instead, he went to a kitchen cabinet and pulled out six ounces of cocaine. I could pay him later, he said.

"Tu me ayudas; yo te ayudo," he said. We're friends; you help me, I help you.

His eyes were bloodshot from the whiskey, and when I inquired about a ride back into town, he tossed me the keys to the Durango and said he'd get the truck later.

My delight at having a fancy new four-wheel-drive vehicle in the snow was short-lived. This was before GPS was available on every phone. Unfamiliar with the area, I took a wrong turn and ended up on a winding rural road. Ahead, I could see the flashing lights of a law enforcement SUV stopped at a snow-covered intersection. I had six ounces of cocaine in my pocket and liquor on my breath.

I tried to appear nonchalant as a deputy approached. I rolled the window down, told him I'd gotten turned around and needed to get to Route 29.

He pointed me in the right direction. "Be safe out there," he said with a smile, patting the side of the truck as he sent me off.

I dodged two bullets that night, escaping the house of a man whose family I'd robbed and asking directions from an officer tasked with solving the crime I had committed. My luck wouldn't last.

A few days later, my new supplier called for his truck, which I dropped off for him in town. My friends and I had plowed through most of the cocaine and only had a quarter of the money we owed him. Hoping to put him off a few days, I told him I could return some of the cocaine and had the money for the rest. We never did pay him. Instead, we had one last party, inviting friends and girls, trying to make it all fun again.

During this last hoorah, one of the guys we had been hanging out with was sharing an ounce with us to say thank you for all the times we had shared with him. There is a weird camaraderie between fellow drug users. Sometimes we stabbed each other in the back. Most of the time we truly supported each other, going to all lengths to make sure we were okay, or at least not in withdrawal.

We were almost enjoying ourselves. It almost felt like the old days. We had cocaine, laughter, and booze—somehow, though, it still wasn't enough to mask the pain, fear, and shame we were all feeling. We knew we were in too deep. We knew this was the end.

Then a phone call interrupted our drug-fueled festivity. Our buddy's pregnant girlfriend was on the line, her voice panicked. Two guys were at her trailer, asking about the gun they had stolen and sold to my buddy, who sold it to me. The person they stole it from had found out and was threatening to call the cops. Now they were the ones threatening, telling her to tell my buddy that they needed the gun back. They wouldn't leave her trailer until he brought them the gun or money or cocaine. I knew then that they were as strung out as we were. This wasn't about the gun, or not entirely. It was about the same insanity we were mired in. It was about the way cocaine warped our brains. They wanted the gun back but wouldn't give me what I had paid for it. They just wanted more.

By now, I had been the villain in so many stories that I wanted to be the hero. I told my buddy to give me the phone and let me talk to them. I said some things, they said some things. We raised our voices. We threatened each other and then agreed to meet.

My buddies wouldn't let me drive there alone. We had created this imaginary war, and we were all ready to do battle. Rather than letting me take the motorcycle, Marco insisted that I take my truck, then jumped in the passenger side. Francis rode with Ernie behind us. We took the rifles, shotguns, and handguns that we usually kept in the laundry room for protection.

We drove twenty minutes north to a semi-rural strip mall with a Food Lion and a massive parking lot. I drove around to the back of the complex, and Ernie's car followed. We unloaded a scoped rifle and checked the pistols. We waited. Then waited some more. Finally, it started to sink in that what we were doing was insane. After another few awkward minutes, I twirled my finger above my head like I had seen in movies, signaling for us to leave. My truck got stuck in the snow so Marco got out to push. Once I was rolling, I didn't stop, and Marco ran over and jumped into Ernie's car.

That was how I ended up alone when, at the last minute, I pulled around the front of that Food Lion parking lot. The same voice that had warned me not to go through with the robbery was back. It was telling me this was a very bad idea, that someone was going to get hurt or even get killed. I don't know why I went back. I felt like I was at war with myself.

The lot was empty, so I got out of my truck and walked to the grocery store to buy cigarettes. Despite smoking off and on since I was thirteen, I had just turned eighteen and had never bought a legal pack. The store was closed. I had been up for days and didn't realize how late it was.

I walked back toward my truck, just as a car came screeching into the lot. The small hatchback pulled up close to me, and two men got out. They started toward me. I had my gun in my belt but was so scared I didn't even remember it. I hurried back to my truck, got in and locked the door. Feeling like a coward, I started it up and peeled out, classic rock blaring from the speakers inside. They ran to their car and followed.

As I pulled out onto Route 29, I watched them in the rearview mirror. They were the source of the gun in my belt, so I had reason to believe they were armed, and now they wouldn't let me leave. In a toxic mixture of fear and rage, I was reliving every time someone hadn't respected my boundaries, every time someone had bullied me or made my life unpleasant. My vision narrowed, like I was going into a tunnel.

They sped up, pulling up beside me in the passing lane, swerving to run me off the road. I tried to accelerate but my old S-10 pickup was no match for their hatchback with its big muffler and flashy rims.

They continued to swerve across the dotted line, toward me, with the passenger gesturing and yelling out his window. I was trying to keep my eyes on the road but also on him. I had swerved over the outside line once already to avoid them slamming into me.

When I glanced once more to my left, the passenger wasn't waving out the window anymore. His back was turned, his arm extending behind the center console. I wondered what he was grabbing and then panicked. A gun, I thought. He's getting a gun.

I pulled my pistol out of the waistband of my pants. I don't remember flicking the safety or racking a round into the chamber. Maybe there was already one in there. I remember screaming, I remember pulling the trigger, firing across my body and out the window.

Then, I couldn't hear myself screaming or even hear the gunshots. I felt massive concussions, I clenched my teeth, as I felt a crushing pressure in my ears and against my eyes. I don't remember squeezing the trigger more than once but then I squeezed again and nothing happened. The gun was empty. I dropped the gun, and it bounced off my leg and onto the floorboard of the truck.

I didn't hear brakes screech. I just saw that they were no longer beside me. I glanced in the mirror. The hatchback had slid to a stop at the side of the road. I turned back to the road ahead and felt tears sting my eyes. I began to cry, which I didn't understand because I felt nothing.

Then suddenly the music crashed back in. I felt the cold wind whipping my face. I wiped my cheeks and fumbled for a cigarette that I lit with a trembling hand. My brain had partially come back online by the time I got back to the house. I needed a story to explain why I had shot two men. I couldn't tell my friends I had done it because I was afraid. So, I insisted I had seen a gun.

Marco didn't care why I shot them. He went into a rage. I felt like a child being chastised. I apologized. I told him I hadn't had a choice (even though I clearly did).

He yelled something and stalked out of the room. Before he made it out, I asked him if we were leaving "como hermanos," the phrase we'd used to signify our brotherly bond. He gave me a cold look and replied, "No. Como amigos." I felt like I had been stuck through the heart. I thought I had finally found family and now I had fucked it up again. I picked up a plastic bottle of Aristocrat vodka and guzzled it straight.

Despite things getting hazy, I knew that we needed to get out of town. Ernie told me he heard on the radio that one guy was dead and the other was fading fast. I was a murderer, a taker of life. If they caught me, I would spend the rest of my life in prison. *If* they caught me.

Francis and I planned to head west. My sister was in Colorado. Maybe we would go there. Maybe we'd go to L.A. and steal a sailboat. He promised he could sail us to Central America and that he had friends in El Salvador. He promised to introduce me to his sister. We were going to be okay—we just had to get away. (We were insane.)

I had a few errands to run first. I went to see my mother. In tears I told her that I was leaving, that I had messed up really bad. She cried. She grabbed all the cash she had on her and shoved it in my hands. She asked if I needed her to go to the bank. I told her no, then walked out the door, both of us sobbing.

I went to see an old girlfriend, to say goodbye, to see a familiar face. She had called me in the early hours to yell that she had heard my description on the news, that everyone knew it was me. I had talked about shaving my long hair so I would no longer match the description but never followed through.

She bought me cigarettes so I wouldn't have to stop on the road. She never would have done that before. She hated when I smoked. Her new boyfriend was there, looking on disapprovingly. I didn't care. I tried to kiss her, but she turned her head away.

When I returned to the apartment, Ernie and I were switching vehicles since the police had an APB out on my truck as well as my description. I gave Ernie the pistol I had used, which he promised to get rid of. We were saying our goodbyes and getting ready to leave. The car was packed so I went to the bathroom to take a small bump from the last little bag of cocaine. I had gone from sharing with everyone to hiding out so I didn't have to share with anyone.

I lifted the bag, shaking, trying to get a key in to grab enough to keep me awake. I nodded for a second and looked down to see my open bag of cocaine floating in the piss-filled toilet. With no hesitation, I reached in and pulled it out. The powder inside had turned to sludge. I could still cook it up into crack, but for now I just wanted to wash my hands and get on the road.

But back in the living room, I looked at Ernie, Francis, and Marco. I felt defeated and tired. I sat down with the bottle of Aristocrat vodka and took a solid chug. I closed my eyes. A minute of rest would be nice before I started my life on the run . . .

"La policía está afuera!" Marco yelled, rousing me from my sleep as he ran through the room. I jumped up and headed to the laundry room, where Francis and I each grabbed the loaded rifles we kept in case someone broke in.

Then we took one look at each other and saw fear. I trembled. We dropped the rifles with a clang. Francis ran out the downstairs door and I raced for the upstairs exit, with the half-hatched idea that if I exited the "wrong" part of the duplex, the police would think I had come out of the unit upstairs.

I pounded up the steps, pausing to briefly peer through the side window. Convinced the coast was clear, I yanked open the door and ran straight into the barrel of an officer's assault rifle.

There are moments that clearly divide life into "before" and "after," and this is one of mine. Sitting in handcuffs in the back of the cruiser, watching the flashing blue and red lights illuminate nearby houses and the neighbors peering curiously out windows and doors, I felt like an observer, like I had already died and was looking on from the afterlife. When those handcuffs closed around my wrists, I had thought my life was over. In fact, it had just begun.

Chapter 2

Stewing in Jail

The detective driving me to the police station was friendly and conversational. It was off-putting considering I thought my life was over after committing serious crimes and being arrested. I was handcuffed, arms in front, with my long black overcoat thrown over my shoulders. They marched me into an interrogation room, sat me down at the long wooden table, then left me to stew. I knew what they were up to—making me so uncomfortable that I would want to talk. It probably would have worked if I hadn't been so empty. I hadn't slept in days, other than my brief slumber before the SWAT team burst in. I'd been living on fried chicken, cocaine, and liquor. I didn't really want to live, so there wasn't a lot to hold over me. Plus, when I looked down at my paperwork there was no murder charge. Instead, there were charges for malicious wounding—I hit both men the night of the shooting but they both lived.

The first detective tried the good cop/bad cop tactic. He told me it probably wasn't all my idea, and that we could figure out a way out of this together. When I told him I wasn't interested in talking, he switched tactics and threatened me, told me how bad it was going to be if I didn't cooperate. I told him I wouldn't talk about anything that had or hadn't happened and he got up in a huff.

Then I remembered. I felt around my jacket to find the cigarette pack full of .22 bullets that had fallen through the hole in my pocket. The box was lying on the bottom of the liner. I fished it out—not the easiest thing with the handcuffs—and placed it on the table, trying to line it up perfectly square and even with the edge.

The second detective, assigned to the shooting, came in and stopped, looking at the cigarette pack.

"You probably want those," I said.

He picked the pack up and heard the jingle. Then he opened it and looked inside.

He looked irritated, like he was going to read someone the riot act when he was done with me. "Thanks. That was, uh, not the best job on our part."

He sat down. I expected him to ask me to sign a witness statement or a form about having been read my rights. But he didn't. He looked me in the eyes and it felt genuine.

"That other guy is looking at you for the robbery, and he needs to build a case. I don't need anything. I have you clear as day for the shooting. So, I'm happy to listen if you want to help yourself or not, since my wife hasn't seen me for dinner in weeks anyway."

Looking back, I remember feeling that the first detective was trying to make this really important thing happen, and trying really hard. The second detective was just doing his job. And I remember thinking, "I like this guy." I still didn't give a statement, just said something cryptic like, "Everything isn't as it appears."

After my final interrogation, an officer loaded me into the back of a car and brought me to the jail. He drove through a giant garage door that shut behind us with a clang. It was like being locked in the Batcave, but not nearly as cool. I was ushered into what looked like a steel and concrete version of a hotel lobby. One of the desk officers processed me. I was expecting the old ink-on-my-fingers experience, but he fingerprinted me on an electronic machine then took my mug shot. After processing, I was sent to strip my clothes off and shower in an empty room. Later, I learned to worry about how disgusting the shower floors were. It would become a theme.

I wasn't wearing boxers when I was arrested—laundry hadn't been at the top of our priorities. I had black dress socks, but when they stripped me out, they said those socks didn't follow jail policy so they took them. I was issued an old, worn-out pair of blue slip-on shoes and bottom and top scrubs with stripes across them, like in the old-timey jail movies. I slid the shoes on my bare feet and pulled the scrubs over my naked body.

Over the radio, the officer escorting me called for master control, the door buzzed open, and I walked into a tiny R&D (receiving and discharge) cell—just a bench, a toilet, and a sink, almost touching each other. I paced one step, turned and stepped back, then stopped, almost collapsing. I sat down and stared at the wall. I started to count the bricks. I felt like a shark, like if I stopped swimming I would somehow die. I was exhausted but running from the cops and having an assault rifle thrust into my face had left me wired and on edge. Yet, I also felt a strange sense of relief that it was all over.

It must have been another hour until the first of my codefendants—Marco—entered the jail. Then another hour for Francis. Then Ernie shortly after. Why had it taken them so long? After a second, I understood. It hadn't taken me much time because I hadn't given a statement. I had chosen to exercise my right to remain silent. They hadn't.

My father raised me on stories of his gangster misadventures. I never knew him as that person, but I knew his past and I idolized him. When I was in middle school, I learned Spanish because I wanted to be bilingual like him. I did drugs, either because I wanted to be like him or because I was hoping that by acting up, I could earn the same attention he gave his twelve-step sponsees. After just a brief lifetime following his path, I was set in my ways. In that police station, I couldn't imagine doing anything other than what he would have done—I kept my mouth shut.

A lot of guys talk about how they stayed true, either to the game or to the people in their circle. However, the ones who tell almost always get a better deal and a better outcome. Everyone at least thinks about telling, either at the time or afterward.

Sometimes the deals reached in exchange for statements or testimony make sense—the prosecutor is saving time and money by eliminating the need for a trial or getting a different person deemed dangerous off the street. So often, though, savvy people do great harm, then make a deal and face fewer consequences than those who simply refuse to talk because they've been brainwashed into a twisted sense of integrity. There is loyalty among people living a criminal life, but not always. Sometimes people look at the person next to them as a means to an end and friendships are cast aside for the benefit of a plea deal.

The image of me that my family and friends saw the day after my arrest.
Courtesy of *The Daily Progress*

When the adrenaline finally wore off, I crashed in the R&D cell. I hadn't slept enough for longer than I could remember. Three times a day they placed a Styrofoam tray of food on the slot in my door. I woke up, ate the food, then went back to sleep. Sometimes I woke up just to use the bathroom, and I felt like I was going to burst. I stayed in that zombie state for days.

The third day was the hardest. I woke up before I opened my eyes. I was warm. I somehow knew that I was back home, that I was next to my high school girlfriend, that it had all been a dream. When I opened my eyes and saw the peeling paint of the cinder block inches from my face I wanted to cry out in agony.

After a few more days of quarantine, they moved me to a dormitory for guys newly arrived at the jail. We would be housed there, reviewed, and placed in the housing unit considered most appropriate for our situations and to avoid any conflicts or gang/neighborhood associations. Fifteen of us shared a small space, with a single shower, a single toilet, and a single sink. Most of us were new, didn't have any money, or hadn't had the chance to put in a commissary order so we didn't have any food, clothing, or hygiene items that commissary sold. Some guys had come from other jails or were being classified into different parts within the jail, so they had shower shoes (so they never had to touch the disgusting shower floors), magazines and books to read, and even food, coffee, and the hygiene staples like soap, toothpaste, deodorant, and baby powder. We were given indigent packs when we first arrived that contained a small toothbrush and clear gel toothpaste that didn't seem to clean our teeth. We were all amazingly excited for the opportunity to get "real" toothpaste, even if we had to use it with our three-inch indigent toothbrush. Not all of the guys shared, but most did. They understood how much it sucked to come in with nothing, so they would give us a small amount of coffee or a magazine to read. It made our days more tolerable.

The first day in that classification block, I sat staring at the phone for hours. I was terrified. I had to call home.

My eyes hurt and I couldn't focus. I had trouble reading a sentence. I stared at the same page of a book someone had left on my bunk, reading the same words over and over again before giving up and lying back down on my bed (which was situated right over the open drain, so it smelled like sewage). I put a warm washcloth over my eyes to try to soothe them. I felt like I had holes in my brain. Maybe I did.

I was ashamed. I didn't know if my parents even knew where I was. (I didn't realize our arrest had been front-page news.) They had long since divorced but I knew they would be united in hating me. I had disappointed them. I had thrown my life away. I had become the addict my father, a substance abuse counselor and figurehead of the 12-step community, told me I would become. I had become one of the clients that my mother, a lawyer, used to represent at legal aid. I had become the client who was so bad she swore she would never practice criminal law again. I hated myself and couldn't imagine anyone feeling differently.

Finally, I dialed my mother's home number from memory, and when she didn't pick up, her office. She answered the phone, already in a panic. Panic was pretty normal for her. And the frantic tears and her attempts to always fix things. One year in elementary school all the kids in my class got invited to a birthday party—all the kids but me. My mother was furious when she heard that I hadn't been invited. Rather than asking me if I was okay, she ranted about how sad it made her. She was angry and threatened to call those parents and tell them how terrible it was that their children had not invited me. I somehow convinced her not to call them and even though I hadn't originally felt the sting of rejection, I now took on her sadness and rage as if they were my problems to fix.

As I gripped the jail phone, she explained that she had talked with a lawyer and talked with the jail and talked with friends and talked with everyone she knew. She was running 1,000 miles an hour trying to figure out how to fix it. But she admitted that she was getting nowhere. I felt the familiar pang of guilt. I had caused her this panic. Then I heard the one-minute warning. There was an end in sight. I promised I would call again, sometime. I hung up on her panic and then felt guilty all over again. She was just trying to get me out of this disaster I created.

Then, from memory, I dialed my father's home number. Wondering if he would answer. If my stepmother would answer. If no one would. When I was little my father told me a story. He had visited a fair once and met a genuine psychic, or someone he thought was psychic. I felt awe that someone could have impressed my dad so completely. This man told my father that his third child would change the world. There was only my half-sister and me, but my dad admitted to living a pretty wild life and believed there must be another child out there, which would make me the third. Now this may seem like a glorious thing to tell a child, and it was. I felt more important than I had ever felt in my short life. I felt seen and valued by my father. I also started to feel a tremendous pressure to live up to this standard. If I was going to impress my father, I was going to have to become a person who would change the world.

Now I was calling him from jail to tell him that I had failed. That I was not the son he thought I was.

When my father answered, his voice was heavy with sadness. When I look back at pictures of my father, even now, what always stands out is the sadness in his eyes. He carried things with him that weighed on his soul. Even in laughter, he had a burden that was never lifted. Over the phone my father kept saying how sorry he was. He mentioned the "sins of the father being visited upon the son." He had grown up in an abusive religious family and under stress he would use biblical language. I had only heard him do this a few times before.

They were hard calls to make, but at the end of them both I felt relief. My parents didn't hate me.

It was about a week before I saw them in person. I was handcuffed and shackled, then a deputy loaded me and number of other guys into a van in the sally port (sheriff's deputies were responsible for transport and custody outside the jail). There was no sally port at the courthouse—instead the deputy just parallel parked next to the lower door. They marched us through the door and into the basement holding cell that reminded me of a dungeon.

One guy had to use the bathroom. Being handcuffed in the front meant it was easy to go "Number 1," but "Number 2" required a creative approach to wiping. I averted my eyes as he did his business, in a small room, with several of us packed close.

After a long wait, deputies took turns leading us individually up and into the courtroom. When it was my turn in front of the judge, I listened to the charges against me. I answered questions. I filled out paperwork for a public defender—the deputy saw me pausing, confused, and whispered for me to just put zero dollars income across the board. After that, I was done in the courtroom and marched out with a deputy holding me by the elbow.

I spotted my parents in the hallway. I wasn't used to seeing them together. They first met and bonded over the shared practice of coping through drugs and alcohol. On their first date, my father borderline assaulted my mother. They didn't meet in a healthy place. As a young kid, I witnessed their fiery conflicts, which seemed to happen even more often after they broke up. When they split, I blamed my mother while also believing my father had abandoned me. Now I nearly cried seeing them together. The officers let me talk with my parents for a moment in the hallway. When it was time for us to go, I lifted my arms, handcuffs jangling, to hug my mother but the deputy stepped in, raised his hand, and said, "No contact." Then I was taken back to the holding cell and then to the van, where I looked out the window and was amazed by the colors of the outside world. Then once again at the jail, I was unshackled and escorted back to the block.

I watched someone negotiate a deal with another cell block, across the hallway from ours. He slid a "fishing line," ripped from a sheet and weighted with a bar of soap, under the bars and across the floor. He pulled back a package someone had tied to the end of the line. He borrowed staples and batteries to light the cigarette he had bartered for. He then passed it around. A single toke from the tiny roll-up was enough to knock us on our asses. It was my introduction to making fire without matches or a lighter. Next, he used the electrical plug and pencil lead to start a small fire so he could solder someone's headphones. Someone yelled at him because he had to have the prongs of the TV plug connected when he arced the lead across them. The guy yelling thought he would blow up the small TV when it popped. Considering we didn't have much else to do, guys were very protective about that TV.

After a few days I met with my counselor and was classified to one of the long-term housing units.

The day I moved, that receiving block was where I discovered how selfish I was.

I was malnourished, pretty weak, and very much feeling sorry for myself. Every morning the breakfast cart rolled in, and the officer, who everyone referred to as a CO (correctional officer), called for us to get a tray of food. On the tray, each person got one small carton of milk (think elementary school) and sometimes a tiny juice carton. The food wasn't bad—there just wasn't much of it. For that reason, guys would keep their milk until later, just to have something to fill their stomachs later in the day or at night long after the last tray had been served.

One of the guys was diabetic, so they had assigned him a cooler to keep his diabetic "crash kit" in. He allowed everyone else to keep their milk there, too.

The morning they moved me out of the block, everyone had already gotten up, eaten breakfast, and gone back to sleep. Not long after breakfast, an officer called me to pack my stuff. I didn't have much. I hadn't been assigned a footlocker, because I hadn't been able to go to the commissary, so I didn't have anything but the mattress, and that was easy to roll. I reached into the cooler and grabbed a juice and a milk that didn't belong to me, and I left.

I drank that milk and drank that orange juice and felt a deep loathing of myself. I didn't ever feel bad when I got an extra tray from the officer or food cart, but I felt terrible stealing the milk and juice from whoever had stored them in the cooler. I didn't know who I had stolen from but I did know that he had just as little as I did. I allowed scarcity to bring out the worst, rather than the best in me.

It was one of the first times I became conscious of feeling as though I was more than one person. One part of me was hungry and thirsty and felt frail and desperate. Another part of me recognized that these were just excuses—and that if I continued to live in a way that involved taking from someone else, I would never be able to look at myself in the mirror.

Chapter 3

Trapped and Deceived

I was five-foot-ten and 150 lbs. when I walked into the next housing unit (HU-1). My face was gaunt, and my eyes were deeply sunken. I looked much older and rougher than my eighteen years due to my diet, habits, and lack of sleep. I was so wasted away that people in the unit called me "Mikey" because "Mikey will eat anything"—based on the famous TV commercial, which doesn't actually make sense, but a lot of things in jail don't make sense. I collected all the greens and scraps of food from other people's trays to try to gain some weight. I was ravenous all the time. I also blew out giant chunks of what looked like brain matter every time I blew my nose. I had been snorting a quarter ounce of cocaine a day by the time I was arrested, and the damage to my sinuses was severe.

HU-1 had more people, more showers, more phones, and even a half basketball court with fresh air from grates in the wall. It had fancy green metal doors and plexiglass windows, just like the newer R&D unit where I started. There was a lot more happening than in the old, dilapidated receiving block I had come from, but it was still boring. I couldn't comprehend how people stayed here for days or weeks or years. Many, like me, were waiting to go to trial or enter a plea. Others had completed that step and were waiting to receive their sentence and find out just how long they would be there. Others had been sentenced and were serving their jail time or waiting to be sent to the Department of Correction (DOC)—or prison. For the most part guys took pity on me, with some even taking me under their wing to teach me the "rules" and what to watch out for. Not everyone had that same mentality, though.

There were two guys who had been sent back from prison, or at least that was the rumor. They were ripped, tattooed, and had scowls. When they worked out, other guys avoided their corner. A few days in I managed to get an extra tray from the guard who was serving—it was common to try to get back in the line or run some kind of scam, because a lot of us were still pretty underweight and didn't have money to buy commissary. Sometimes they would just take pity and give out the extras.

As I sat down with my tray, smiling at my good fortune, one of the tatted guys came up and stood way too close. He looked down at me and said, "Next time you get an extra tray, you give me something or I'm going to take it."

I don't know how or why I said the right thing: "Nah, bro, I'm good."

He sneered and then just walked away. Someone later explained to me that a lot of jail and prison is theater and if you aren't scared and don't play along, people will just stop acting. Of course, this isn't always true. Sometimes it's not acting, and the consequences are severe.

Being locked up was a weird series of expansions. First, I was locked alone in a cell, then in a small dormitory, and then in this large housing unit. Eventually I would be sent to prison with more than a thousand other people at the institution. Jail was a barren warehouse, for short sentences and holding someone prior to their trial. Prison was a warehouse, too, but one where people were locked away for years or decades. In jail we had nothing to do. In prison there were jobs, classes, and the ability to live some semblance of a life rather than just rotting away.

Being locked up is also about grieving loss. There is the loss of liberty—being locked in a small cell for days or weeks. The loss of connection—away from loved ones, friends, and community. The loss of power—people tell you what to do, sometimes for no reason at all, and punish you if you don't listen. The loss of privacy, including having to use the bathroom and shower in front of people, especially at dormitories where there isn't a single space anywhere where you can be alone or enjoy quiet.

My advantage was that I didn't have far to fall. I had been sleeping on the floor of my codefendant's apartment, packed into a small space with six other deranged people. Jail felt almost familiar, or at least not as much of a change for me as for some people.

One of the saddest things was just how many of the men I saw in jail seemed relieved to be there. Jail wasn't comfortable. But, for some, it was familiar. Most of the guys I talked to had been in and out since they were kids. They grew up in institutions, and some felt safer being locked up than at home. Some guys just didn't know how to handle the pressures of being free. Outside, they had too many options and responsibilities and would do something small to return to the simplicity of an institution.

I felt grateful as well as guilty at mail call. Five nights a week, the officer stood at his desk and read names from the stack of envelopes he had brought in. Each time, he read my name over and over, and each time, I was handed envelope after envelope. Other guys lined up dutifully, day after day, with hope in their eyes, never to hear their name called.

Because our arrest had been front-page news as well as my mother's outreach efforts, I was more connected than anyone else in jail, or later in prison. Old friends, distant family, and people I barely knew reached out. Letters, phone calls, and visits sustained me and started to bring me back to life. If so many people believed in me or saw some value in me, maybe I could believe in myself. But I wasn't ready to yet.

Anisa was one of my oldest friends. Even when we were younger, she impressed me by being quirky and unapologetically herself. It was a joy to know her. I hadn't imagined she could bring that same energy into the jail. But when she came to visit and we talked via corded phones through glass I smiled and even giggled. Anisa also responded to my complaints. After I wrote to her that my cell was stark, with no color or softness, at mail call one night I opened an envelope from her and found it stuffed full of rabbits. She had taken the time to cut dozens of pictures from newspapers and magazines, telling me I should decorate my cell with them so it would feel more comfortable. I was still generally numb at that point, but in that moment I was overcome by a wave of emotion. What she did was such a big thing to me. It was a direct line to my heart at a time when I felt empty and undeserving.

Later, when I complained to Anisa that the food had no flavor, she packaged up a dozen individual bags of spices, labeled them, and sent them in. I got a sternly worded note from jail officials that I was not to have people send me small bags of green herbs.

Guys in the jail continued to be mostly supportive, too. They saved me extra food even after I had gained a bit of weight back, continued to give me tips, and generally talked me through being okay. Some guys schooled me more than others, though not always in a good way.

Walter was a short, kind of sleezy, but charismatic guy. When I was transferred between housing units in the jail, he somehow followed me. He then managed to get moved into my cell. He was broke when he was arrested but he was a hustler and good at poker. So, with a little backing, he built quite a collection of stamped envelopes, ramen noodles, toothpastes, and deodorants. It's funny what we consider "jailhouse rich" or worthy of envy inside.

Walter pretended to take an interest in me and care. He taught me his hustles and games, pointed out the unit's politics, and helped direct me around certain situations (often violence). He had spent most of his life behind bars, usually for short stints of a few months or a few years. Whatever else he knew, he knew how to make the best of jail.

In between "lessons," he told me about his situation. His girlfriend had kicked him out, his mother wouldn't talk to him anymore, and he had nowhere to go when he got out. Now, this should have been a huge red flag. But I was young and naive. He was looking out for me, and I wanted to look out for him. He made all sorts of promises, about how he would go collect money that people owed me and send it to me so I had a nest egg for my years in prison. At one point he even offered to "make all of this go away"—a comment that became extremely relevant later.

I didn't believe anything Walter said. I definitely didn't believe that he would collect any money for me. I wanted to get him a place to stay on the outside because I felt like I owed him—he had put me up in poker games and schooled me to the ways of the jail. I struggled to say no to people.

The problem was that deep down I wanted to believe he could send me money or fix everything I had broken. I wanted him to have some magic solution. Looking back I see that, if there had been a button I could press to make all of it go away, I would have pressed it. I wouldn't have cared how much it cost. I wouldn't have cared how many people it hurt. I only wanted out. I would have done anything to be free.

I had been bouncing through life, trying to fill the void I carried. I hurt myself, caused hurt to others, and never felt in control or able to take accountability. In jail, I was like an animal in a trap, with a powerful impulse to gnaw off my own leg (or someone else's) to get out of it.

On Walter's behalf, I contacted a friend and asked if she could put him up when he got out. She agreed. I felt like I was paying a debt and doing a good thing. Little did I know that "favor" would change the course of my life.

When Walter was released my friend picked him up and the next time we talked she made it clear that she didn't like him. He was rude and she didn't trust him. He was staying with her in the small home she was renting on a farm outside of town, and she was just waiting for him to get on his feet and get out.

Well, he did get out. One day he snuck over to the farm's barn and hooked the farm truck up to a trailer loaded with power tools, jacks, and other expensive items. He loaded everything else he could find into the bed of the truck, jumped in, and drove over the mountain to a pawn shop. He unloaded everything and went on his way. When the farm manager saw the truck missing, he called the police and they began investigating.

I found out when the police showed up at the jail. They asked me about Walter and what he had done. They interrogated me: Had I known his plan? Had I been a part of it? My chest was burning, and my face was hot. I put my friend in a terrible spot—I was fairly certain the landlord would kick her off the farm. Now they were accusing me of organizing or even participating in the whole thing.

It got worse.

For months, I had been on the waiting list for transfer to the treatment block, the one part of the jail with a focus on rehabilitation and actual classes, support groups, and speakers. Many guys were there because they wanted to look good for the judge at their sentencing. I just wanted help. When I was finally moved, I was excited about learning and doing something positive, anything other than just sitting around, wasting away.

Only a few weeks after I had started programming, the largest group of officers and administrators I had ever seen showed up on the block. With more staff members than incarcerated people crammed into the relatively small space, they pointed fingers and looked down at a face card, trying to identify someone. Then they all pointed to me, put me in handcuffs, and ransacked my stuff before taking me back to one of the same R&D cells where I had started my jail journey.

The next day, the door to my cell buzzed open. An officer met me at the door and directed me to the legal meeting room, a plexiglass booth with a small table and two chairs. The detective from the robbery case was waiting in one of the chairs. He didn't stand up when I walked in. There was no good cop this time. He asked me questions, made accusations, and then took me over to the magistrate's office where I was charged with six new offenses: three counts of conspiracy to commit capital murder for hire and three counts of obstruction of justice. My original charges around the break-in had been upgraded from grand larceny (stealing) to robbery (using force or threat of force).

In addition to stealing from the farm, Walter had been arrested for breaking into a home. He was arrested, and police found the truck and trailer. They retrieved items from a pawn shop, as well as a whole new load of stolen items. When he was arrested, Walter made them an offer: "If I tell you about a guy who hired me to kill the witnesses in his case, will you cut me a break?"

Despite Walter's prior charges (and the fact that he had made this story up multiple times before), the prosecutors cut him a deal. With his record, his guidelines called for more than ten years for everything he had done, but he would serve less than two. In return he would testify against me. I was charged with crimes that, if convicted, meant I might never see the free world again.

Chapter 4

Isolation Was the Best Thing

I was alone. After months of dormitories, roommates, and constant hustle, I was two doors down from the R&D cell I had started in. It was the same routine. Three times a day, I heard a clink when my tray slot was opened, a small plop when the Styrofoam tray of food was placed there, and a clink when they closed it after I grabbed the tray. They let me out for a shower once a day. Then straight back to the cell. That was it. It was simple and left a lot of time for thought.

In a way, total isolation in that R&D cell was the best thing that could have happened to me.

Between drugs and jail, I had never been able to stop spinning. I had been surrounded by people who weren't accepting responsibility or thinking in positive ways. Now that I was alone and "under investigation," the jail administration had cut off all outgoing communication. I could receive mail but not send it. I couldn't make calls and couldn't have visits. Like living in a vacuum, nothing I said or did made it out.

The first week was nerve-racking. I kept looking around, feeling like there was something I was supposed to be doing. I was scared and I was powerless.

The second week I started to accept it. Over the next month it became routine. I exercised and practiced yoga. I read books that people sent me. I meditated. I wrote letters that weren't going anywhere. I slept. I felt like a monk. Being alone with my feelings, my thoughts, my guilt, and my shame, I had no choice but to face what I had done. I had hurt so many people. I had hurt myself so badly. I didn't yet understand why. I didn't understand how I had become that person. I was a ball of screaming pain that had been lashing out at the world but that was now locked alone in a room. I heard my screams and echoes of my past screams. It compounded. It broke me.

In R&D, the cells were built around a central space and had giant plexiglass windows so all of us—guards and everyone inside—could all see one another. That meant I was never actually with other people, but I never had privacy either. People came and went. I saw them hauled in, patched up from the hospital. I watched someone slit his wrists in the cell across from me. I watched several women, likely brought in for being drunk in public, dance and take their tops off. Through it all, I didn't speak to any of them, just pantomiming to communicate across the plexiglass divide.

Three months I was in that R&D cell. Then, one day, the superintendent called me into his office. Walking in, I saw the box where each of my unsent letters had been placed—hundreds of them at that point. He told me to sit in the chair opposite him. It felt strange to speak out loud and have an actual conversation. Then he said, "This has gone on long enough." He told the officers to move me to a housing unit. This confused me. I hadn't gone to trial yet. Nothing had changed—it was just out of the blue. Then I found out why. A local attorney—for whom I would one day work when I got out of prison—had made a strong case that what the jail had been doing—restricting mail especially—was illegal since they didn't have a court order.

I didn't know what to expect as I carried my stuff to the old side of the jail. I soon found out. It was 100 degrees—it felt like there was no air. Paint was peeling off the walls. My cell was tiny—originally designed for one person, now crammed with two. When I lay on the bottom bunk, either my feet or my head was six inches from the toilet. I was miserable. The first day in the cellblock, I naively tried to stop a fight and caught a few good shots in the process. It was a reminder that I was no longer in the peace of my own isolation.

I understood the tension. It was hot. We were locked in a small cellblock, and at night locked in tiny cells, with no outlet for our emotions. We didn't get outside. We didn't get fresh air. We didn't even get an outlet for activity except rec one hour per week in a large gymnasium with a single basketball for everyone—except that rec was canceled about as often as it happened. We compensated by doing countless pushups, morning and night, just to have somewhere to put our energy.

Even early in jail, I had no problem taking responsibility for what I had done. I *had* broken into a home. I *had* shot two people. So, when the time came, I pleaded guilty to the crimes I committed—the robbery and the shooting. I pleaded guilty with no agreement about the sentence. I had caused harm, and I was going to accept what came. A trial was set for the charges of conspiracy and obstruction of justice. Finally, I wasn't just waiting—I was waiting for something specific to happen.

The day of the conspiracy trial came sooner than I expected. That morning, after a surprisingly good night of sleep despite fear of what might happen, I put my jail scrubs on. I brushed my teeth and washed my face. I was handcuffed and shackled and transported in a van to the courthouse where I was walked into the upstairs courtroom to face a trial for my life.

The deputy walked me into the courtroom. The judge's bench was situated at the rear, several steps above the rest of the room. A stenographer sat to his left, and two tables, one for the prosecution and one for the defense, were positioned directly in front of the judge's platform. The jury seats were empty, since I had elected for a bench trial, so no jury had been empaneled.

Here, as often in cases like these, the courtroom is divided. The left table in front of the judge and the pews behind were for the defense—me and my lawyer and people there to support me. The pews were full of friends and family. People smiled at me encouragingly as I walked by in my handcuffs. The other side had mostly empty seats, with just a few people I didn't know.

"All rise," called the bailiff as the judge entered the courtroom. We stood up. "Please be seated," he announced. We sat back down.

The Commonwealth's attorney—Virginia's name for a prosecutor—made an opening statement. Just after he wrapped up, my lawyer whispered to me, "This guy is terrible. What he just alleged doesn't even assert the required elements for the crimes you're charged with. I don't want to give you false hope, but I don't see how this doesn't go our way."

I wasn't exactly feeling good, but I felt a bit of relief at that point, and even more when the people called to testify against me kept making odd, contradictory statements. On the stand, Francis—my codefendant in the robbery case—argued with the prosecutor and even threatened him in a bizarre tirade. As far as Walter, the "star" witness, even the prosecutor had a hard time taking him seriously. I couldn't believe that I had been charged on the strength of Walter's accusation alone.

The prosecution finally rested. Then my lawyer made a motion for summary judgment. Essentially, this argued that the prosecution hadn't met their burden of proof and as a result, we didn't even have to put on a defense. The judge could grant the motion, and the trial would be over. Legally, I'm pretty sure it would have been the right decision, just based on the prosecution's opening statement.

The judge took a moment to consider. Then denied the motion.

It was our turn. There wasn't a lot of evidence. The administrator for the jail, called by the prosecution, had already testified that Walter and I had never lived in the same unit and couldn't possibly have had contact. (This wasn't even correct and gives you an idea of the ludicrousness of the case.)

Then it was up to me. My turn to get on the stand. My chance to say, "I didn't do this."

Before the trial, my lawyer had advised me that I didn't have to take the stand, that he was pretty sure the judge would rule in our favor. But he went on to say that he thought I should. I wanted to take the stand, too. I was scared. But also self-righteous—this wasn't right.

I kept my cool until the prosecutor implied that my friend, who had put Walter up, was somehow part of a grand criminal conspiracy. I raised my voice and said something I most definitely should not have. I was angry that I had put my friend in a terrible position. I was angry that they had charged me based on the word of someone who had a track record of lying and setting people up just like this. I was angry because I felt powerless and scared. I was angry because deep down, I felt like a complete piece of shit. I had created this—I had put my family and friends in a courtroom where I was fighting for my life when I should have been in college or off making the world a better place.

I managed to calm myself down and answered the rest of the prosecutor's questions. When I sat back down at the defense table, my lawyer patted me on the shoulder. He whispered, "You probably shouldn't have said that. But it's okay, you did what you had to do."

And that was it. Now my life was in the judge's hands. My lawyer and I had elected for a bench trial because we had no idea what to expect. I later learned that juries can be absolutely terrible at evaluating evidence, especially when it relates to people's credibility. As the judge deliberated, I was walked outside the courtroom, where the deputy let me talk to my father and friend. I was still handcuffed but it was almost casual—they even let me use the public bathroom rather than taking me down to the holding cell. Then it was time: We all filed back into the courtroom.

The judge banged his gavel and there was a very heavy, very long pause. The judge said, "Let's get to the ruling that's much easier—the obstruction of justice charges. There is no evidence of an action against the witnesses, so I find you not guilty on all three counts."

Another long, heavy pause.

"On the conspiracy charges, though . . ."

My heart caught in my throat. How could he possibly think—

The judge continued, "It's a lot more complicated, but in the end I just can't believe the testimony against you beyond a reasonable doubt. I find you not guilty on all charges."

The courtroom erupted in cheers. My lawyer turned and shushed them. He was not amused by the cheers. The judge was annoyed. The Commonwealth's attorney was livid.

It was over. I almost couldn't believe it. After all of the buildup, all of the fear, all of the catastrophizing, the judge had found me not guilty. Now I just needed to wait for sentencing on the charges I had pleaded guilty to. It would all be done soon. It would be okay.

It didn't go as we had hoped.

Chapter 5

The Sentence

Standing in front of a judge, sweating, with my heart racing, knowing that my life was in his hands and that my fate would be sealed with the strike of a gavel, was one of the most humbling experiences of my life. I felt small.

By the last week of August 2003, I had been in jail for a little more than nine months. I had pleaded guilty. I had dealt with legal twists and turns. I had endured ninety days of isolation without a visit or phone call. I was ready to receive my sentence and get on my way to prison and whatever the future held. My lawyer had explained that the guidelines called for between eight and thirteen years with a midpoint of ten. He bluntly told me I deserved ten years for having done some "serious shit." I had made peace with that number.

Finally, after all the waiting: sentencing day. An officer walked to our block and yelled through the bars, "Crosson, put on your scrubs. Time to go." I was again handcuffed and shackled, then led to the sally port where I was again loaded, along with three other men, into the back of a sheriff's van. At this point, transport was the most exciting thing in my life. It was a chance to see the outside world, even if it was just through the window of a locked van. Despite my anxiety and fear, I felt awe, transfixed by every color, every detail, every aspect of life on the outside.

We pulled up to the courthouse. The deputy parked next to the main entrance and, waving onlookers back, unloaded us. Once inside, we four walked past offices and back to the holding cells, whose giant metal doors looked like they belonged in a doomsday bunker. Our leg irons were taken off as we entered the cells, but we were still handcuffed. The cell was cramped, with an uneven bench and a shiny metal toilet that looked out of place amid a sea of concrete. As all the times before, one of the other men had to use the bathroom. Sharing that experience again, with no room to get away and not many places to look away, was not one of the high points of that day. Looking back, though, maybe it should have been.

At last, I heard a key slide into the heavy lock and turn over with a metallic groan. An overweight deputy with kind eyes stood at the door and said quietly, "Crosson, let's go."

I stood up, thankful to no longer be wearing the leg irons and "black box" that was used to secure my handcuffs to the chain around my waist for transport. I walked to the door, where he took me by the shoulder and led me down the cramped basement hallway, up the steps toward the courtroom's entrance. He stopped before a smaller door to the right.

"Do you need to use the bathroom before we get started?" he asked.

"I don't. I mean . . . I think I do," I mumbled.

He pushed the door open then turned his back, giving me a sense of privacy even though he had to leave the door open. I was so nervous that I struggled to start. Once I did, I peed for what felt like minutes. He chuckled. "I guess you did have to go." Washing my hands was a process made awkward while handcuffed—though not as awkward as wiping was for the guy in the holding cell.

The deputy grabbed my arm again and guided me through the large, double doors to the main courtroom. I glanced to my right, to the first two rows of people behind the prosecutor's table. My eyes found cold stares from people I didn't recognize. These were the people I had harmed and their relatives. On our side, behind the defense table, were faces I did recognize: former classmates, my parents, friends, and even one of my favorite teachers. A few smiled as our eyes met, others cried. Many looked as numb and stricken as I felt.

I shuffled forward to the defense table. As I sat down, my lawyer clapped me on the shoulder, smiling tightly. He looked me in the eyes and nodded. Then we both turned back toward the bench. Moments later, after we all stood for the judge to enter, the Commonwealth's attorney addressed the court. He announced a motion to modify the sentencing guidelines for my case.

The judge asked my lawyer if we wanted a recess to discuss. My lawyer said yes. "Let's talk," he whispered, and motioned for the bailiff to lead me into the hall, where we could talk privately.

Looking over the motion, my lawyer explained that the prosecution wanted the court to enhance the sentencing guidelines. Guidelines are designed to give suggestions consistent with sentences across the rest of the state. Eight to thirteen years would become ten and a half to sixteen and a half, with a midpoint of thirteen. My lawyer said we could object, but that we would probably lose. He also liked that the judge had just been looking at the eight- to thirteen-year guidelines and thought if we didn't object he wouldn't have a lot of reason to give the new ones any more attention. I had been expecting a ten-year sentence, and thirteen didn't sound too much worse, so I agreed. We wouldn't argue against the motion.

Back in the courtroom, the Commonwealth began by calling witnesses to testify about the impact of my actions.

It was terrifying to see one of the men I had shot, to see the scar where a bullet had entered his jaw yet somehow left it intact. As he testified, I was blanketed in shame, wanting to hide my face. His voice was calm and flat—and did not prepare me for the impact of the next witness.

An elderly lady walked from the back of the courtroom to the stand. She moved slowly and with dignity. Her age and demeanor lent her a gravitas, and the courtroom was respectfully silent.

After the Commonwealth's attorney asked her name, she recounted the night she was told her grandson had been shot. She paused often, sometimes wiping tears, as she talked about the horror she experienced, the terror she felt.

She talked about driving to the hospital to see him, not sure he'd be alive when she got there.

If I thought the testimony from the guy I shot was uncomfortable, this was agony. But instead of hiding my face, I forced myself to look at her and listen. I saw her anguish as she relived those moments. I forced myself to sit with shame and sadness and hopelessness and to acknowledge that I was the cause.

Something in me broke. I had prepared a speech in which I'd accept responsibility and apologize and ask for leniency but after watching the grandmother testify, I couldn't bear to ask for anything. I didn't deserve anything.

Instead of what I had prepared, I spoke off the cuff. I turned to my victims and their families and apologized. I apologized to my own family and friends for failing them. I was so, so sorry.

Then, turning to the judge, I asked for help. I said I knew I had done wrong and needed to go to prison, but I wanted to get better.

He asked what kind of help I needed.

I said, "If I knew that, sir, I wouldn't be here. I need addiction help, I need all kinds of help. I see all these guys in the jail with nothing to do and no hope and no future," I told him. "I want them to get help. I want to get help. I want to get better."

He scoffed, as if dismissing my request, and read my sentence, a numerical laundry list representing each of the twelve felonies to which I'd pleaded guilty.

"Five years with five suspended . . ." he began. "Twenty years with fifteen suspended . . ." Only when he finished rattling off numbers did he acknowledge my request for help. "And I order you to be evaluated for two years of outpatient treatment at the conclusion of your sentence," he said.

My attorney looked confused, and so did the prosecutor. "Your honor, how much time is that?" my attorney asked.

"I don't know. I just told you," the judge replied.

Everyone in the courtroom murmured and looked around at one another. I was glad I wasn't the only person who thought this was bizarre. The judge directed the stenographer to recount the sentence. The stenographer did the math and announced the combined figure.

"One hundred thirty-eight years with 106 suspended," she said. "An active sentence of thirty-two years in prison."

Behind me, I heard a collective gasp and a woman's wail, maybe my mother.

I was conscious of the "split" again, experiencing multiple, seemingly contradictory reactions.

Part of me was angry. "This isn't fair!" an inner voice screamed. "I was supposed to get ten years!"

Another part was resigned. This judge—this person appointed to a place of power—had validated my deepest fear, the thing I always thought was true: I was unworthy. Something was fundamentally wrong with me. I deserved this.

Both reactions felt true at the same time.

When I looked at the people collected behind me, I still remember one face. Simon, a classmate from school, who was staring at me with his mouth open, in shock. I smiled at him, or I tried to. I wanted him to know it would be okay. I certainly didn't know if it would. Then everything became a blur.

"Damn, Crosson, that's a rough one." That was a deputy charged with transporting me from the courthouse. Somehow I was back in the sheriff's van, heading back to the jail, with no memory of how I got there.

At the jail, the COs seemed sympathetic as if word about my unexpected sentence had already reached the jail when I arrived. One asked if I had anything on me, meaning contraband. I shook my head, expecting a strip search, but he allowed me to forgo that humiliation, despite it being standard procedure for reentering the jail.

Back at the cell block, as I sat in my own miserable, stunned silence, another officer walked up to the bars and told me to pack my stuff. My sentence was so long that someone in the administration—I never found out who—was afraid I would harm myself. I was being placed on suicide watch.

I was going to be held in the medical unit, in a single cell with a plexiglass wall that gave officers a clear view of me at all times. Without a word, I brought my mattress from the cell block and placed it on the concrete slab bench that doubled as a bed. I dropped my box, full of belongings, on the floor. I sat on the bench, unmoving, for a few minutes or maybe longer. The numbness had sunk so deeply, I couldn't function.

Eventually, I reached into the trash bag and fished out the small AM/FM radio that was the only electronic item we were allowed to buy in the jail. I turned it on, switched the dial to WNRN, Charlottesville's local independent radio station. I heard the bang of a hand drum and the bars of a guitar.

"Cyrus Jones, 1810 to 1913 . . ."

I knew this song. It hadn't ever meant anything. This time, I started to feel something. Some frozen thing in my body was thawing.

". . . Cyrus Jones lived forever."

More. Something was building, rising up in my chest now, almost to my throat.

"Gravedigger

when you dig my grave,

could you make it shallow

so I can feel the rain."

The sobs that had been building inside me broke free. I shook and rocked, battered by waves of grief and guilt and a deeper pain—a pain I had spent so many years running from and trying to hold at bay. I cried for what felt like hours, wailing in a way I didn't know I was capable of. My life was over.

"Gravedigger, when you dig my grave, could you make it shallow so I can feel the rain."

Chapter 6

What Is Wrong with Me?

I was in prison with people who had killed, stolen, abused, and neglected. I don't remember one of them who was happy and healthy at the time of their crime and woke up deciding it would be a good way to spend their day. When someone commits a crime or causes harm, there *is* trauma, poverty, learned maladaptive behaviors, mental illness—or often all of the above. Rehabilitation, also known as healing, is looking at our origin story and untying the knots that led us to do the things we did. Real change is about acceptance and accountability.

Opening wounds and facing painful experiences with fresh eyes is devastating. Rather than listening to the simple narratives handed down from our parents and wider communities, we have to dig through pain to find the truth. Often this makes us the black sheep—willing to challenge the story that others are most comfortable with. In my case, that narrative was that I was just a kid who decided to throw his life away. People have asked me if I'm writing a book because I want to tell my story. No. I am writing a book because, through it all, I'm still trying to understand what my story is in the first place.

For most of my life I thought I was broken or defective and that I didn't belong. As a child I thought everyone else had it figured out or knew something that I didn't. If I could just learn, or copy them or find out the secret, I would be okay. Every mistake, every new challenge that I failed reinforced my inadequacy. It culminated when the judge sentenced me to serve more than three decades in prison. It was final proof that I wasn't enough.

I don't remember big chunks of my childhood from any age. It was only in prison, listening to people share their stories, when I realized that most people had more memories of their own childhoods than I did. I didn't understand why.

Some memories stand out brightly, though. My mother and I went on one vacation every year for my whole life, driving three hours to Virginia Beach, where she would attend a professional conference to maintain her bar membership. We went to the beach and ate crab legs and I'd visit Flipper McCoys, where they had the biggest arcade game collection I had ever seen. It felt like a healthy, childhood experience.

Another couple worked in the same office as my mother. They joined us on the trip one year. We all rented bikes. Their son Jason and I enjoyed sailing down the boardwalk on our rented bikes until, with a loud clink, my chain slipped off. We stopped and tried to pull it back on. We were kids, though, and didn't know how to do it. I just assumed I had done something to break the bike.

Jason and I started pushing our bikes back to the rental place. In another family, a bike slipping a chain would be an opportunity to learn or a memorable experience to make jokes about. When my mother found out, she began seething with rage. When we got to the bike shop, she demanded a refund, saying that my bike was defective. The guy behind the counter calmly told her that wasn't how it worked, and she really started flipping out. There was screaming and threatening and the cops were called or were going to be called—I don't really remember. I just remember the shame I felt and how sure I was that this was my fault. Not only had I not figured out how to calm her down, but if I had been more careful the chain never would have slipped off. I imagined my mother hauled away in handcuffs because I hadn't ridden the bike right.

Here's another. My parents were not happy for years. Eventually my father left. My mother went into the full throes of depression, I started feeling like it was all on my shoulders. I had to make sure she was okay, that she wasn't sad, that she didn't explode in public. I had to become the adult. I was seven.

The memory from that time that stands out is the day that she wouldn't get out of bed. I walked into her room and she was lying in the bed, not moving, not answering me, not engaging with me at all. Years later I could still close my eyes and see that scene. I never felt much about it, though, until many years later, when I read the book *Room*. It's a dark and disturbing psychological book that somehow also manages to be brimming with hope. When I read the passage where young Jack said, "Today is one of the days when Ma is Gone. She won't wake up properly. She's here but not really. She stays in Bed with the pillows on her head," I began to shake. I sobbed, streaming tears, because once I could see the pain, confusion, and sense of abandonment in this fictional character, I finally could see it in myself. No young child should have to bear the burden of not only his own, but his family's well-being.

To say I grew up with a poor understanding of boundaries and expectations is an understatement. I didn't know what boundaries were. The only boundaries I saw were when my father left or my mother exploded. I didn't think I was allowed to have wants and needs, so I didn't know what I wanted or needed. I still struggle with that today.

I had weird, enmeshed friendships as a kid, where I tried to become just like my friend because I thought they knew the "right" way to do things. I had unhealthy romantic relationships: I couldn't see where they stopped and I started.

I was in love with a girl from kindergarten until second grade. Then another girl from third through fifth grade. Looking back I wonder if I was just a "romantic at heart" as people affectionately called me, or if I was copying some behavior I didn't understand.

Sadness has always been how my mother manipulates, before or after she explodes. It was her inner child's coping mechanism. About fifteen years into my prison sentence, I was standing in the visitation room with my mother and a friend. She had just bought me a sandwich from the vending machine and was heating it up in the microwave. Both the vending machines and microwaves were on the other side of a red line that marked where incarcerated people had to stop. While my sandwich was heating up, my mother, the friend, and I were standing at the line, talking. Then a woman visiting someone else walked by and was about to open the microwave that held my sandwich. Rather than saying, "That one is occupied," or just letting the woman see for herself, my mother exploded. She shrieked, "Don't touch that!" The woman jumped back, and the whole visiting room fell silent, all eyes on my mother. The woman's face tightened and started to grow red. I did my best to apologize and calm her until my sandwich was ready. When we got back to our seats, I told my mother it wasn't okay to do things like that. She started to sniffle and slumped, pulling herself into a self-hug. Then she asked why everyone was being so mean to her.

I was so used to reading her moods, either to try to cheer her up or head off an angry outburst, that it became second nature. I was a precocious kid. In elementary school, I started running errands for my mom, typing up documents, filing deeds, and carrying checks to the bank downtown. The ladies at the courthouse and the bank got to know me well.

I learned the smile that would get me an extra lollipop at the bank or the question that would get me special attention at the courthouse. I became a master manipulator. It was how I survived.

I also learned to manipulate my mother when I realized she was ashamed of her rage and her behavior. It would be so much simpler if people were just one thing—just evil or just nice. I know now that most of what she did was because she didn't want to see me or herself or someone else in pain. Yet, much of the pain I remember from childhood came, directly or indirectly, from those things she did.

I recall being a teenager, walking on the red bricks of the open downtown mall full of cute shops and big crowds. I was angry about something she had done. So, I provoked her. I said something I knew would make her angry enough to hit me in front of everyone. She slapped me across the face, then the light in her eyes went from fury to panic. She looked around, worried about who had seen. It was how I regained power. Most people talked about how much they liked my mother. I wanted to show the world the other side of what she was capable of. I was angry. I was tired of both feeling like a victim and feeling like it was all my fault.

When I look back, I just feel sadness. I don't hate my mother. I know that deep down she is just a scared, hurt child lashing out the only way she knows how. I didn't understand that then. I just wanted a way to stop wearing her pain as my own.

Growing up with her rage, I promised to never let my own anger out. I didn't want to embarrass myself or make anyone else carry my burden. The pressure of my rage bottled up to the point that in the rare moments it slipped out, people would stop and stare.

In prison a kid tried to jump in the shower ahead of me. Even as blood pumped through my hands and I felt my face grow hot, I tried to say, casually, that wasn't how we do things. He muttered, "Fuck that shit, man," and turned back toward the shower.

Now fully shaking with rage, I put my hand on his shoulder, spun him around and stared into his eyes. I felt so anger for more than just that moment. It was a stored, compressed energy. I was ready to hurt this kid over something as stupid as a shower line. He lowered his gaze, side-stepped out of the shower, and went back to his cell.

Someone who had known me for years said, "I've never seen you like that, bro. You okay?" I wasn't.

The first time that rage truly came out was when I pulled the trigger. The combination of fear and anger and sadness was like a volcano exploding, like energy rushing out of the earth and scorching the sky. It is one of the reasons I am so adamant now about feeling our feelings and not bottling them up. No emotion is a "bad" emotion, but if we don't feel them, they fester and can come out with all the destruction of a natural disaster.

What I also know, or at least what everyone tells me, is that there was a time—some have said as early as five years old—when my light went out. I stopped being this bright, happy, playful kid and withdrew into myself. I became scared, neurotic, insecure. Something happened to me, but I have no idea what. I have cried and prayed, just wanting to know "what happened to me," believing that would somehow help me be okay. I have had terrifying flashes of emotions and memories that seem almost dreamlike.

Elementary school Jesse, still with a spark in his eye.

In the darkness of lost memories, one night stands out. It was winter and I was young. I was in a house that was freezing because the power had gone out. A family member invited me into their room and told me we would help each other stay warm. They said we couldn't sleep under a blanket and we couldn't wear clothes, because it would cause us to lose body heat. Instead, we had to touch, skin to skin, and shiver our way to warmth.

Even as a little kid I knew that was stupid, that it didn't make sense. I felt angry. The rest is blank.

My New Life

Chapter 7

Entering the System

Two weeks after being sentenced, an officer came to the bars of our cellblock and called out, "Bags and baggage, Crosson!"

I was surprised, and grateful. Once a person in Virginia was sentenced to a term longer than a year, they were classified with a DOC number. Most were transferred to a prison to serve their time. However, the wait list for transfer was months, or in some cases years. So, quite a few guys in the jail never got transferred and instead had to serve their entire sentence at the jail.

An officer took me to the long-term storage closet and pulled out the clothes I had been wearing the day I was arrested. They were dress pants, hiking boots, a button-up shirt, and an overcoat. (I hadn't been able to decide whether I wanted to be dapper, a gangster, or just comfortable. I had started hanging out with an old Irish mob guy and he told me dressing well alleviated suspicion. But I was so strung out I couldn't do it consistently.) It felt so strange to take off the scrubs and put on clothes with buttons and a belt. The officer then handcuffed me, shackled my ankles, chained the two together, and loaded me into the transport Crown Vic.

It was about an hour drive to Powhatan, almost due east from the jail where I had been held for ten months. I stared out the window as we drove across the countryside. I couldn't stop watching the people and the daily lives that were going on. Other than transportation to the court, I hadn't been outside once. I hadn't seen the sky or felt the breeze or even seen the colors. Everything seemed brighter and bigger. It was like coming out of Plato's cave and seeing the world as it really existed.

Powhatan had three prisons all on the same plot of land: the general population unit, the medical unit, and Receiving and Classification, where I was going. The original prison had opened in the 1890s as part of the South's answer to the abolition of slavery. No slaves to work the fields? We have incarcerated people for that on a place literally called "State Farm." The medical unit was new. The receiving prison was one of the facilities where everyone entering the system was evaluated. Counselors plugged age, charges, criminal history, and jail infractions into a formula to determine security level and good-time earning level—the number of days per year off your sentence that you could earn back for good behavior.

It was daunting to enter a new institution—like the first day of school, with the same unknowns, the same cliques, the same politics. As someone wisely once put it, prison is a lot like middle school, just with more knives. As we drove up to those tall, stark brick buildings surrounded by several layers of fences, I recalled all of the conflicting stories I had heard in the jail: "You're going to love it there!" "Watch your ass—someone's going to want it." "It's like a country club." "When the stabbing starts, make sure you get away and keep your back to the wall." People were describing two very different places, and I couldn't figure out which one was real. Turns out, neither.

When we arrived, I shuffled my shackled feet out of the car, like an old-time vagabond with my overcoat and bag of ramen noodles, oatmeal packets, soaps, toothpastes, and deodorants from the jail commissary.

I shuffled to the entry gate and the guard gave me two options: I could leave all the food outside with him and he'd feed it to his kids, or I could take it inside, where the food would be thrown away since I wasn't allowed to bring anything but hygiene items.

I took him at his word and left most of the contents of the bag outside. Looking back, I wonder how many thousands of ramen noodle packets he got that way. I wonder if he really fed them to his kids or if he distributed them to friends or even sold them in the prison. It's wild how different the rules are from prison to prison. In some receiving centers you could bring anything in with you. In others only hygiene. In others, hygiene and shorts. I lost all of the food I had transferred with, so I went to bed hungry every night the first week—just because of which receiving center I had been sent to, by chance. They gave us three meals per day but there wasn't nearly enough food to be full, dinner was before 5 PM, and we weren't allowed to bring food back to our cells.

I was ignorant about the system. Now I know that if I had taken the bag inside, the incarcerated workers would have figured out a way to get those commissary items back to their cells or possibly even gotten them to me. It would have meant a lot more to them than to the guard.

I met with a counselor, took a brief mental health evaluation, and had a quick call with my family to tell them I had been moved. Calls from the prison required a pin number, but mine wouldn't arrive for days or weeks from the telecom company (which, by the way, charged something like $7 for a fifteen-minute call back then). The prison provided everyone with one free five-minute call to let family and friends know where someone had ended up.

I also received my state number. Technically it had been assigned previously but no one told me. For the foreseeable future I would not be Jesse. I would be Jesse Crosson #325421. I wrote it on every envelope I mailed out, on every request form I submitted, and every commissary order. I was a person but I was also a number.

A group of eight of us had come in together, and we sat on metal benches waiting for each person to go through the process. Once we were all done, we walked together, all carrying a bag of clean linens, down a dark hallway, through a large, gated entrance to the cell blocks, and up to the cells they assigned us. That was where I met the guy I would be living with.

Short, heavy, with white hair like a wall around his bald spot—he didn't look like he belonged in prison. I wondered what he could possibly be in for. He seemed like a smart and reasonable guy, but I was wary. I knew that cheerful people can have rage in waiting behind a smile. Later I found out he had strangled his girlfriend then gone about his life, leaving her body under their house for weeks before she was discovered. He claimed to have no memory of strangling her. The idea of this guy I lived in a tiny cell with, leaving a body to decompose under a house, didn't make sense. His story was one of many I heard over the years that just didn't add up or fit into easy boxes like evil or crazy.

The receiving prison at Powhatan was transient, like jail, but it had a library and a chow hall (we had eaten in the block at the jail). The unit was three massive stories with tiers around the walls and an empty center space. Tiny cells with doors made of metal bars circled the tiers. A short railing around each tier didn't prevent people from falling—or being thrown—from the second and third tiers. The cells were built for one person, but we were all doubled up. Sitting on the toilet, my knees touched the bunk. Sitting on the edge of the bunk, I could reach out and touch the wall in front of me. There was no HVAC. There were giant steam pipes running through the cells for heat and sliding windows with bars on the outside to let in fresh air. The sinks only had cold water. It was loud and eerily interconnected. Even being in the cell, I could never just be in silence or feel alone.

We were in our cells almost all day so I continued my jail routine: mostly reading, writing, sleeping, and doodling. The one change was that after ten months of being locked indoors, I could finally go outside for one hour each day. I was ecstatic. The first time I walked in the sunshine and fresh air, without handcuffs or shackles, I wandered around, entranced but also a little overwhelmed by the brightness and the colors and the activities. I stopped to stare at the clouds. Then I jumped from observation to action—working out even harder than I had at the jail, playing handball on the uneven brick wall, and walking around the small track talking to different people. It wasn't long before I got into an argument at the weight machine and instinctively stepped back into a bladed karate stance I had learned as a kid. Four years of karate, with sparring sidekicks and backfists, weren't much use against people with hundreds of street fights under their belt. But during that first argument during outside rec, the guy didn't take a swing at me, so maybe the training didn't hurt.

It was also the first time I experienced an earthquake. I didn't even know we had fault lines in Virginia and I was scared as hell when the building started shaking and the steam pipe rattled like it was going to explode.

After about three months, I had gotten used to Powhatan Receiving but the other guys I was with kept telling me that "real" prison was going to be different. I didn't know what this meant. Then one early January morning, I found out. The officer came in early and called a list of names, popped open a number of cell doors, and sent us all to Property. An officer took all the things I had collected during my time at Powhatan, packed them into a cardboard box, and taped it shut. We were shackled and handcuffed, then sent to line up in the cold morning air. It was winter and the sun hadn't risen yet, but they sent us out without coats anyway. Powhatan Receiving didn't have any. After transfers, the other prisons were supposed to send the transports' coats back but they never did, so we just had to deal with 20 degrees in thin jumpsuits.

We shivered our way to the bus and even after the heat kicked in we kept shivering while they drove us to the central bullpen, a meeting area for all the transports that day. Handcuffed and shackled (so popping in to use the port-a-potty was an adventure), we were led from the bus we were on to vans headed to our next destinations with all the efficiency of cats on catnip. Eventually we all made it onto our correct transports, still shivering.

Four or five of us were in the van headed to Nottaway. One of us had already been there. He had been shipped to a higher level for disciplinary reasons, had stayed out of trouble, and was now on his way back down. He swapped war stories with the officer driving us, asking about certain people with the officer answering, "Oh, he got jumped and they had to send him off." "He's still in the law library." "He stabbed so-and-so up over a boy." Hearing violence and chaos discussed so casually unsettled me. Still, for me, living in survival mode wasn't a new experience.

Eventually we pulled up to a massive sally port at Nottaway and were unloaded. I felt grateful (briefly) for the heat in the strip-out booth. If I had to get naked to squat, cough, and be searched, at least it was in a very warm space.

Then with the shackles off, we were marched to the property department, carrying our cardboard boxes, where I met a very different kind of officer.

At Powhatan, I had started smoking roll-ups—loose tobacco, purchased from commissary, rolled up like joints and smoked in the cells or other designated areas. While waiting to be transferred I was told that I wouldn't be able to bring any open containers of any sort to a level 4 or above prison. Since

Nottaway was a level 4, I had rolled a bunch of cigarettes and hidden them in various books and in my belongings, hoping they would evade notice. I wasn't very good at hiding things yet.

As the property officer looked through my stuff, he pulled out one roll-up after another. At last he asked, "Why the hell do you have a bunch of loose cigarettes in here?" I sheepishly told him about the rule and he laughed. "I ain't never heard of that one myself." He was so amused by my attempts to hide contraband that he said he'd look out for me since I "obviously must be desperate." He walked away from the counter, went in the back storage area and brought me a pack of unopened Marlboros that had been confiscated from someone. He slid them over the counter to me and said, "To hold you over."

He also helped Ghost, who had come on the transport with me and who would be my roommate at Nottaway. Prison commissary sold property items including a radio, a tape player, as well as a TV. Because playing music or TV without headphones was prohibited—it could lead to problems—we were required to purchase and keep a pair of headphones for each electronic item we had. They usually let people slide with just one pair. Ghost didn't have any headphones so, by policy, the property officer should have taken his TV and radio until he bought some. Instead, the property officer went to the back, found a pair of confiscated headphones, sanded off the old name and number, and then engraved Ghost's name. This was about as far out of policy as I had ever imagined.

Virginia doesn't have the kinds of racial politics of other states, where people have to pick a group and stick with them. There were definitely some old-minded individuals of all races who did not like to see one of their own mixing, but that was more of a personal bias than a system-wide thing. Ghost, my new roommate, was white but had grown up in a nearly all-black neighborhood. His wife was black and they had several kids together. A few days after getting there I was talking to a guy who accused Ghost of not hanging out with white guys and said something racist about Ghost's wife. It reminded me that there was a lot of anger and a lot of hatred behind the walls.

About a week after I got there, Ghost was called back to court so I was in the cell alone. I had no property: no TV and no radio. I had arrived with only my college textbooks and even those had been taken for review. So, I didn't have a lot to do other than read the books that people lent me, work out, talk on the phone, or do any other daily activity in the common area of the housing unit, or pod, as it was also known.

Every morning, between 5 and 6 AM, an officer would yell over the loudspeaker, "Stand by for chow." If we wanted to eat, we had to get out of bed and stick a hand out the door of our cells and wave to get the guards' attention. Only then would they open the door. This was partly for our protection; the guards wouldn't just open all the doors because anyone who was still sleeping wouldn't be able to defend themselves.

We had five minutes to get dressed and get out of the cell before all the doors were closed again. Then we waited. Sometimes for a minute, sometimes for an hour. There weren't enough seats so guys sat on the floor or on the steps in the middle of the unit, which most officers promptly yelled at them for doing.

One morning we came out of our cells, and it was too quiet, even for the early morning. Quiet was one of the scariest things in prison. Whenever you heard the steady buzz die away or walked into a room that was too quiet—something was coming.

The doors all closed and we were settling in to wait when the quiet was broken by two voices: Raul and Bang. Raul was a short, light-skinned guy from Cuba. He had that strong Cuban/Florida accent—think "ey mang" instead of "hey man." Bang was taller and quite stocky, and dark-skinned to the point of being almost perfectly black.

Their voices started off low then got louder until Bang stepped back and said something like, "Fuck that." He lifted his fists to his chin, like a boxer, and that's when Raul stepped back and pulled a Rambo knife out of his pants. The knife was so big it almost looked comical, but this was no laughing matter. Bang stepped back farther and reached into his pants, pulling out a lock in a sock—a swinging weapon made of a padlock (or in this case two), inside a long sock.

Raul took another step back and grabbed the lid of a trash can, one of those commercial lids with an elevated hump and a flap that you could push your trash through without lifting the lid. In his hands, it became a shield. Raul advanced and started swinging his knife at Bang, who jumped back with every swing while whirling his own weapon. When he finally swung that lock in a sock at Raul, Raul lifted his makeshift shield. With a bang against the lid, the sock split, the locks went flying, and suddenly Bang was holding an empty sock in front of a man with a sword and shield. When you make a lock in a sock, you're supposed to run the sock through the hole in the padlock—not just put the lock in the sock because, as Bang found out, it'll rip. From where I was squatting down next to my door, I thought, "I'm about to watch a person die."

Bang, to his credit or his insanity, dropped the empty sock and brought his fists up to box this Roman legionnaire in front of him. Raul took a few more swings with his knife, advancing steadily—

"Chow call, chow call. Two minutes to get out for chow," burst out over the loudspeaker. The officer in the booth hadn't seen any of the fight. Everyone rushed for the door, happy to be away from the looming bloodshed. It was best to see nothing and say nothing.

Walking to chow, I imagined Bang's blood all over the pod, like a horrible scene from the worst horror movie. That's why I was surprised when I sat down for chow—they made us fill one table and one row at a time—and Bang sat down right in front of me across the table. I looked around and there was Raul, at the back of the chow line. The tension between them was palpable when they avoided each other as they got up for milk from the dispenser.

Another pod came in to fill up seats at the opposite end of the chow hall, then it was our turn to leave. We went back and were locked in our cells for the rest of the morning. That's when one of the few incarcerated workers allowed in the pod during morning hours ran back and forth between Bang's and Raul's cells, making peace between them. Some arrangement was reached, and their dispute was never discussed again. Was it all theater or just good conflict resolution? I didn't know, but what I did learn was that this prison dynamic—civility punctuated by extreme conflict followed by resolution—was more or less normal. I accepted it, maybe because even before I was arrested, this was a pattern in my life.

I had experienced some chaos at home but didn't fight much growing up. In prison I got into a few scraps. Despite karate as a kid and wrestling in high school, I just didn't have the instinct to hurt people. If I had to, I could get someone to the ground but I usually walked away, partly out of caution and partly out of fear. After the shooting, I was even more profoundly aware of my capacity for violence—and afraid of it. I had an ego and a lot of fear but I was hoping I could avoid trouble.

Then one night, I came back to the pod from the chow hall. Unlike after breakfast, we were allowed to stay out of our cells after dinner. If any of us wanted to go back into our cell, the guards would open the cell door to let us in. With the good officers we had time to grab something from the cell and come back out before they shut the door.

This time, I spotted a bunch of people gathered around my cell. A guy was reaching his arm into the slot of my cell door. Old heads in prison tried to teach me not to let anyone into my space—and that meant my cell as well as my personal space. So I reacted.

"What the fuck is going on?" I shouted. I grabbed the shoulder of the guy who was reaching into my cell to spin him around. He stuck his arm out between us to keep a distance and told me to back up. Much later, I watched him break a guy's jaw with one punch, so I should have been glad he didn't hit me. But I was triggered—both scared and angry—so I stayed there, just out of reach of his arm, my eyes locked on his. Then someone hit me from the side—a clean shot on my chin that knocked me to the ground. When I warily got up, a circle had formed around me, blocking the guard in the booth from seeing—and trapping me alone on the floor. No one threw any kicks, though. One guy eventually even helped me up.

At this point I was shaking. I had no idea who had hit me. I didn't know who to fight. I didn't know what to do. Someone came up behind me and walked me back to a table to talk. The group of men formed again in front of my door. A guy at the table where I was sitting got up to mediate. He walked over to the group and briefly conferred, then came back with the guy who had been reaching into my door.

"I was just trying to get the dice," he said. "They went under your door. You didn't have to make it all that."

"You were in my space," I said, through gritted teeth. "You were wrong."

The guy nodded. "Yeah, you right. Aight, you gonna fight LB to settle this."

I thought LB was the one who had hit me. But no, the one who hit me was my older neighbor, and they didn't think he could stand a fight. So, by some logic they replaced him with LB, a few years older than me, about my height, and around 240 lbs.—I was maybe 160 at that point. We waited to fight until the next cell break, when doors could be opened for five minutes before being shut again for the remainder of the hour.

When they called cell break, I waved my arm, the officer opened my cell door, and LB and I walked into the cell. Feeling tense, I squared up and threw a punch. He dodged. We went back and forth like that for four or five swings, then he ducked in and grabbed me and picked me up. I had been a decent wrestler, but a wrestling sprawl is hard to do when backed into a bunk. He hoisted me up into the air, my head hitting the ceiling. Then he swung me downward like a sack of potatoes. My head hit the sink, my head hit the floor, and it all went black.

I thought I had learned to wrestle in high school—prison changed the rules.

When I woke up, my cell door was shut. I had no idea what time it was and couldn't, at first, remember what had happened. My brain was foggy, and my skull hurt. Then LB appeared on the other side of the door. "We thought you was dead," he said. "Then we heard you moaning, and we thought your skull was cracked. I ran out before they closed the doors, but I've been checking on you."

I managed to get to my feet, dizzy. I walked to the door where LB had placed a row of crackers, some aspirin, and a can of ginger ale. "Eat these, drink this, and don't go to sleep. Don't die on me. I can't handle another body."

I took the supplies he had brought, opened the crackers, sat in my chair, and stared at the blank wall in front of me. I felt sharp pains radiating through my head and I ached all over.

Someone brought me a book to read but I had trouble concentrating on the words. Someone else brought me more food. Every time I looked in the mirror, my face looked worse. The skin around my eye was red-black, with blood pooled deep in the socket. The back and side of my head were reddish black. (I didn't even know that was possible.) I looked as if someone had rag-dolled me into the ceiling, the sink, and then the floor, which is exactly what had happened.

For a few days, people continued to bring me food so I didn't have to go to the chow hall and walk in front of the officers. When I finally went to chow, someone lent me an orange hat to wear. Someone else gave me oversized sunglasses. I felt ridiculous but I had to keep the guards from noticing. A black eye or split lip meant you got put in the hole. When they asked who you were fighting, you had a choice: Tell them and maybe get a lesser charge and probably still get locked up, as well as being labeled a snitch. Or don't tell them, and definitely get locked up but keep your prison cred alive. You could be held "under investigation" for a charge for a longer time than if convicted of that charge. There are additional, unofficial punishments for not cooperating. Once I was held for four days without my soap, toothpaste, or any of my property because the captain was pissed I hadn't talked. It took the sergeant on the next shift to go out of her way to get me stuff. She was horrified but not surprised that the shift commander had instructed his officers not to give me anything.

I somehow slid by after the fight with LB. Only one counselor noticed. She had called me to her office for a routine meeting and asked me to take off my sunglasses when I was talking to her. I remember the grimace on her face when she saw my two black eyes. I told her I got elbowed playing basketball. She clearly didn't believe me but didn't say anything else. I wonder how many times she saw someone with bruises or marks, obviously from violence, and how many times she felt powerless to help.

I got a little bit of respect, because I had gone into the cell to fight. I lost some respect because I got beat up so badly. But LB ended up doing the same thing to a lot of people while I was there. He wasn't great with his hands, but he was so stocky that once he got a hold of someone, they almost always went for a ride.

The day after our fight, one of the bigger guys in the pod pulled me aside and told me I needed to work on boxing. He offered to teach me to stick and move. He said that LB never would have been able to grab me if I had jabbed and moved. That wasn't much of an option in a small cell, with my back to the bunk. The same guy who offered to train me ended up getting into a fight with LB and, despite his size and training, got slammed unconscious on the pod stairs. So it didn't work for him either, even in an open space.

The threat of violence wore on me. I always thought it was coming. Eventually, I made peace with the fact that it would come or it wouldn't. Instead of violence or big scary things, one of the hardest parts started to be the down time. Having nothing to do and having to wait. Waiting for chow. Waiting for mail call. Waiting all week for visitation. Waiting for the few opportunities or pleasures of the day. Not knowing how to pass the time in between. I kept in motion, because I didn't know what else to do. I went to chow when they called it, went outside when they called for rec, I read every book and tried to learn every tabletop game.

There was also big-picture waiting. When I first received the thirty-two-year sentence, everyone told me it wouldn't stand up to an appeal. I hoped they were right. I didn't want to believe I would spend almost twice as long in prison as I had been alive. But along with the process of hoping came more waiting. Waiting for my appeal to be filed, then waiting to hear back. Waiting for the appeal to the state supreme court, then waiting for the response to my habeas corpus petition. I had so little to do and I was always waiting. The days stretched longer and longer. At first, all I wanted was a chance to go home. Over time, the waiting began to tear me apart. Then I just wanted an answer. I didn't care if they said I wouldn't be getting out because at least I would know. I needed to know. I needed to stop waiting more than I needed a path to freedom.

Some part of me was in denial that this was where I would live for more years than I could imagine. Another deeper part knew I had a knot inside me that I had to unravel.

Chapter 8

Getting into the Routine

Pweeeeeeep! went the whistle.

"Stand for count! All inmates on your feet! Bottom tier, stand for count!"

It was 6 AM. I don't remember which day because this happened every day—the same shrill whistle and a voice yelling the same thing.

Then two officers with clipboards walked from cell to cell, first along the bottom tier, then the top. They counted how many people were in each cell, checking off their list. Newer officers stopped at every door and scrutinized each cell. The more experienced officers walked with a certain flow that allowed them to never break stride. Occasionally they had to go back to check because someone hadn't gotten out of bed yet, had been obscured behind their roommate, or wasn't in the cell at all because they were out on a medical run, were at work, had been sent to the hole, or were absent for some other reason.

Most guys went back to sleep after being counted. I usually waited until my roommate got back on his bunk (not a lot of room for two people in a cell that's really just the size of a bathroom), then I brushed my teeth and started the stinger for coffee.

Someone had long ago figured out that if you connected an electrical cord to a piece of steel wool, wrapped that steel wool around a pen tube covered in cloth, connected the other end of the steel wool to the neutral end of the plug, and dropped it into water, you could convert electricity to heat, boiling the water. The design was passed down and called a stinger, for reasons unknown. It was helpful because while the pod's common area had a hot water spigot or hot pot, the sink water in each cell only got lukewarm—and we were often locked in the cell for hours, days, weeks, or even months. The same concept made an oven, with one difference. For the stinger, water kept it from popping the breaker. For an oven, dozens of strands of steel wool were required to disperse the electricity as heat and keep the circuit breaker from popping. The strands were run in loops inside of a cardboard box, which was lined with stripped-down soda cans to reflect heat back on the food being cooked and to keep it from setting the box ablaze.

The stinger boiled water in less than a minute. I'd pour it in my coffee cup and mix in instant coffee. Then I would slide my chair over to the door to read by the light of the overhead pod fluorescents streaming in through the door slot.

I read a lot of different books over the years, about two or three per week. I tried daily reads and inspirational titles. Finally, I found *Radical Acceptance* and it resonated so much that I picked it up nearly every morning for a decade, reading a few paragraphs or pages before getting on with the day. It was the single best book I had found to put my mind in the place I wanted it to be: present, grateful, and grounded in my body.

After count cleared, the booth officer opened the doors and we waited for chow. Eventually the officer called chow and opened the pod door. I fell in line and we all walked to breakfast. In the chow hall, I picked up my tray and got some milk from a giant dispenser. I usually also filled up a coffee bag or peanut butter jar with milk so I could have some later in the day. Milk and boiled eggs were the only free protein they consistently provided so I drank a lot of milk and ate more boiled eggs than I care to remember. Sometimes I questioned whether I had a healthy relationship with both, or whether I needed an intervention.

After eating, I hustled back to the cell. But first I had to get my milk and any fruit I brought back through the shakedown line outside the chow hall. I slipped the container of milk or fruit down the leg of my pants and looked for the most out-of-shape officer. This officer patted my arms and my waist but could not bend all the way over to check my legs. After a while of this, they just kind of left me alone. The officers knew I wasn't a "troublemaker," and some even called me the "apple-pie guy" because they knew not only about my baking hustle (more on that later) but knew full well I had to be getting the apples from the very chow hall where they were shaking me down. Prison has that kind of "we'll punish you for breaking the rules but we also expect you to break the rules" vibe.

I always tried to get back to the cell and use the bathroom before my roommate. Not sure if it's a scientific fact, like women who live together syncing up their periods, but we all seemed to use the bathroom right after breakfast. Somehow I always seemed to end up living with someone who took forever, so it was easier for me to use the bathroom first and then go back out into the pod, taking a book and some paper and a pen to write.

When chow was finished for the whole compound, work call was announced over the loudspeaker. I worked a lot of different jobs, some that had set schedules and some that were more fluid. For example, maintenance meant they called me when they needed me, sometimes in the middle of the night. For the law library, I went in at the same time every day.

If I didn't have to work, I'd usually go outside for rec if the yard was open. I went through periods where I couldn't get a job and went outside often, supplementing that exercise with extra workouts in the pod. As I got older, the workouts hurt more, took longer to recover from, and inspired me to slow down to one workout per day.

Coming back in after rec, I either rushed to try to get in the shower (lots of fights around this limited resource) or take a birdbath in the cell's sink, accepting that I'd be smelly.

There was another count at 11 AM. Same whistle. Same voice yelling to stand. Same waiting for the guard to come by.

This is when I usually meditated. The experience was sometimes peaceful, sometimes terrible, sometimes overwhelming. But it helped me develop the habit of staying present and connected to myself.

After count I went to early chow call. That was for people going to school or work because lunch could take hours and mess up schedules. It was when I'd see guys from the other side of the yard and we'd catch up. When I was working maintenance, I'd then stand by the fence to wait for the supervisors to bring in their carts and pick guys up to complete work orders. We would head off to all corners of the compound. It was a small thrill to be able to stand on the roof and look off into the distance or get into the unsecured areas and work with tools that no one else was allowed to use.

After work, we headed to dinner. Sometimes our supervisor got us food from the staff-side dining hall. Food for staff was dramatically better than food for the population. It was also totally against the rules for him to give us anything like that. Any time we could get even something small from staff-side we celebrated the special experience.

Then it was back to the pod for another shower—this time with less rush or pressure since everyone wasn't coming back at the same time.

Then another count. Another whistle. Another time to stand and wait for them to pass.

Summer meant the rec yard might be open in the evening, while in winter months programs were the only option. At first I didn't see any reason to attend programs but over the years I got tired of having so little to do. So, I went to programs. I led programs. I taught classes. I did whatever I could for growth, novelty, or a chance to give back.

At some point in the evening they would do mail call, with a night shift officer walking around the pod and stopping at each cell door to hand out whatever letters and magazines had been delivered and processed. Even years into my sentence I was grateful to still get all the mail and support I did. A lot of guys never got any.

Then I'd lie back in my bunk, read and respond to letters, watch TV, and go to bed early after—you guessed it—another count. Going to bed early meant my roommate might leave the light on. I always asked for that. "Leave it on as long as you want," I told him. "But don't let me fall asleep with it off and then turn it on later." That would always wake me up.

The next morning, I got up and did the day again. And again. And again.

Four years at Nottaway then thirteen years at Buckingham. Almost a generation of time spent on two small plots of land doing the same thing.

In the beginning it was numbing and hopeless. I fought the insane rules and regulations, only to be beaten down by the system. Then I fought myself, feeling that I should be doing more or somehow making things better. Then I gave up. I accepted it. And by no longer wasting mental energy on *wishing* things were different, I was suddenly in a position to *make* things different.

It still got boring. It still got old. The real benefit, though, was that there were no expectations. For most of my life I had been defined and driven by what other people wanted or what they thought I was supposed to do. In prison, there was none of that. I could lie around all day if I wanted. I could self-destruct. I could achieve and work and grow. It was the first time when I felt fully free to explore. If I made mistakes and fell, I had no choice but to pick myself back up again. It was the first place I started to become who I wanted to be—and start living the life I wanted to live.

Chapter 9

No One Is Just One Thing

The night my stepmother told me who my roommate at Nottaway was, I didn't sleep. On the top bunk I tried to lie still even though my body wanted to toss and turn, or get away. The next morning, I screwed up my courage, and said, "Greg, you remember how I told you my stepmother was going to write to you? Well, she looked you up and—"

"You did your homework, huh?" He laughed. It was a terrifying laugh from this little old man I had come to see as a helpful teacher. It was the laugh that told me that what my stepmother had discovered was most likely true.

I arrived at Nottaway a little more than a year after I was arrested, after jail and then Powhatan Receiving. Nottaway was my first major prison. There I listened to the older guys who told me to get a job. It would make my time easier, make it go by faster, and give all sorts of benefits. I applied for every job possible.

I put in to be a houseman, an in-pod cleaning job that ranged from scrubbing the showers to stripping, waxing, and buffing floors. It was the most basic job with the fewest perks, but the easiest to get. I put in to work in the school and was told I wasn't eligible because I had been convicted of violent charges.

I put in for the woodshop, a factory run within the prison by a semi-private industry that sold the material to other state agencies. The woodshop job was one of the most coveted because their pay rate was almost double all other jobs that paid from $0.27 to $0.45 an hour. That's why I was surprised when they called me for an interview and even more surprised when they told me I had gotten the job. I was too much of a risk to tutor people at the school but was trusted with sharp objects and power tools.

I found out when an officer came to my door and told me to pack up. Reading off a sheet of paper, he told me I was moving to Upper N, which was the woodshop worker pod. I loaded my meager belongings into a laundry cart with a wheel that wouldn't run straight and followed the officer down the long boulevard to the opposite side of the compound. I loaded the cart into the elevator then ran up the steps since incarcerated people weren't allowed to ride elevators (though later my fellow maintenance workers regularly broke that rule). When I rolled into Upper N, I was struck by how different it was. The last pod had been loud and dirty and full of people lounging around. This one was pristine, quiet, and nearly empty. The last pod had never been quiet.

Some of the cell doors were open. They were a lot more lax here about cell break, which I was used to happening for only a few minutes every hour on the hour. The cell I was going to was one of the few that was closed. The officer escorting me spoke to the officer in the booth and the door popped. I saw a little old man in the center of the cell, facing the wall locker. His legs were crossed. He had a cigarette in one hand and a cup of coffee in the other. He was watching the five-inch TV in front of him. As I rolled the cart up to the cell, he stood up, came to the door, and shook my hand. It didn't feel like a prison handshake, more like one I'd get at a business meeting.

Greg Barker was a highly decorated US Army officer who had served multiple tours in Vietnam. An educated man, he had lots of varied life experiences and was reserved but had a great laugh when it came out. He grew to be an avuncular figure in my life. Actually he taught me the word "avuncular."

He also taught me to shave. (I hadn't yet been able to grow a beard when I was arrested.) He helped me with schoolwork and gave me daily word lists and reading assignments to improve my vocabulary. He was, in many ways, the first mentor and father figure I found in prison.

But my stepmother later told me was that I was locked in a cell—daily—with a man who was not only in prison for a particularly gruesome murder but who had also been investigated for a dozen more and had been labeled a serial killer. Additionally, she told me that he had come up with a fabulous defense that it was all a CIA coverup because of what he had discovered while working for a CIA front company after Vietnam. I had been learning lessons from a madman.

Despite the shock of this and the lack of sleep that first night after my stepmother told me, over time I began to feel comfortable with him again. I never forgot what he was capable of but I also recognized that no one is just one thing.

Realizing that compelled me to help Greg when no one else would. Greg was getting older and, among other things, had an inguinal hernia that was getting worse. The medical department wouldn't give him a hernia belt or even let him buy one. They admitted that there was a risk of the hernia strangulating, which would endanger his life, but they didn't deem it worthy of attention.

My relationship with my mother was complicated, but I always knew that when I called about an issue, she took action. As soon as she heard about Greg's situation, she grew angry that they were mistreating the person I lived with. She wrote to Nottaway's medical department in her capacity as a lawyer. She also mailed in a hernia belt that she had purchased with her own money. Essentially she told the prison officials: I represent Mr. Barker and if anything happens to him after I have provided a hernia belt free of charge, you will be liable.

It was totally against policy, but that day they called Greg to medical and gave him the hernia belt, along with an official note in his file that it was an approved device. My mother had again shown up in her best capacity. She had made it possible for me to help someone.

Again, no one is just one thing.

Chapter 10

Unexpected Teachers

Greg wasn't my only unexpected teacher in prison.

Not long after he was transferred, I got into a fight over something stupid. Someone owed me money. He didn't pay me. I said something to someone about it. The person I said something to owed money to the guy who owed me and wanted to stir stuff up, hoping we would both be sent to the hole. Just normal prison drama.

The guy who owed me money felt like I had been threatening him through other people, so he ran into my cell, and we started swinging. After a few punches and a poor double-leg wrestling takedown attempt, the booth officer spotted us. The other guy was out of the cell by the time the response team arrived, and I couldn't go anywhere because it was my cell. They locked me up "under investigation," because I wouldn't admit that I had been fighting or tell them who I had been fighting with. The watch commander questioning me yelled and told them to put me in the hole. He told me I was going to regret it, which meant no property for four days. No toothpaste, no soap, nothing to do. Finally, someone at least gave me sheets, a washcloth, and some state soap.

Prison rules said that if you are convicted of a charge, the review committee could take your job. Because I was under investigation (it was later dropped and I was released), I was told that they were taking my job because I wasn't available to work. However, I had a medical pass—I had previously hurt my back—and they couldn't fire me while I was under investigation if I had a medical reason for not being able to work.

So when I was released, I was about to head back to work in the woodshop but discovered that my state boots were missing. All my property in the cell had been packed up after I went into the hole, but not my boots for some reason. The woodshop required that we wear state boots for safety, so I went to the laundry and asked for another pair. They wouldn't give me any. I handed them the property slip that showed that my boots hadn't been packed up. They didn't care. I couldn't get boots so I couldn't go back to work. At that point I just gave up.

When I was released from the hole, I was moved into Lower C. It wasn't a work pod like Upper N, so guys there had a lot less money and a lot more problems. I got to know people—I talked with my roommate and met some guys to work out with. Then I met Karl. He had frizzled hair and an odd, thoughtful demeanor. He had taught Shakespeare in prison GED classes because he wanted people to know that learning was about the human experience. His students almost always started off scoffing at the idea of Shakespeare but within a few weeks they were arguing about the role of Polonius in *Hamlet* or talking about Macbeth on the rec yard. Karl was quirky, complicated, and funny. He had done great harm and was capable of doing great good. He was flawed just like everyone else, except probably smarter and more honest than most.

We first crossed paths in the pod, exchanging just a few words only because he lived with one of the guys I worked out with. Eventually, we were sitting on the stairs leading up to the lieutenant's office, both waiting to interview for a houseman job. That in itself was a ridiculous process: "Can you sweep? Yeah? Okay, you have the job."

We talked, and Karl noted, "I see you doing your thing. You read, study, exercise, and go back in your cell. Education is great. I studied for a long time. I learned a lot—I damn near have a PhD. One day, though, you'll realize that life is about people and that none of us can live on an island."

It was the first time we had talked at length, and I was surprised by the depth of his observations and his perspective. I didn't know how to respond. He was pointing out what I had been feeling, almost like he was looking into my soul—I had focused on growing and learning over my first years inside and felt isolated. I didn't have great social skills and I didn't know how to connect with people in the way it sounded like he was talking about.

Over the next year and a half, Karl became my regular sounding board, even when he was moved "across the yard"—to the other side of the prison—and we could only see each other during rec time. We skipped our workouts, stood at the fence to talk, gave each other "homework" assignments, and generally helped push one another forward. Once, he assigned me to write an essay on what freedom meant. It was the first writing I did in prison that made me feel proud to reread.

One of the most memorable days from my time in prison was the second Christmas I was at Nottaway. Karl and I both elected to go outside despite the holiday and the weather. It was sleeting and windy and we were the only two people on the rec yard. As we talked and laughed, the sleet started seeping into our prison-issued cloth jackets. We grew colder, until our teeth started chattering. It was a two-hour rec period and they were supposed to let us in for a gate break at the hour midpoint, but since we were the only people out in the yard they didn't bother. Shivering, we grew silent and miserable. Finally, after sustained silence, Karl said something, poking fun at the insanity of what we were doing. Standing outside, freezing, when we could be inside drinking coffee. It broke the spell—we were still cold, but we no longer cared. We started laughing. It hit me then: I was happy. Happy to be there despite the freezing cold, or maybe because of it. I felt connected to a friend, and I felt alive.

At some point, Karl got transferred and paroled out. Just like that, my friend and teacher was gone. We lost touch. Communication after release almost never lasts.

I didn't find my next teacher until I had been incarcerated for seven years, a year after I was transferred down a security level to Buckingham Correctional Center. The universe had at the ready an assembly line of mentors for me to come across—with just enough time in between to start applying the lessons in my life that each had imparted.

My first mentor had been the alleged serial killer, and the next had been a teacher with a penchant for Shakespeare. I didn't know what to expect next. It definitely wasn't Ricky.

I was at Buckingham, settling in and acting as a pod tutor when I ran into someone with an untreated mental health issue. Actually, he attacked me, screaming, "He's looking in my mirror!" while I was getting hot water for coffee. Ever since this guy had moved into the pod a few weeks before, he had been vacillating between talking to himself in a corner of the pod and aggressively confronting people for imagined offenses. I happened to be the one he targeted on a bad day.

His first punch, clean and unexpected from the side, put me on the ground. I was not primed for a fight so part of me was still confused and trying to figure out what was going on. Plus, it was hard to fight from my back with him standing over me raining blows and just as hard to get up without getting kicked in the face or catching a clean overhand punch. Eventually, I managed to get to my feet and throw a feeble groin kick. By the time I was in a position to really fight back the officer blew the horn and the response team came rushing in the door.

We both went to the hole, and after my hearing, where I was found not guilty of fighting, I was released to the pod across the hall from where I had been, in a cell with Ricky.

Ricky was an awkward, lanky kid, several years younger than I was, with a lazy eye and a loose smile. He had bad stick-poke tattoos and was one of the wisest people I had run across.

He smiled and laughed a lot. He had a bizarre family story. He told me about his dad being a wild biker, doing drugs and crazy things while his mom stayed at home and pretended none of it was happening. His dad also taught him martial arts and meditation.

During the day, Ricky was always reading, meditating, or sleeping. Then, one night I woke up to see him pivoting and punching and kicking with a Zen-like intensity and focus. He had been staying up most nights to be alone and practice in peace.

The next day, I asked him about his nighttime practice, and he confirmed what he had been doing but was hesitant to say more. I never understood whether he was genuinely shy talking about it, or if he was trying to make his practice seem even more mystical. Eventually I wore him down and he started to teach me some of what he knew. By this point I had added boxing to my experiences with karate and wrestling, but every time we played, this little 130-pound kid could tie me up like a pretzel and hit me with twenty punches before I could get off one.

I trained with him. First a style that resembled karate, but more smooth-flowing, then Wing Chun, a "soft" style made famous to Americans by Bruce Lee in the '60s and '70s. Then I started meditating with him. Then reading the books he suggested. That small cell in C3 pod at Buckingham Correctional started to feel like an incubation chamber, where I was becoming something new, or something more.

Martial arts drew me in. I had always been fascinated and even more so after being attacked across the hall. It was hard to be on high alert all the time and for me to flip that switch from trying to de-escalate to just hurting someone or putting them down. More training meant more ability and more confidence.

But it was the meditation that changed my life. After Ricky got me started, I meditated every day until I got out of prison. I had always been an anxiously reactive person. I was always trying to predict other people's thoughts and actions, to conform to what I thought they wanted or needed. I was like an echo to everyone and everything around me.

With meditation, I watched myself slowly become a different person—a person with the space to feel my feelings and hear my thoughts without immediately reacting to them. I credit meditation with fundamentally changing who I am as a person.

Then Ricky went home. He had had a relatively short sentence. I was happy for him, but I worried. I was losing a good friend and a teacher. I felt selfish and flawed because I didn't want him to leave. I was afraid I wouldn't continue to grow without a teacher to push me forward.

I heard from Ricky after he got out, when he signed a birthday card that a mutual friend sent me. He signed it with a drawing of a phallus. Drawing phalluses was surprisingly common inside, sometimes written as "pen 15" instead of an image. I haven't heard from him since, like most people I met in prison.

I used the phallus drawing idea years later. When I was working in the law library, we workers would send out case law and request forms using the institutional mail system. That meant I could fill a manila envelope with whatever I wanted and have an officer deliver it to anyone on the compound. On occasion I drew a phallus on a blank sheet of paper and had it sent to someone I knew. Then at mail call, I watched that person receive it, open it up, stare at it in confusion, and then inevitably laugh out loud. That always made me smile. I never said I was particularly mature, especially in prison.

Chapter 11

Seeing Things as They Are

"Come on, Crosson," the officer said, banging the door open and waking me up. Unexpectedly, he walked right through the doorway into my cell.

Startled, I sat up in bed, tense, glaring at him then behind him, trying to figure out what was happening. Standard procedure in the hole was that the officers tapped on the door, and I had to stand with my back to the tray slot with arms held behind me. The officers would reach through the tray slot to lock the handcuffs around my wrists. Only then did the officers open the door and walk me to the bed to put on the leg irons and escort me out of the cell.

This time the officer just walked through the doorway holding the shackles. He didn't give an explanation.

Standard procedure in the hole was never broken, even when the infraction was trivial—in my case, possession of contraband pancake syrup. Anything that's allowable in the chow hall becomes contraband the moment it passes out the chow hall door. Syrup is of special concern because it can be used to make wine (as well as tasty cakes and desserts).

But I just figured I had a visitor. Before I went to sleep I had just gotten news that my father made it through surgery without complication. I wondered who would be sitting on the other side of the glass, yelling through the small holes in the grate to talk to me. Maybe my father, who had somehow miraculously recovered from the procedure in Costa Rica in time to get back to the United States to see me. How long had I been asleep?

After chaining me up, the CO walked me down the stairs and out the back door. Wearing my orange jumpsuit and jingling with every step, I did the slow prisoner shuffle down the long, empty boulevard toward the front of the prison. I automatically headed to the special housing visitation room. But the officer escorting me turned away from the visiting room. As we walked past the door of medical, the prison psychologist stepped out to say, "Bring him to me when you're done."

He walked me to the main entrance for the prison, past the painted sign that read, "No inmates beyond this point," and through the heavy mechanical door to a small sally port, where I saw my mother and stepfather.

"Is it my dad?" I asked.

My mother nodded, and I started to tear up. Intellectually I understood that my father had died, but I didn't really feel it. I didn't really understand that I would never see him again. I did what I always did when things got hard—I dissociated. I was there but I wasn't there. Like operating on autopilot.

Up to that point, I had spent my life chasing my father, trying to get approval or attention that I didn't realize I needed. He was bigger than life and sometimes that made me feel comforted. Other times it made me feel small. When I was a young kid, I didn't remember him being around—he was working and going to grad school at night. My mother was the one who kept things moving. She was always running errands and doing chores while he got to be the fun dad and take me to play T-ball and explore on the weekends. Then when I was seven, he left us. I thought it was because of something my mother had done, and I blamed her. I felt abandoned and angry. I didn't know how to put all that into words back then so I shut down. I felt ashamed of my feelings. I didn't think I was allowed to feel that way. That was the first time he left.

My father always straddled two worlds. As a long-haired hippie dad, he told me bedtime stories. Half were about my stuffed animals: The stories would always start with my climbing the tree behind our house. I would go up and up and up. Eventually I would climb through the clouds and walk out onto a cloud meadow where all the stuffed animals lived with a river and a bridge over it. It was my safe space as a kid. The other half of the stories were about riots he had led, crimes he had committed, and the five tons of marijuana he had been caught with but never gotten any significant time for. Even before he got clean, my father went from landscaping to counseling to help people in recovery. I heard later that he led group sessions only to sneak out and shoot cocaine in the bathroom. Did the next session's attendees ever notice a little extra zeal, I wondered? How did those who were inspired by him react as he slowly slipped back into the swamp of craving?

He finally got sober when I was two. It wasn't easy. My father had tried again and again to stop but never made it long. During a period of separation from me and my mom, he went to the remote shack he was living in, stuck a shotgun in his mouth, trembling, and couldn't bring himself to pull the trigger. He was too afraid to die so he had no choice but to live.

Once sober he quickly took on the role of a twelve-step figurehead. He sponsored countless guys locally and was tapped to speak around the state, around the country, and eventually around the world.

He left my mother and went straight into a relationship with the woman he had been having an affair with, the woman who would become my stepmother. She was a much younger, attractive woman from a more traditional, religious Southern family. My father was capable of being a bit sanctimonious.

Split between two homes, I tried to think positively (two Christmases!). But in the background, tensions were brewing. Even though I had never gotten high, I got caught with weed in middle school, and he took me with him to twelve-step meetings—to keep an eye on me. Then, after the very first time I experimented with alcohol and drugs, he kicked me out. Immediately. I got the message loud and clear. His principles came first. They were more important than everything, including his relationship with me. That was the second time he left me.

We continued to see each other occasionally at planned visits, but the damage had been done. We only really reconnected when I called him after my arrest. Then I lost him for a third time.

Shortly after I got to prison, he asked if I would be okay if he moved to Costa Rica. I was less than two years into a thirty-two-year prison sentence. We had just reconnected, and I couldn't imagine my father being thousands of miles away. I felt so much shame about the harm I had put him through that I couldn't ask him not to move just to make me feel better. He promised that he would come back and visit. (He did, a few times.) That we would play chess by mail. (We never did.) My relationship with my stepmother improved as my relationship with him withered away. She worked half of each month as a nurse practitioner in the US and would visit me before heading back. She became my main point of contact.

We couldn't use the normal phone system since he was out of the country. They allowed us one call per quarter from the counselor's office. I looked forward to and enjoyed the calls but couldn't shake the feeling that I had lost my father again. I couldn't explain how, but I felt it.

Two years after he moved to Costa Rica, while I was in the hole for contraband syrup, this was the news I heard: My father had wandered down to the river by his house and collapsed. Someone found him, shirtless and without shoes, lying in the muddy grass. Sierpe, Costa Rica, is rural and at the time lacked medical facilities—other than my stepmother offering services as a nurse practitioner at a small local clinic. He was airlifted to San Jose, where doctors discovered a blood clot, which was treated. Upon further testing, the doctors informed him that he had a faulty heart valve. He was otherwise in very good health so they suggested getting a replacement—a pig valve because it would last longer than a mechanical valve. They suggested this because they anticipated that he would live for a very long time.

After I got the news, officers in the hole were gracious and allowed me extra phone calls during the day (we were normally only allowed a few phone calls per month, and only at night). While everyone assured me that my father would be fine and the surgery was standard procedure, I knew he wasn't going to make it. Even with the extra calls, I was mostly alone in that cell, trapped with my thoughts, fears, and certainty that the surgery was going to go badly. Add to that the shame of not being able to be there with him—and now being in the hole for some fucking pancake syrup.

Finally, the amazing operations manager at the prison set up a phone call with my father the day before his surgery. An officer brought me over to the admin building, decked out in my orange jumpsuit and shackles, then the operations manager instructed the escorting officer to remove my shackles, which was totally against policy. She told the officer she had it from there and marched me back to her office, where I plopped down in the chair next to her desk. She dialed the collect number that connected me to my father in his hospital room.

On the other end of the connection, I didn't hear the voice of my father. I didn't hear the man I had idolized. Instead, I heard the frail voice of a scared man. I heard someone panicked and uncertain, in no way like the person I knew and remembered. The phone call didn't make me feel better—I grew even more sure that he wouldn't make through the surgery the next day. I thanked the operations manager. She had allowed me to have what I was sure would be the last conversation I would ever have with my father. That meant the world. I walked back to the front of the admin building, getting strange looks because I was decked out in an orange jumpsuit but unescorted and without shackles. There the officer cuffed me back up to take me back to the hole. Then I shuffled back down the boulevard to my cell.

I didn't sleep. All night I had visions of my father and his different stories. Rebelling as a teen against his drill instructor father by acting up, dressing in black like Johnny Cash, and becoming a gangster (albeit a sort of hippie gangster). Then rebelling by joining the Air Force and getting kicked out (somehow wrangling an honorable discharge) and going to college. Rebelling by protesting the Vietnam war through both peaceful methods and "by any means necessary." The rebellious fire with which he moved to Costa Rica—convinced that he could change the land, its people, and its economy. He hired local workers to help around the property or to take on some random quixotic project, and he always insisted on paying them twice the going rate. He then cashed out his retirement, bought a farm, and operated it like a commune intending to provide free training and support for future farmers. But that night I kept coming back to the image of my father in a hospital room, on the operating table with his chest ripped wide open, again and again.

I was still awake until the next morning when someone knocked on the cell door. The psychologist was there. "Your dad is fine," she said. "He made it through surgery." She had wanted to make sure I knew.

I had been so sure he wouldn't make it. I felt almost guilty, as if I had created something negative. Finally, I slept. That's when the CO had jolted me awake, walking into my cell with handcuffs and leg irons. That's when the COs walked me to my mother so she could tell me that my father was dead.

I don't know how long I sat with my mother and stepfather in the sally port. I couldn't really tell time in the numbness that had washed over me. The guards let me give my mother and stepfather a hug made awkward by the handcuffs and shackles, then I waddled away from the room where they let us meet. The officers took me into medical, where the psychologist was waiting.

"What do you need, Jesse?" she asked. "Do you want to stay in the hole, or do you want to get out?" I had already been "released" by classification but actually getting moved back to population could take days or weeks.

"I want out."

"Where do you want to go?"

This was not a question they ever asked. Nottaway prided itself on not giving people the power to choose where they lived or who they lived with. I think the psychologist felt guilty. She had told me that my father was fine. She was right. He had emerged from surgery without complication the evening before. Then he went to sleep and never woke up.

"I want to go to the nonsmoking pod."

She immediately picked up the phone to call the records department. She didn't ask them to move me to A3—she *told* them. I had never heard her take this tone and it was clear the person on the other end hadn't either.

They slow-marched me back to the hole. Once the shackles were off, I grabbed my few things and stuck them in the laundry bag I had been allowed. It would be a few minutes or hours before the move happened, so I took out the few pictures I had of my father.

There he was, alive, smiling, working hard. Yet, he wasn't anymore. I would never see him smile again. I would never hear his voice or feel his hug. I would never be able to show him how sorry I was. I would never be able to address the anger and sadness I felt about the times he had left.

I tried to cry. I thought crying would make it better. But no tears came. Instead an officer opened the door and told me to take my bags upstairs to A3.

My father's memorial service filled up the auditorium of the local community college. One of our shared friends quieted the room and brought on a lot of tears by singing "Amazing Grace." Other people spoke about the impact my father had on their lives, or on the lives of their loved ones. Few people talked about the complicated stuff.

Not that I was there. I only know about the service secondhand, because I wasn't able to go. There is a system for approvals for bereavement furloughs, but I didn't qualify. In any case, if I had qualified, I would have had to pay the salary for two officers and the gas for transport to take me to the service for an hour before others arrived. I wouldn't be able to hug anyone or shake hands. I would have been able to sit with family, but I would have had to leave before the actual service began.

It was a year and a half before I could really grieve.

It was right after I was transferred to Buckingham. After four years at Nottaway, I had stayed out of trouble and lowered my security level. That same psychologist who checked on me after my father's death and who made sure I got moved called me over to say goodbye. She told me she was proud of all the work I was doing and how far I had come. That felt good to hear.

I went through the whole transfer process, packing my stuff, selling or gifting what I couldn't take with me, getting handcuffed and shackled, riding the bus, then finding myself in front of property officers at Buckingham. Nottaway property had been lax across the board, not just in giving me a pack of cigarettes and giving my roommate a pair of headphones. I was surprised when the Buckingham property officers started throwing away things that were on the border of contraband (and generally permitted). However, I didn't think too much about it. These were easy to replace.

Then they started sorting my photographs, making two nearly equal piles. The officer pointed to one pile. "Crosson, we're going to have to take a lot of your pictures." Nearly every photo in that pile was of my father.

One of the few pictures of my father to survive the prison transfer.

One photo was of him in Costa Rica smiling next to a crocodile. Another, him holding woodworking tools in his workshop. In another he was on his way into town. In every photo, he wasn't wearing a shirt. Once he had moved to Costa Rica, he had basically taken off his shirt and shoes for good.

"These are all semi-nude. You know better than that, Crosson."

The officer was telling me that the last pictures I had of my father, the last connection I had with him, were going to be taken because they were considered pornography. I couldn't fucking believe it. They had never enforced the rule even close to that way at Nottaway.

I tried to keep my cool and ask how she thought this was fair. From the other side of the table, with a metal screen between us, she tsked and said, "Policy is policy. You know that." I felt the anger start to build. I started to shake in rage. I locked eyes with the second officer, who looked away quickly. But when the officer sorting the photos turned away, the second officer reached into the discard pile and swept a few of the pictures into the "approved" pile.

"Sorry, bro," he whispered.

I didn't stop shaking until I got to the cell they had assigned me. My new roommate had come on the bus with me, and I told him I needed to use the bathroom. The doors at this prison could be manually opened and shut, so it wasn't a big deal for him to step out. I hung a sheet over the slot in the door for privacy. I sat on the toilet, and I cried.

It started small at first. Then the tears grew bigger. Then I was shaking and sobbing and angry and crying. I hated myself so much. I had thrown my life away. I had lost my father. I would never see him again, and I hadn't even been able to go to his funeral. Now I didn't have the pictures from the last years of his life. I finally felt it all.

I was never religious, but I have read religious books over the course of my life, seeking understanding and a perspective that made sense to me. That's why Ecclesiastes has always been my favorite book of the Bible.

I spent my life seeking a place in the world. I was seeking acceptance, rescue, and redemption. I was seeking a system that made sense, a system that was fair and just. Rather than grand promises, Ecclesiastes talks about the meaninglessness, about how sometimes life just isn't fair and doesn't seem to make a lot of sense.

I had a friend in prison who always read the obituaries. He said it was his way of "winning," because the people in the obits had bought houses, had families, and lived full lives while he had been in and out of prison—but *they* were dead and *he* was alive. It wasn't the healthiest habit but I liked the guy, and I always listened when he came over to share.

One day he walked over to me with a huge grin. He was waving something he had cut out of a newspaper. He showed it to me, ecstatic at what he called the first-ever honest obituary. It read something like, "Bill was a real son-of-a-bitch. No one liked him. He won't be missed. He leaves a lot of broken things behind. He was funny at times, though." The obit wasn't all "roses and rainbows," as this guy called it. The obit was "a real take" on who the deceased person had been.

A lot of things clicked for me then. Thinking about all those glowing accounts about my father from his memorial service—I realized that my father never got a "real take," outside of my own reckoning. Yet, his complicated nature is part of why I loved him and part of what has helped me better understand myself.

I always craved his approval. I always wanted to be like him. Yet I never understood that his greatest desire was for me to be better than he was. I had been trying to live up to his expectations—or rebelling against them. Now that I understood in my heart and in my bones that he was gone, I realized I was the only one responsible for the direction of my life. I had to make my own decisions and bear the consequences of them.

Deep down, at its core, this book is a letter to him, for all the ways he didn't see me, all the ways I want to show him who I was and who I am now. I want him to see me putting in the work, day after day, to be a little bit better.

Chapter 12

What Violence Taught Me

The first time I saw bloodshed in jail, I felt pain, wanting to do something, anything to stop what was happening. That impulse got me into trouble more than once, usually because I tried to intervene, as if I felt responsible. Over time I learned to numb myself, to look through violence or walk by it—essentially walling off my human sensitivity. Prison was slowly making me less and less myself, less and less who I wanted to be. I had to make a choice.

Some of the most frequent questions I get on social media about prison are about fights, stabbings, and other violence inside. I understand that people are curious and that it's human behavior to feel drawn to the extreme. I don't like feeding that part of our experience, though. I don't like to tell war stories. I especially don't like to glorify violence or the people who unleash it. However, it's an important part of my story and, oddly, an important part of my life. Sometimes we just have to tell the story, as long as we make sure not to add something that didn't actually happen or take away something that did.

In jail, people got into little scraps—a black eye or a busted nose. In prison people got into small "respect" fights—not all out, just guys settling a dispute. Then there was the scary violence, often with multiple attackers and weapons.

Some were a combination: dumb fights over nothing that escalated. Joe and another guy were fighting over something stupid that one of them had said. The other guy didn't like how badly Joe was beating him, so he grabbed him, pulled him in close, and bit Joe's nose, ripping one side off his face as if he was tearing off a piece of steak with his teeth. After the fight, but before they were caught, someone managed to bend a sewing needle and sew Joe's nose back onto his face. The prison nurses were impressed, and said they wouldn't have been able to do better. That was a Wednesday.

In the nonsmoking pod, two guys had an argument. One guy thought it was over, went back to his cell and lay down. The other guy nursed his anger. He waited until the doors opened again, went into the cell with a lock in a sock, and beat the guy's face until he was almost unrecognizable. He then walked out, threw the lock in the trash can, and read a book in the pod like nothing had happened

A few minutes later, the bloody-faced guy came out of his cell holding a pencil and a belt with a metal tip at the end. He advanced on his attacker, swinging that belt and holding the pencil like a knife. The other guy picked his chair up and used it to ward him off as if he were a lion tamer. Before long they were slipping because there was so much blood on the floor it looked like they were fighting in gallons of red paint.

The booth officer called a 1033, which is radio code for a fight. Officers ran in, holding cans of Mace before them, and split the two up. No one wanted to touch the guy whose face was bashed in—he was still leaking blood like a fountain. They walked him out the door and someone put him in cuffs. They locked the pod down, sending us all to our cells and shutting the doors.

The property of the two guys was packed into plastic bags and set out in the hallway, where there were no cameras and no one watching the bags. And so of course someone from the pod across the hall rifled through the bags and stole a TV. The housemen in our unit cleaned up the blood and then they opened the doors and called us to chow. That was a Thursday.

There were also gang fights or gang disputes. Like the time Yella told on someone. His gang told him not to come out of the hole. He came out anyway. They waited for him to sit down alone at chow.

South, the set leader, walked around the railing and punched him in the face while one of the younger guys reached over the railing and stabbed him in the back repeatedly, puncturing his lung. The leader then kept swinging until Yella was a mess on the floor.

The officers thought it was just a fight so grabbed Yella and South, put them in cuffs and dragged them out of the chow hall. They rushed everyone out, including the guy who had time to drop his knife in the tray slot and slide out. It wasn't until Yella collapsed on the boulevard that they noticed the blood bubbling out of his back and called an ambulance. That was a Friday.

There were incidents that highlighted just how different my life could have been. Like when Happy had arrived at the first prison where we both landed. We were about the same age, had similar charges, and both had thirty-plus-year sentences. The difference was that I had people encouraging me to get an education, exercise, read, and better myself while he had people warning him that he had better make an example out of someone—that he had too much time to let anyone think he was soft.

It was the classic mentality: be predator or be prey. It wasn't necessary but he believed it was. So, while I was working and studying and growing, Happy stabbed a guy over something he wasn't even involved in. He used a friend arguing with someone as an excuse to make a name for himself. He let that place define him. He caused more harm, and now he might never go home.

To be clear, I wasn't always just witness to violence. At times I was the victim, a willing participant, or the perpetrator. With the exception of the following story, I never started a fight but I was in quite a few that I could have (and should have) walked away from. Jules was a ranking gang member in my pod. He also regularly lied and scammed people out of things, using his weight as leader so he didn't have to face consequences. I'm not really sure how he rose to his position because he didn't have much in the way of leadership qualities.

He and I had words, very publicly, over a disagreement involving a magazine he wanted to borrow. The last thing he said, loudly, was, "I'll take all your shit." The next day I came in from rec and found my cell tossed. The locked locker was untouched but almost everything else was gone. Most of it had belonged to my roommate but it didn't matter. This was a major violation.

As I looked at my ransacked cell, I grew both scared and angry. I quickly consulted with a few guys, telling them what had happened. One of them quietly left and came back with something up his sleeve.

"You need steel?" he asked, offering me an icepick wrapped in a sheet.

I understood the logic. I was about to fight a gang member, which meant I was probably going to get jumped. If I stabbed him up badly enough maybe I could keep them at bay, or if they did come after me at least I'd have a weapon to hold my own.

"No, I'm good," I said. Even if I got jumped, I didn't want to be responsible for maiming or killing anyone. I had come close enough before. I would roll the dice and see what happened.

An hour or so later Jules and his crew came back from school. I had to wait until he was alone. He got a parlay gambling ticket and went to fill it out, bent over the trash can. This was my chance.

I ran up behind him and with a big ridiculous yell, jump-kicked him in the ass. My hope was to drive his head into the wall and knock him unconscious.

It didn't work.

Instead, he bounced off the wall, turned around, looking bewildered. Then he saw me and got his face screwed up in anger. We started throwing punches. We grabbed each other and fell to the ground. I ended up with a bit of his hair in my teeth, and he ended up scratching me with his nails. It was a pretty pitiful fight.

At one point I looked up and saw his whole crew coming. I flinched, hoping I'd be able to roll Jules over on top of me so they would kick him (or maybe not kick me so hard). Being on the ground with a group jumping you is about the worst place to be.

Out of nowhere, Mookie stepped in. I didn't really know the guy, other than he was a giant of a human being and that he "played fair" with everyone. He didn't stand for bullying or people claiming phones or showers. He would always step in to fight for the smaller person getting picked on.

In this case, he singlehandedly stopped an entire gang set from stomping me. Then it was only another moment before the officer in the booth opened the front door and other officers started rushing in.

But Jules and I had already stopped fighting and made it to opposite sides of the pod. The COs looked around to see who had been rumbling. I was sweating and breathing heavily so they picked me. Somehow, they also picked Jules and took us out to the watch commander's office.

My saving grace was that before we made it out of the pod door, Jules started yelling: "It wasn't me. He attacked me. I didn't do shit!"

With handcuffs on I looked over and saw the shock on the faces of his set. He had told on me in front of everyone. Ranking gang member, holder of the code, and he had violated publicly. Even so, we both got sent to the hole, charged with fighting.

For him, it got worse. He was the bank. He was supposed to hold all of the set's money. They would give their guys supplies when they needed it, do deals together, and disperse profits. Except that he had dipped into the bank, spending almost all of it on his own gambling and drugs.

Once the money came up missing, his homies sent word to him that if he came out of the hole they would kill him. I didn't know this yet, though. I found out from one of his homies who was in the hole with me. At first I expected retribution. But after a day or two of seeing him at rec, he whispered through the fence: "You lucky. If he hadn't done that shit we would have had to get you. Fuck that dude, but he was one of us."

Now here's the worst part: Jules hadn't stolen from me like I thought. It was my neighbor and another guy. They had seen me having words with Jules and came up with a plot. My roommate had a lot of money and was constantly in debt. They figured they could go take all of his stuff and blame Jules. They thought we'd be too scared to do anything so they would just get away with it.

Well, I did something and they got away with it anyway.

It made me all the more thankful that I hadn't been willing to pick up a piece of steel. I saw too many people do it out of fear or because they believed they had to. I was young and didn't know what courage was. I should have walked away from the robbery. I should have run away before the shooting. Sometimes courage is putting down our egos and being willing to go the other direction.

Of all the violence I witnessed, though, there is one event that even still sticks out. It was a watershed moment. It happened on the rec yard at Buckingham Correctional Center. I had been in for about five years at that point, and I didn't like what I was allowing prison to shape me into.

We were lifting weights when someone nudged me to turn around. Two guys were jumping someone. They had knocked him unconscious and were taking turns stomping on his face. It wasn't a fast stomp then run—they were taking their time. His head was no longer shaped like a head. I was pretty sure they were going to kill him.

My role, according to prison lore, was not to look too closely, not draw attention to what they were doing. To make morbid jokes and go about my day because it wasn't my business.

But this time, something inside of me snapped. I wish I could say that I went and stopped them or somehow saved this guy, but I didn't. What I understood, though, was that if I let this place and the rules of this place define me, I would become someone I couldn't live with. I may have had to limit my reactions and the steps I took while I was there, but I would never internalize those rules. I would never allow prison to shape who I was as a person. I saw far too many people lose themselves to that trap.

I realized I had a choice. I could either be a thermometer or a thermostat. I could be defined by the temperature around me or I could choose to set the temperature. After that I was a lot more likely to intervene, especially when it was possible to de-escalate things. I began to understand that most of the time neither person in the conflict actually wanted violence. They just didn't want to lose face in front of the crowd. It was easy to give people an out and almost every time they would take it.

Violence is a reality. We can't deny it or wish it away. In reflecting on my history and my trauma, I realized that I needed to find a way to make friends with violence, to take away the emotion and make it a tool I could use when absolutely necessary. I didn't want prison to define me but I wasn't going to stand by and let someone hurt me either.

One of the things I was most proud of during my time was participating and teaching in a fight club training program. It was totally against the rules and we all could have gone to the hole or been punished with a loss of good time. It was also one of the most significant and positive things I ever did. Funny how training violence can actually lead to greater nonviolence.

A small group of us loved martial arts. We all wanted to learn and push ourselves. So, we started to share our knowledge.

I had practiced karate and wrestled, boxed, and trained with my roommate Ricky. Other guys had boxed or gone to MMA gyms before getting locked up. We started slowly but worked our way into training several times a week and let other guys come around. There were strict requirements, though. You had to be willing to push yourself—the "coach" would take guys through a grueling workout and if they quit, they couldn't come around. You had to stay out of drama and you had to leave your politics at the door. You had to put down your ego and work for the group.

Before long we had an odd collection of people with all varieties of crimes and life experiences. We trained together and even put on matches, with cornermen to throw in the towel if it got too bad. People thought it was all about that fight and whether someone won or lost. That couldn't be further from the truth. One guy always beat me boxing and I remember when I landed my first-ever clean hook on his jaw—it was worth all the beatings. It wasn't about winning. It was about growing and improving. It was about the countless hours of grinding and training. It was about the camaraderie: We ended every training session by taking a knee in a circle and "building." We talked about what we were dealing with or where we were struggling. We would each lift up someone else in the group, talking about where we saw improvement or where they needed to be held accountable. We had some of the most honest and vulnerable conversations covered in sweat, and sometimes blood, kneeling together on the rec yard.

I learned some lessons from this: First, it is vital to push outside my comfort zone and learn something difficult because that learning transfers across experiences and disciplines. Second, those who share difficult challenges with me will become connected to me in a way that other relationships cannot match.

It also helped me accept that there are things in life we can't escape. Sure, we can try to minimize contact with those things, and we can try to build a bubble around ourselves. But violence is a reality in this world. If we don't develop a relationship with it, we will be controlled by it. Jordan Peterson is a polarizing figure, but he has a quote that sticks with me: "A harmless man is not a good man. A good man is a very dangerous man who has that under voluntary control."

In the past, I was traumatized by seeing violence in action or I was consumed by the unaddressed violence within myself. It paralyzed me or I lashed out at others. It was only after I developed a relationship with violence that I was able to begin to find and maintain peace in myself and in the world.

Chapter 13

Making Lemonade

"Crosson, Masters, Woodson—y'all are all on work duty tonight."
    We three looked at each other, unsure what this meant. We had been called for off-hours projects before but that could mean 6 PM, midnight, or 3 AM.

"The walkway to A/B buildings needs to be re-poured. Supervisor Banker is going to bring in a concrete saw and some sledges. Y'all are going to bust out that section overnight. Try not to have too much fun."

Being volun-told to bust concrete overnight when I would have much rather been sleeping wasn't the best news that week but it also wasn't the worst. Almost every job description included the line "other duties as assigned," which pretty much meant we could be called to do anything at any time—and refusing could mean losing our jobs.

I had finally managed to work my way into a maintenance job about twelve years into my prison sentence, and it was pretty sweet, at least as far as prison jobs went. Our hours were flexible, we got to use tools that no one else was allowed to, we got to go places no one else could go, we learned meaningful skills, and we spent time with our supervisors, who treated us as actual human beings because they had to spend so much time with us. Proximity has an amazing power to reduce prejudice and break down barriers. I worked on the electronics crew—think cable TV, cameras, and computer networks. In addition to my regular schedule I got called out at all hours of the night and day to fix something so a supervisor didn't have to be called in. I was supposed to get overtime pay for these extra projects but I'm pretty sure I never did. Though more than once officers bought me a soda or candy from the vending machines in their lounge for fixing the TV system during the NBA finals or some other special. I kept that job until I was shipped off of Buckingham.

Supervisor Banker was the butt of many jokes among workers and other supervisors. He was a giant of a man, and one of the jokes was about how he folded himself out of a tiny import coupe every time he arrived at work and how he folded himself back in every time he left. The other jokes were usually about how he took things far too seriously. He did not find either of these topics funny.

Once evening came and night shift took over, the officer called me from the booth and told me to get to work on the walkway job. I headed out and found Banker and the other guys standing in front of A/B building, at the end of the main boulevard that connected buildings within the prison. It was a wide concrete walkway facing the front of the building, with lines of cells coming out at an angle on each side. We were working overnight to minimize the number of incarcerated people walking through the area, to limit their potential access to the concrete saw, a Class A tool that no one was supposed to touch or operate without supervision. It turned out we didn't need to worry because Banker had forgotten to fill it with gas.

The procedure for him to get out and get gas would have been a nightmare. He would have had to send us all back to our housing units, march the saw and sledgehammer somewhere to secure them, go back out through security, find a gas can and gas, get special approval to bring it in, go back through security, call us back out from our pods, and go to work. So, he decided we didn't need it. Anyone who has worked in a bureaucracy, especially in the bureaucracy of prison, knows what it is to make do with what's available. I can't tell you how many hot electrical receptacles I changed with a pair of fingernail clippers because getting a screwdriver or shutting off the breaker would have been too much trouble. Prison is definitely not OSHA approved.

We took turns with the sledgehammer, working to perfect our swing and figure out how close to the edge we should hit to break off as big a chunk as possible and not waste time with dead thumps that reverberated up our arms. Even with gloves I felt my skin start to burn. By the end of the night the calluses were ripping off both hands.

We started off joking and talking. After a while, we grew quiet, almost mechanical, swinging until we ran out of breath or strength, then passing the sledge. There's something incredibly comforting about silence and action with people I trust. That need to fill the silence is so often a sign of friction or uncertainty.

Over time I did meet people and develop friendships, just not many. Making friends in prison is like anywhere else. We meet people at work or doing shared hobbies. Grahm and I met playing soccer. D-Nice and I met playing cards. Qawee (former gang leader who became an imam) and I connected because not only had we done time at the same prison but we shared a love of exercise, training, and homemade cheesecake.

Some of those friendships continued even through transfers and releases, which is how I ended up picking Grahm up from prison, writing a front-page story about it, and then giving him a motorcycle.

I was able to write for *C-VILLE Weekly*, the local paper, about picking Grahm up from prison. Newspaper photo by Eze Amos, C-VILLE Weekly

Other relationships faded at the gate, as soon as our lives became so different. Someone coined a term that I love—an archived friendship. It's someone that we've run a full cycle with. We've met, we've connected, we've had experiences, and made memories. Now we're off living our own lives. That friendship is like a perfect memory, sitting on a shelf somewhere, because we aren't creating any more memories or having any more interactions. We can take them down off the shelf and relive them over a cup of coffee or a phone call, but they are not growing or developing further.

I have a lot of archived friendships from prison. At one point I thought that was a personal failure, or something that I should have put more energy into. Then I remembered that no friendship exists in a void. Sometimes, especially in prison, they exist based on shared circumstances. Other times friendships are based on a deep connection that doesn't rely on commonalities. I have run into people after more than twenty years and immediately fallen back into that place of connection and closeness. It's a wonderful thing.

I also find that friendships change as I change. I'm not the kid I was in high school. I'm not the guy I was when I committed my crimes. I'm not the anxious eighteen-year-old I was when I walked into prison. I'm not the person I was the day I graduated from college inside those walls. My life has changed dramatically and therefore I have changed dramatically. It only makes sense that my friends and the people I want to share my time and energy with change as well.

Early the night of the boulevard project, the kitchen supervisor said he would have one of his workers "take care of us" because we were working so late and promised a special "lunch" at midnight. These situations were always hit or miss. Sometimes fried chicken and special meals from staff-side were delivered to workers. We were not quite so lucky.

Around midnight the kitchen side door opened with a clank, across the boulevard from where we were working, and an officer brought us each a crumpled brown paper bag. Inside were two boiled eggs and a juice pack. We were underwhelmed. Then we sat down on the concrete walkway and looked up.

The sky was full of stars.

It was hard to see the stars in prison. We were rarely outside of the building at night, and when we were, the bright lights polluted the sky. But, from where we were, there was enough of a funnel between the big lights and the building wall that we could see more stars than we had in years.

I had been in prison for almost fifteen years at that point. I would occasionally see the night sky when being rushed from night shift at the law library. This night I just sat there, looking up and taking it all in.

We had started ribbing and shit-talking again when we took a break for "lunch." Once we looked up, we grew silent as we reveled in the human experience of feeling small next to something so massive and beautiful. Those moments, being next to nature, always feel so humbling and so enriching.

I had been living a hopeless, empty life when I was arrested. It felt like the final straw, like my life was over. I expected to be forever cast from the experience of being human. I thought I would never again feel joy or safety or security. Over time, I had every experience possible behind bars. I found people who made me laugh until my stomach hurt. There were people I bared my soul to. There also were plenty of people I have no desire to ever see again. I never imagined I would be sitting under the night sky with people in prison and feel profoundly connected.

Chapter 14

Ignorant to Education

Four years after I got to Nottaway, my security level dropped, and I was transferred to Buckingham. Both prisons had been built with the same blueprints, so walking the new compound felt both alien and familiar. Despite minor cosmetic differences, I knew the place, even if the cast of characters around me had changed.

Knock, knock.

I called out and a face appeared at my cell door. A short, young guy said hello and started asking me questions. It was the standard "new guy" interview. What's my name? Where am I from? Do I know so-and-so?

After a few minutes, he tilted his head, looking pensive, and asked, "Are you the guy who shot those two on Route 29?"

"Yeah," I said, nodding. "That was me."

"Oh shit . . . You know old boy's just down the hall?"

I felt my chest tighten in panic. I had steeled myself for this possibility but still felt unprepared. Back when I was in the jail and held incommunicado, officers had taken pity on me and let me walk around when they weren't supposed to. They had also shown me two mug shots. I recognized them as the two men I shot. The officers described them as "frequent flyers," though I'm not sure that was a fair description. I knew it was theoretically possible that we could someday end up on the same prison yard together, but policy dictated that the perpetrator of a crime and the victim should not be housed together, and so I assumed it wouldn't happen.

The guy I had been talking to said he would be the in-between, and see if the guy I had shot—the one with the scar on his chin—and I could make peace. I took him up on that offer. I told him to express my sincere apology and ask if there's anything I could do. I meant it. That guy had been along for a ride with his cousin. He hadn't been a bad kid. I felt terrible about what I had done. I also told the in-between to say that I wanted to apologize but that I would defend myself if needed. I would come to rec the next afternoon, unarmed and ready to talk if he was open to it.

That night, I couldn't sleep. I'd been hearing about how the guy I shot was telling people about his scar and saying he would kill me if he ever saw me. The next morning, I headed to the chow hall, where, unlike Nottaway, people from all different units ate together. I walked along the railing and toward the slot in the wall where we had our chow trays passed to us. Then, to my left, I saw that familiar scar. I was standing fifteen feet from the guy I had shot.

I got my food and sat in a corner as far away from him as I could get. I kept my eye on him, though. He was smiling and joking with someone, not at all on his guard, so I was pretty sure he hadn't gotten word about me yet. He looked young, goofy. In that moment, I sensed that his threats about killing me had been just posturing. He wasn't a bad guy. He was just trying to live up to some image he thought everyone else expected from him. Like I had been.

That afternoon I went outside to rec, as I had said I would. At that point I was 160 pounds, almost as small as I had been coming into prison. The year before I had injured my rotator cuff so I couldn't lift and so I had taken up running and boxing—my shoulder could deal with the stress of hitting pads but not the strain of lifting. So, there I was, trying to do pull-ups again for the first time in a year. Buzzing with nervous energy, I kept looking at the gate. A figure walked out, but it wasn't him.

Halfway through rec, the officer in the tower called my name. He told me to go back to my unit. As I walked into the building, a sergeant stopped me and asked, "You Crosson?"

I nodded. He told me to go pack my stuff. I was immediately worried that I was about to be shipped somewhere else. I had waited four years to get away from the last prison. Buckingham promised more rec, more programs, better food, and more time not locked in the cell. It was a huge step up from where I had been, and I wanted to stay.

I was put in cuffs and taken to the hole, but I wasn't given any of my property. About an hour later, officers put me back in cuffs and shackles and led me over to the administration building, then into the office of the assistant warden.

I sat silently across from the assistant warden for long minutes as he theatrically looked through a file, saying, *hmm* a lot. Finally, he put down the folder—with plenty of pomp and circumstance.

"Do you know why you're here?" he asked me.

Someone had overlooked this situation in the paperwork, I thought to myself. "I'm pretty sure I do," I said out loud.

"So, what are we going to do about this?" he asked.

I was dumbfounded that he was asking me. They shouldn't have brought me to Buckingham in the first place.

"It says you shot him."

What am I supposed to say to that, I wondered. I kept quiet.

"We can't have you here together. So, I'm going to send you back to the hole and have him transferred next door. Then you can come out."

It was my good luck that there were two prisons right across the street from each other, and I was doubly lucky that the guy I had shot had stayed out of trouble long enough that he had fallen to a lower security level—so he was the one who qualified to get transferred.

Back in the hole, I waited. A few hours later my door popped, and I was sent to grab my bag of property and return to the same cell I was first assigned to when I arrived at Buckingham. Once I was on the yard again, guys started saying stuff about him. That he had snitched on me and that he had backed down. They called him names.

I could have joined in, but instead I told everyone that he had done the right thing. He wanted to go home just like I did. He didn't want to hurt me any more than I wanted to hurt him. He was brave enough to put his ego aside, really look at the situation, and take the path that led to the best outcomes possible.

I learned a lesson in maturity from probably the last person I ever would have imagined.

Another person in prison helped transform the way I saw myself. Ever since I was a little kid I've been driven by feelings of inadequacy. I've never felt like enough. I've always felt that I had to be improving and doing to not just be okay but, more fundamentally, to be worthy of love. I never knew where this drive came from.

I was about sixteen years into my prison time when a counselor at Buckingham called me into her office and told me to shut the door. I closed it and waited nervously. I didn't know what to expect.

She said, "I'm going to self-disclose here, Jesse. I don't normally do this. But you and I have a lot in common. We don't settle. That means we will always push ourselves further—in my case, I went to the best school and got the best grades. But it also means that we won't be satisfied. We don't get the same feeling of accomplishment other people do. We keep asking what's next."

I felt seen. I felt grateful that someone understood what I hadn't ever been able to put into words. No, I was never satisfied. But as the counselor said, I never settled either. I wasn't ever at peace—and I wasn't ever stuck in one place. That's why, for all my faults, whenever there was an opportunity or a chance to learn, I took it.

Shortly after I went to jail, my mother set me up to enroll in college courses. I was grateful for a place to put my time and energy, because the jail was just a depressing warehouse full of people waiting. At the same time, I battled with insecurity and nerves. I didn't feel worthy of college. I didn't think I'd be able to complete work on the same level as other students. But there was a door open in front of me, so I walked through it. That has been the key to so many of the successes in my life: taking direction from others and walking through doors into rooms I didn't feel like I belonged in. I took college courses when I didn't feel like I could. I wrote articles I was sure no one would read that eventually got published. I reached out to people who I never imagined would respond—and I call them friends today.

College was a profoundly rare opportunity in jail. No one else there was taking courses. In fact, they had to write a policy to allow me to do so. Even once I was transferred to a prison of 1,100 people, only five guys, at most, took correspondence classes at any one time. At one point, a local community college started introducing first- and second-year courses in the prison, and more people were able to sign up. Still, there was no financial aid or student loans available and classes cost more than guys made in a year at a prison job. So, the ones taking classes were mostly those whose families had money, a few people using their VA benefits, and the very few who had successfully navigated the extremely difficult grant and fellowship process.

Some classes were hard. Some were easy. Some really left an impression.

My Philosophy 101 professor went out of his way to answer all of my questions. He responded—pages and pages of handwritten notes—to my essays and every little random question in each paper I submitted.

I remember the moment calculus started to make sense to me (or at least that I remembered and understood where to apply all the proper formulas).

I remember the English professor who said I had "real promise" and how that inspired me to write an essay about the power of language—and express my deepest desire to be able to write something that could make another person feel and understand and experience as if they were there.

Education fundamentally changed how I saw myself and how I lived my life. I spent years completing assignments by hand, mailing them to Ohio University, waiting for a response before I was allowed to send in my next assignment. Once one class was completed, I waited until my mother could gather more money so I could take another. I had to have exams proctored at the prison by the principal of the school program, who would sit with me in the library or in an unused classroom while I took my test. I had to wait months for the special approval to get the calculator required for my math class.

I wasn't thinking about being a college graduate. That was never on the radar—very little about the "future" felt attainable or real. I just wanted something meaningful to do with my hours and days. I was living in a place that was almost devoid of stimulation and opportunity, so I grabbed on to college and held on with all the strength in my soul.

After a decade and a half of essays, assignments, and exams, I put on a cap and gown, one that was used for the GED and vocational graduations. I walked into the prison gym as part of a long line of men, and we sat in seats that had been assembled in rows. I looked for my mother and my not-by-blood but better-than-by-blood grandfather Bill in the audience and saw them sitting near the gym wall. Bill had tears in his eyes and his lip was quivering. He nodded to me, and I felt my heart swell. Bill wasn't *really* my grandfather; he was my stepmother's father and the best human being I've ever known. He showed me what unconditional love is. When my father died, he had written me a letter and then visited me. "You may have lost your father but you won't lose me," he said. Then he showed up week after week, month after month and year after year.

The principal read out the list of those who had earned their GED. Those men lined up in front of the stage—some lucky enough to have family watching from the audience—shook the principal's hand and accepted their diplomas before filing back to their seats. Then the names of those who had graduated from vocational classes—plumbing or electrical—were called. Then, the principal said there was a special presentation. The director of education from the central office walked to the microphone. She held up my college diploma and started reading from it. I heard ". . . do hereby confer on Jesse Luke Crosson . . ." and didn't hear much else—she read a long time but it built up tension, like an Oscar speech, with the closing music adding to the experience.

When the director finished, I walked up to the stage to thunderous applause. I spotted my grandfather crying hard. I was almost crying myself. I looked out at my fellow incarcerated people and on their faces I saw hope. I saw pride. I saw unity, and I saw aspiration. I started to feel proud of myself, then I pushed that pride back down, ashamed for feeling special. What had I done? Simply what anyone would have done if they had the opportunity. It was both one of the best moments of my prison experience and one of the hardest, because if I couldn't bring everyone else along with me, I felt I didn't deserve it.

In a strange twist of timing, I heard my name again from the stage a few minutes later. I walked up to get another piece of paper, this one from the electrical apprenticeship program, which was the academic side of becoming a journeyman or master tradesman.

My grandfather Bill, my mother, and I when I got my degree.

I had never taken the electrical vocational class, which was a requirement to enter the apprenticeship. So, I had basically "lied, cheated, and stole" to get into the program. Per the DOC, you could take only one vocational class per security class level designation, even if you had been at that facility for years. Because I had already taken a different vocational class, I wasn't allowed to take the electrical one. On paper, it was the State of Virginia rationing resources but this had consequences: If you wanted to continue your education, you might not have the chance—or, like me, you had to actively manipulate the situation to create the chance.

I had negotiated behind the scenes to get a maintenance job to fulfill the on-the-job-hours requirement. Then I was lucky enough to have a teacher who would work with me. Four years later, I had completed the book work for the apprenticeship and the required hours through my position on maintenance. I still had to take the written journeyman's exam, which I was able to do several months later. That teacher broke quarantine rules to get the DPOR rep, the person responsible for proctoring the exam for the agency that licenses tradesmen, into the facility so I could have the opportunity to earn my license. It was an awesome thing to have an educator willing to fight for his student. He is a teacher I will always remember.

That day I picked up both a college degree and an apprenticeship certificate. It was important to me to make progress on at least one "white collar" and one "blue collar" path. I had no idea what the world held in store for me. I didn't know when I'd be getting out of prison. Being a worrier, deep down I often feared that I would never get out—that I would die before my release or some world war would lead to us all being euthanized. What I did know was that it is always better to have options than plans. Plans can be thwarted or fail, leaving us with nothing. Options are limitless. They create more options that build off one another until we are faced with a broad array of choices. Instead of looking at how an opportunity fit into my plan, I looked at whether a decision created more options or fewer. I just wanted as many options as possible.

That's why I saw education as my out. It's part of why I read so much and why I always read one fiction and one nonfiction book. I wanted to learn, to experience a richer world than I lived in—and sometimes enjoy an escapist comfort.

I asked for books as Christmas gifts. I also ordered them from discount booksellers, and checked out as many as I could from the library. I unofficially studied economics, psychology, history, and pretty much anything I had access to. I read news magazines to keep up with the world. I did obscure brain-building exercises because I hoped they would help me understand and retain more.

Academic learning has been valuable. It helped me create a framework for the world. More importantly, though, it started my understanding of my place in the world. It gave me permission to start learning the things I wanted to learn and following my whims without judgment. But, ultimately, intellectual learning is limited. Sometimes it even seems stale and abstract.

What I needed more than anything was a way to *be* in the world. That's why I studied psychology. That's why I went to therapy and meditated. That's why I read every self-help book available. I never forgot when Karl told me, sitting on those prison steps, that no one is an island and that education will never be enough—because life is about people.

I became a different person as a direct result of the education I pursued. College and writing and the electrical apprenticeship gave me the ability to believe in myself. I started to see myself as capable and worthy. I started to see that my peer group could continue to expand.

It wasn't the diploma. It wasn't the journeyman's license. It wasn't the $50 check I received when I had my first article published. It wasn't any of the external things.

It was the daily work that translated to a belief in myself, in the belief that I could do more and be better.

It took effort and opportunity. Knowledge is power but uncoupled from the will to use it, it's like a cart without a horse. It broke my heart to see others in prison who had opportunities but not the will or the "want" to pursue them.

On the other hand, I saw guys who did all the work. They read and studied and bettered themselves but got no recognition and never received a hand up. When they got out, they went back to their families and neighborhoods. The families and neighborhoods were the same, but they no longer fit in. Some people who got out were able to continue their growth and expand their lives. Many got drawn back into old patterns.

As they say, talent is evenly distributed, but opportunity is not. That was when I began to realize how big of a difference it would make for people to have the same basic opportunities that I had.

Chapter 15

Selfish to Service

One year, as a kid, my dad asked me what I wanted to do on my birthday. I wanted to help two elderly brothers my stepmother knew, who were having health issues and struggling to chop their own firewood and make repairs to their house.

We showed up early and knocked. One of the brothers partially opened the door, visible through the crack. He eyed us, untrustingly. We told him we were there to help. He looked behind him, acknowledging his brother, or maybe looking for him, then he looked back at us. When he saw my stepmother his face relaxed. He smiled.

We spend the morning and afternoon chopping wood, running plastic over leaky areas of the roof, and exchanging pleasantries with the brothers who sat on their porch, seemingly amused to watch us work.

It ended up being one of my best birthdays. It wasn't about me at all. And at the end of the day, I felt more full than I had when I woke up.

I learned a very important lesson about what actually made me happy. But I never seemed to apply it. Instead, I started chasing whatever made me feel good. Whatever made me feel validated. Whatever numbed the pain. Ultimately, that path led me to prison, a shell of the birthday kid I had been when all I wanted to do was help people.

In life, I tended to jump without a parachute, so my extremes were very high and very low—more so than the people around me. Many times during my lows I have wanted to not exist. Nietzsche wisely said, "He who has a why to live can bear almost any how." I found that to be true. In a funny way, prison saved my life. If I hadn't found meaning, I would have killed myself at one of the low points along this journey.

Prison was certainly a low point, at least at first. It was also where I started experimenting and trying to see what I actually wanted to do with my energy and my time. There were lots of different ways to do time. Some guys lived on the weight pile, lifting every rec period while doing pushups and napping much of the rest of the day so their bodies could heal. Other guys worked a factory or a kitchen job, spending all their waking hours outside of their cells trying to earn a paycheck. Some guys got high and ran the hustles they needed to come up with the money to buy the drugs. Other guys just watched TV and wasted away, eating commissary, and shutting themselves down.

I tried each of these and none worked for me. Then I rearranged the puzzle pieces and found a role for exercise and work and relaxation. And eventually I found my why, thanks to Big Baby.

Big Baby looked a lot like a much younger version of John Coffey from *The Green Mile*. He stood six-foot-six and after spending so much time on the weight pile, he had bulked up to 270 pounds. The prison boxing tournament was coming up, and he wanted to get down to his fighting weight, which meant running, cardio, and just "touching" the weight (like benching 315 pounds for fifteen reps, or deadlifting 405 for twenty-five reps) to keep his strength. If you don't know those numbers, it is an absurd and scary display of strength.

He was a giant, stoic figure, and I didn't know how to read him. He often sat in the corner watching everyone else. Sometimes he ran a dice game, but he would never shoot in anyone else's game. He shut down drama and antics with a word—and I never saw his word questioned. I had heard stories about his capacity for violence. That's why he surprised me when he asked, almost shyly, like an ashamed child, if I would be willing to help him get his GED.

He had been trying for years and still hadn't made it past the TABE test, the first of the three steps to getting the GED. He had almost given up hope, until someone had recommended that he ask me.

One of my earlier mentors had told me to never give something away for free. He explained: "People who have never gotten a fair deal won't trust something that's free. They'll think it's a trick. So charge them something, but make sure it's something they can afford to give."

So, rather than asking for money, I told Big Baby that I would help him get his GED if he taught me to box. He immediately agreed, and asked if we could start that night.

It was a long road. Big Baby was fine with most categories, but his math scores kept him from moving forward. That's where we focused, though at first it seemed hopeless. Each new mathematical concept was a challenge, and as humble and polite as he was, he sometimes lost his temper at himself and wanted to give up. He never did, though.

Then there came a time when I thought he would quit. We were stuck on algebra's distributive property. For weeks we went over the same processes and it just didn't make sense to him—until the day it did. I remember the smile, the absolutely radiant, joyful smile on his face, when it clicked in his brain.

I gave him one problem using the distributive property, and then another, and then another. He got them right every time. We finished that session with a great deal of relief and excitement.

The next day Big Baby had forgotten it all. With each problem he couldn't answer, I watched him grow frustrated. I felt myself getting frustrated. Then he took a breath, and said something that will always stick with me. He said, "If I got it yesterday, I can get it again." That was it. Final. No more feeding the frustration. No feeling sorry for himself. No beating himself up. He made a decision that he was going to get it again—and just kept going.

Up to that point, I'm not sure I had ever in my life made the simple decision to just get over something and keep going. I may have been teaching him for his GED, but he taught me one of the single most important lessons of my life: We can choose how we react even in the most frustrating or stressful situations.

He did finally get the distributive property again. He got everything. A month and a half later he came back from school, dressed in his state blues, with tears of joy running down his face. He hugged me in the middle of the pod, then picked me up and swung me around like I was a child. He had passed his GED. That was a great moment. I got to see the unreserved gratitude and happiness in him come out. His reserved stoicism was out the window. It couldn't possibly get any better. Then he was asked to be graduation valedictorian.

This was enough that his family came to see him speak at graduation. Life had been rough for him as a kid, and life was still rough for his family. They hadn't come to visit in all the years he had been locked up, but when they heard he was going to be giving the speech for his graduating class, they made it.

He practiced his speech over and over with me, other soon-to-be graduates, and random people in the pod. It might have driven us crazy if it hadn't been so heartfelt. He even made the entire group of his fellow almost-graduates listen to him rehearse on the day of graduation. Then he was on stage giving the speech. Then he was hugging his family. Then he was heading back to the cell, still crying, and so full of joy and life. Of all the things I had done in my life, *this* was one of the most meaningful. This was what I wanted to do with my time and my energy.

I had always wanted to be a good kid and have a positive impact on the world. But up to now, I had pinballed between being profoundly selfish and a people pleaser. Often I ran up against situations I didn't know how to cope with, and I acted poorly. Watching Big Baby graduate showed me that there was truly nothing better I could do for myself than to show up for someone else. It would be a privilege to watch them grow and achieve.

Sometimes I went a little too far. At several points, both when I was still in prison and after, I decided my role was to sacrifice for others and take care of others rather than myself. It played along with my people pleasing. It was putting myself at the center of things I didn't need to be at the center of. It was just another way to ignore the pit of emptiness I felt inside me, and continually trying to fill it with external things.

Not long after Big Baby graduated, he was offered a tutor position in the GED program. He accepted, and he quickly became an inspiration because everyone remembered how he had struggled. His promotion inspired hope—for me as well as others.

Shortly after, I was told to pack up for my transfer to Buckingham Correctional. I carried my bag and baggage on the bus, back to the bullpen, and finally to the new prison. I knew I wanted to continue teaching. I didn't know where that would be or what it would look like. I didn't know a lot of things. A transfer like this was a mixed bag—a new place, losing a bunch of property, having to find my place all over again, and lots of unknowns. It was a mid-level prison—the best option—because it was loose enough that we could move around but had enough violence and "real problems" that the staff wasn't nitpicking little stuff. They also offered a lot more freedom and many more opportunities.

My father spoke fluent Spanish and used it at any chance he got. He never offered to teach me or practice with me, and so I took Spanish classes in middle school. After eighth grade I went to summer school. My teacher was an attractive, brand-new college grad, who said we could speak about anything we wanted as long as it was in Spanish. With that motivation, I started speaking Spanish very well.

One of my favorite things to do whenever I transferred from prison to prison was to go onto the rec yard or into the chow hall and hang around Latinos and not let on that I spoke Spanish. It's always entertaining what people will say when they think you don't understand.

Newly at Buckingham, I was at rec, on the dip bar, when one of the Latinos waiting to use it complained in Spanish about how I was taking too long.

I gave it two or three rounds then heard him say, "Este pinche guey." (This fucking dumbass.) I responded, "Siempre son esos pinches gringos." (It's always those fucking white guys.) At first I thought no one had heard me. They kept going for one beat, then two. Then they all stopped and turned to look at me. The one who had called me a fucking dumbass was wide-eyed, like he had been caught with his hand in the cookie jar. The rest laughed. It was as good an intro as any.

When people saw scenes like this, they asked me to teach them Spanish. Like tutoring someone for the GED, it was just as awesome to watch, as they first wrote, then spoke, then actually understood a new language. I taught TJ and Bronson and eventually an entire Spanish class followed by a beginner and an intermediate Spanish class. This teaching thing was more fun than I had realized.

My journey continued with a young man that people called "Shooter," because we had all seen his arrest on the news. (It wasn't unusual for us to comment on someone who made the news and then twelve to eighteen months later watch them walk into the prison, once they were done with court and sent to DOC.)

Shooter was smart but his education had been lacking. He had both a high school diploma and a GED (due to the jail not properly checking his records). He could take a trade but because he couldn't pay out of pocket, higher education wasn't an option. I saw his potential and knew he was motivated, so we decided to hold mock college classes. Using my past materials and experience in undergrad, as well as textbooks and material sent to him by a sponsor, we started his journey.

Initially Shooter thought like a kid who had never been pushed or encouraged in school. He didn't think critically, he was emotional, he jumped to conclusions or repeated other people's arguments without looking at their substance. He couldn't write a paragraph and there were a lot of small things to address. But, over time, his natural curiosity won over. He started to read more, to study more, to explore more. He began to see himself and the world in a much broader and deeper light.

With one-on-one tutoring, Shooter essentially received the first two years of an undergrad education. He didn't get any diplomas. He didn't get any awards. That almost made it better. He wasn't doing it because his parents wanted him to or because it was expected of him. He was learning and growing because he genuinely wanted to.

I'd still like to see Shooter go to college one day, maybe get a professional degree. It doesn't matter what I would like, though. He finished his fifteen-year sentence and is out running a small blue-collar business, making lots of money, dating a pretty lady, and has a young child. It is awesome to see him thrive and continue to find himself. He is a far cry from the kid he was when he first walked in.

I never imagined the final place I would learn how to give.

The prison had a drug problem. Visitors were being strip searched and denied visitation because they were suspected of smuggling drugs—it didn't matter that nothing was ever found. Even with visitors being stripped, people were still overdosing. Guys lost themselves, sold their belongings, and even sold themselves.

Then one day, two guys knocked on the door of my cell. I shouted a response and they walked in. These "office hours" visits were pretty routine after a few years at Buckingham. I was approached daily about an academic question, a therapeutic issue, or just general problem-solving. Sometimes people wanted to hang out, but more often people wanted an answer, needed to vent, or wanted to be heard. In this case Eddie and Josh wanted help. It was common knowledge that they were strung out and trying to get clean. They were also known to have money, so guys were eager to give them dope—to keep them strung out and the money train rolling.

Eddie and Josh got straight to it. "We need help. Will you walk with us to make sure no one puts anything in our hands?"

"That's not how this works," I said. "I can't be with you 24/7, but I can support you."

"You don't get it," Josh said. "I can't even go to the hole because someone back there will send me something."

I asked, "So, do you need a space where there's no one around? Or where you're only around people not getting high?"

That was a small piece of what led to the most successful peer support mental health program in the state, the Shared Allied Management (SAM) program.

I hadn't ever had a grand plan. Going to school, working, teaching, tutoring—it was all piecemeal, done solo and without guidance or support from anyone else. Besides, I never knew when the person I was working with (or I) would get transferred or moved.

After I coordinated with a few guys, we met with the head of the mental health department. We laid out our idea of a supportive place where people on the same page about life and trying to get clean could live. He said he would "run it up the chain." Soon we got the news that the state had approved a budget for "a pilot peer-support mental health program." Off the record, we were told that we didn't have a "drug problem" but that there *was* a mental health crisis and that they had already been kicking this idea around.

Despite the state's denial of reality, something good came out of it. The SAM program was born. Well, sort of. It was slowly forming and morphing and struggling to figure out its way. A number of us were selected to be mentors and, in recognition of their original interest and contribution, Eddie and Josh were invited to be residents.

We basically made it up as we went along (my first experience with a startup). Mentors weren't even official titles at this point. We were volunteering while working at our normal jobs. Originally, I was the activities coordinator, but before long I was working directly with guys. We did journaling, one-on-one check-ins, and I acted as the intermediary before calling a QMHP (qualified mental health professional). The mental health staff were stretched thin and more often than not our guys, even the SMI-2 (the most serious mental health designation), just needed to be seen and heard, which we could do as well as anyone.

The biggest challenge for me was learning to temper expectations. I had hoped we would help everyone return to a life of normalcy. What I realized was that "normal" is different for everyone. Some guys in the program grew by leaps and bounds. They started as residents and were eventually hired as mentors. For other guys it was a win if we could get them to shower every day. By changing my framework, I learned to celebrate all the wins and address all the challenges.

Over time our program became the most successful one in the state. We were regularly sent "problem" cases—guys who couldn't stay out of the hole, or who were constantly in trouble for harming themselves or others. We worked to provide the stability they had never experienced. It wasn't anything radical. We received some training and had activities. But most importantly, we just treated everyone as a person. We listened. We set boundaries. It was only radical in its simplicity and its humanity. The experience was profoundly frustrating at times but also one of most meaningful I have ever been a part of.

Then I had the idea of starting a garden. I had never seen a garden project in a prison but I figured, why not? If the administration says they're all behind this, I may as well try.

I reached out to friends on the street, found a church willing to donate seeds and supplies, and started working the political system to get permission. Surprisingly, the project was quickly approved, but we still didn't have a garden. Yet.

No one had been able to agree how the donated materials would be vetted or who would bring them in. A prison is like any other bureaucracy of a dozen different departments except worse. In prison, we couldn't call or email, we could only contact a department by submitting a request form or if we were lucky enough to catch the head as they walked around the compound.

Finally, the investigator (who actually had nothing to do with it officially) stepped in. He was a complicated and far from popular figure. In this case, though, he went above and beyond. He went to the warehouse where the gardening supplies had been delivered, loaded up a cart, and pushed them into the prison himself. I'm still not sure if he got permission or just figured he'd ask for forgiveness later.

The next thing I knew, we were laying timber, building raised beds, and digging in the dirt. Then what had been a dusty, unused section of yard had tomatoes, peppers, watermelons, and pumpkins. I saw myself in those vegetables. Planted in an inhospitable, poorly tended environment, yet with daily watering and care, they grew up strong and vibrant. I just hoped my story wouldn't end with being eaten by a hungry gardener.

The SAM program was adopted statewide. The guys who still contact me from inside say it's not what it was. In some facilities staff pulled the reins tighter, preventing guys from maintaining trust with the residents. In others the mentors were given less autonomy, and jobs began to be awarded based on favors rather than merit. Many mentors don't invest in their guys. Many residents stopped believing in the system and the programs. It became just another bureaucratic thing—good in name and intention, ineffective in application.

Even if the SAM program hasn't maintained the same momentum, I had the gift of realizing what I wanted to do. I didn't know what it would look like or when it would happen, but I wanted to live a life that was about giving back and was about healing where I had harmed. I even plotted out a career journey. I wanted to write, I wanted to work with people one-on-one, and I wanted to do public speaking. It sounded like a pipe dream at the time.

Chapter 16

Hurt to Healing

Elwood was mostly jovial until he lost his temper. Then it was like a switch had flipped. One night he got into a tear-down drag-out fight over buffing the pod floor. Someone was trying to be a bully and pushed him too far. He had grown up in the foster care system. He described the "games" they would play, where the biological kids got to eat and the foster kids had to keep working. He described the physical, emotional, and sexual abuse he witnessed and experienced in cold, detached detail. As a mentor, I sat in too many prison cells listening to stories like Elwood's and crying, feeling the absolute cruelty that humanity is capable of.

I listened to guys cry as they told me about the things they had done, the shame they felt, and their belief in their unworthiness, even worthlessness. Every so often someone could break from the expectations of prison—the play-acting—and be honest and vulnerable. D-Nice talked about how shooting could be about trying to kill but more often it was about fear, just trying to be safe, scaring the other person to get away. It wasn't "gangster" at all. That had been my experience, too.

At first, I felt emotionally safer in prison than I had as a kid. Once I grew out of my shell, though, and started connecting more deeply with the people around me, prison grew more emotionally than physically painful—even with the fights and the physical trauma I experienced inside. I have always been sensitive and tied up in the experiences and lives of people around me. I have wanted to help and heal them. In prison I was surrounded by broken people who had often done terrible things and had terrible things done to them. I was surrounded by people who had been cast out of society without direction or the services they needed to heal and change. I was surrounded by people in terrible pain.

Over my years inside, I saw firsthand that prison didn't help in the ways we assume it does and it doesn't ultimately protect public safety in the ways we need. Tough-on-crime policies operate on the premise that crime is a rational decision made in a vacuum—and that couldn't be further from the truth. It's easy to judge people from our perspective or expect them to do what we would do. It takes a lot of work to see what others have been through and the ways they have been shaped and affected. The system is set up to punish people. More often than not these are people in pain who made mistakes because they grew up around dysfunction and didn't have anyone to show them a different way. I dreamed that one day we could have systems to help people be accountable, heal, and change. That's what public safety actually looks like.

And so, becoming a mentor wasn't a difficult decision. It wasn't even a question. I knew it was arrogant (and unrealistic) to feel responsible for everyone else in prison. But I needed to ease their pain because that was the only way I knew to ease my own pain.

Over time and with many failed attempts I learned that I couldn't actually save anyone. I could care for them, nurture them, and plant seeds that might one day grow. But people can only save themselves. I can work to inspire and give hope. I can especially work to create opportunities, but the last step and the result are out of my hands.

As a mentor I heard one heartbreaking story of trauma after another. It helped me see just how often pain and trauma acts like a disease that infects one person who then spreads it to another. It also helped me recognize that in the right (or wrong) circumstances, we are all capable of almost anything.

People in the SAM program often asked me, "What is the most important thing I can do to change?" I didn't have it all figured out, but I told them that our job is to stop the cycle, by working to heal so we don't pass that pain and trauma forward. Sometimes this means forgiveness. Sometimes it means distance. It always means doing something very hard . . . actually feeling all the things that we have been saddled with.

A few years into my correspondence college program, I chose psychology as a major because I was desperately seeking to understand where I had gone wrong—and how I could have become the person who did the things I did. I had sought out mentors and people to teach me because I didn't trust myself and I didn't know where to start. When I finally realized it was time to give back, that I was ready to be the mentor, something had shifted in me, thanks to the right support and asking myself the right questions. Mentoring others helped me ask them the same questions I had been asking myself. It let me share my experience and struggles. It also helped me better understand how my own issues manifested.

As I began mentoring others, I was also fortunate enough to find another mentor of my own. He at first was a teacher, then became something like a friend. He was someone I deeply respected, who was doing the same work.

Not long after my young meditation teacher Ricky went home, around 2010—eight years into my prison journey—I had a random conversation over the phone with a family friend who happened to be around when I called home. She suggested I speak with her husband, James, who I had met but never really gotten to know. Apparently, he had been practicing the same form of meditation as I did for more than thirty years. He took it very seriously, she said, almost in a teasing way. She was happy to connect us.

He and I set up a phone call, talked, and then set up another call. We spoke on the phone every week (barring lockdowns and emergencies) for the next eleven years. We continued to talk even after I got out.

He walked me through the Mumonkon, the book of 100 Zen koans—questions or riddles that cannot be solved or answered by the thinking mind, such as what is the sound of a single hand (often mistranslated as "what is the sound of one hand clapping"). We worked through more koans and looked at other meditation practices.

Working with James on both meditation and Gestalt therapy, reading self-help books, developing friendships, and recognizing the absolute power of someone believing in me planted the seed that helped me grow to believe that I was really meant to live in a different way. I slowly began to see myself in a different light. It was a long road, but I was grateful to start somewhere.

One of the biggest kindnesses James did for me was write a poem—for me. This was after he lost his wife of forty-plus years, the person who had put us in contact, the mother of his children, his partner, and his best friend. He wrote a poem about how I was sharing the road with him. Being a friend. Walking through the dark times and the good. It was one of the most meaningful things anyone had ever written to me. Unfortunately, I no longer have the poem. James had sent it through the for-profit prison email system and I have no record of any of those emails.

After James lost his wife, he struggled and struggled and struggled and somehow came out full of light. He wasn't the only one who did that.

One night, while I was locked in the cell, an officer came to the door, called my name, and left a letter on the tray slot. The return address was from my grandfather's ex-wife. It was written on flowery paper with a very formal signature. It informed me that their child had taken his own life.

After my step-grandfather Bill lost his son to suicide, he gave up hope. He later told me that he fixated about ways he could end his own life and make it look like an accident so his wife wouldn't know. For a long time, he couldn't live with himself. Then, over time, through agony, he could.

He told me that he didn't know what the switch was, but over time it flipped. He was already a saint of a human being, but he somehow grew deeper into his love and care for people. It was as if his pain had cleared out more of himself so that he could hold more love for others. He took the worst thing to happen to him, the worst thing many of us can imagine, and he used it to make himself a better person.

Through James and my grandfather, I learned something powerful. I saw that grief and loss and trauma can shape us in terrible ways. They are often the root of our suffering, our bad habits, and our problems. They can also be the root of our deepest strength and our deepest kindness.

Both James and my grandfather gave me the courage to begin to look at my own trauma, to ask questions and be open to the pain. I began to believe that it would lead me to a better place rather than destroy me. I had a lot more questions than answers, though. I thought starting the journey would mean figuring things out but, for a long time, I only came across more and more questions.

However, now that I could look around with my eyes wide open, I started to more profoundly feel the limitations of where I was. I started to feel like a rat gnawing on the bars of my cage. For the first time, I was starting to grasp the inhumanity of my circumstances and imagine what it might look like to be free.

Chapter 17

Excuses to Accountability

I've always hated the term "hardened convict" or even "convict." Language has power. What we call someone affects the way we see them and they see themselves. Some guys preferred "convict" and adopted the label because it sounded tougher than "inmate" and definitely better than the DOC's newest term, "offender." Even with all the prejudices, there is no better way to describe the fallacy of "once a criminal" than to describe the room full of "hardened convicts" crying their eyes out during the final Victim Impact class.

The Victim Impact Program was the only part of the prison system that put me directly in contact with the harm that I had done. It was the only program that required me to talk about and be accountable for the crimes I had committed. This is absolutely ludicrous. Accountability is the first step to change, and prison needs to be a place of change. More than ninety-five percent of the people who are incarcerated are going to get out one day, and if we as a society don't build a system of change, that shows we care less about long-term public safety than short-term optics. Our current system is good at warehousing humans. It presumes that traumatized individuals, with limited perspectives and often major issues around mental illness and addiction, are going to start living different lives (the kind of "good" life that they have never been exposed to or imagined they were worthy of). This is magical thinking. This is dangerous thinking.

The final Victim Impact class was a room full of men sobbing as they listened to a woman, in the front of the room, tell how she had been put into a wheelchair by a drunk driver. Then her mother told us about hearing that her daughter had been hit and not knowing if she would survive. She cried and described being overwhelmed with panic by the side of the road while the fire department used the jaws of life to try to free her daughter's broken body from the car.

It was the beginning of accountability. It was, for some, the birthplace of empathy. It should have been mandatory for everyone.

This class wasn't available until seventeen years into my sentence. The department waited seventeen years to even talk about harm and accountability. If I hadn't started to do the work myself and build my own structure, seventeen years could have been far too late.

Guilt and shame were burdens I carried for a long time in prison. Throughout my young life I felt defined by those feelings. Sometimes it was because I failed to take care of my mother. Sometimes it was a general feeling—like a heavy jacket that I wore, day in and day out. I felt like it had always been there.

Later in my life I could trace the cycle in my teenage years: I felt guilty, then felt depressed, then felt hopeless. I coped however I could, often doing something that I would feel ashamed of the next day, deepening the cycle. I didn't fully understand then what was happening, so I couldn't take steps to change it. I didn't know how.

Once I committed my crimes, the weight of guilt grew even heavier. I felt suffocated and lost. I couldn't see any way to ever get back out. I carried that guilt and shame for a long time. I was a ping-pong ball bouncing through the universe, reacting with emotion and action, with no real intention or direction.

That guilt and shame, along with the depression and hopelessness I struggled with early on, were why I reached out to a QMHP (qualified mental health professional) as soon as I got to prison. There was a stigma against mental health and asking for help, but I didn't care. I had to do something. I couldn't keep living the way I had been.

Then, because I didn't feel guilty *all the time*, I asked one of the many QMHPs if there was something wrong with me. In my mind, any enjoyment or moment of peace was a disservice to the people I had hurt.

She kind of chuckled. And then she explained something that changed my life.

"Jesse, guilt is an instruction. It's a flashing red sign that tells the rest of you that something is wrong, that some action needs to be taken. That's it. Once you take that action, guilt has no further purpose, and holding on to it actually keeps you from changing and moving forward.

"Shame on the other hand . . . shame is about how you see yourself. It's about your trauma, your fears, and your insecurities. That's a whole other topic for a whole other day."

I needed to hear that more than I knew.

It helped me understand that accountability and healing didn't look like sitting around feeling guilty. It looked like doing things a little bit better, day by day by day.

Shame was and is a different journey. Sometimes I felt like I was making progress and healing or at least soothing those old wounds. Other times I felt like it was, as she said, "a whole other topic for a whole other day."

That conversation with the QMHP was early on in my prison experience. It gave words to what I had already been doing, but didn't know how to explain. There's a line I borrow that says, "The only thing you have to change is everything." I have found that to be true.

I continued to see QMHPs wherever I was. I read every self-help book. I mentored and tutored other guys. Later I started daily meditation. I even worked to change my body and my environment—focusing on fitness and keeping my space clean for my mental health and overall wellness. I was possessed by the need to change, to heal, to be different. Underneath it all was a need to not be weighed down by the shame and the pain.

Guilt, and the perspective of that QMHP, helped turn my prison experience into a healing boot camp. I had caused great harm. I had followed a path that left me feeling like the broken shell of a person. Early on in prison I felt just plain empty. In removing the distractions of instant gratification, drugs, and the world, I could listen to my guilt. It gave me a path to move forward and a way to build myself back up. I could be accountable, I could take action, and I could evolve.

It was by no means a straight path. I tell people all the time that it was two steps forward, one step back. Sometimes it was two steps forward and eleven steps back. However, it was a path, and I kept on it day after day.

So many of the good things and good paths in my life have been due to a simple formula: I accept when I don't know something; I find someone I admire in this area; I ask what they recommend or what worked for them; then I put my head down, day after day, and do the work. Learning to trust the process saved my life.

Then one day a magical thing happened. I woke up and talked about the crimes I had committed and I didn't feel the same wrenching in my chest and the same insatiable drive to punish myself. I felt almost okay.

I asked myself why I no longer felt that mass of guilt and heard a voice answer, "Because you're not that person anymore."

People had told me the ways I had changed. They had praised or encouraged me. It felt good, but the good feeling never lasted. I always thought: "If they actually knew how fucked up I was, they wouldn't feel that way."

But when I heard that voice—a deeper, more honest version of me—it made all the difference in the world.

I used to believe that I would become a new man and that all of my patterns would change in a flash of enlightenment. It wasn't nearly that easy.

Those old patterns were still lurking, just waiting for me to be under-resourced and stressed. When I faced new challenges, when I didn't sleep enough, when I put too much effort or interest into external things, my stuff came up again.

Just because I was able to work through the guilt of my crimes doesn't mean I had worked through the shame of my childhood. That was something I still carried and still sometimes struggle with. I didn't fully understand it at that point in my journey. I still don't fully understand it now, though I'm getting glimpses and flashes as I continue on in therapy.

Losing my father when he was in the righteous arc of his life and as I was beginning my path toward redemption felt unfair. It reminded me that we're not traveling some storybook route. We're hacking our way through the jungle, sometimes finding easier paths and other times being scraped and beaten all to hell.

I can't live my life in the "right way" from some big perspective. There is no formula that balances or fixes the past. All I can do is the next right thing. I can live and love and throw myself into this moment because there will be a day when I no longer have that opportunity.

Losing my father gave me a great motivation to live. It also helped me to be more accountable. Every time I faced a challenge I had three options: I could take my ball and go home, I could grit my teeth and hold my breath and just get through it, or I could see each challenge as an opportunity to learn, grow stronger, and expand who I am. I have tried all three approaches. Only the last has allowed me to be stronger after challenges, rather than weaker.

Chapter 18

Closed-Off to Connected

I was sitting in the old side of the jail a few months after my arrest. It was all peeling paint, dripping water, and stifling heat. Craig, who I had known and hung out with on the street before he lost his mind and killed two people in a drug-fueled haze, was telling me about his "girlfriend." I thought they must have been together before he got locked up, but no. She had seen his story in the paper and reached out. Because all visits were through glass with a phone pressed to their ears, they had never even been in the same room together. Yet, they were "in love" and talking about a future together. At first, I genuinely wondered if it was a prank or a delusion. Craig would likely avoid the death penalty, but was guaranteed to spend the rest of his life in prison. How could someone have a relationship while incarcerated? More importantly, how could someone on the outside even feel like they were in a relationship with someone who was incarcerated?

Outside of prison, people share space and time and experience with romantic partners. Inside prison, we do that with roommates. That's why roommates are one of the most important relationships inside. A good roommate makes prison more than bearable. A bad roommate is a curse like none other.

I'm not saying that roommates are sexually intimate, though there is a lot more of that going on than most guys inside like to admit. Prison is a place of homophobia and judgment, so sometimes people's need for connection and intimacy is met in secret, behind closed doors.

Even platonic roommates have a lot in common with intimate partners. There's no sex but there is every other bit of the interaction of people who share space. We looked out for each other, cooked meals together, and took turns doing dishes. Even with guys I really got along with I experienced (and caused) irritation and conflict. We had to negotiate and bring things to resolution. Being locked into a bathroom-sized room with another human being, sometimes for weeks or months at a time, leads to really good communication or a whole lot of fistfights.

Over the years I lived with a cast of characters. Early on there was Walter who tried to set me up for conspiracy charges. There was the firefighter accused of starting fires. There was the old man who had killed his wife, put her under his trailer, and just gone on with his life. There were so many people that I can't remember them all.

The worst roommate I ever had was Omar. He was close with a guy whom I talked to every day. I assumed that meant he would be a good guy. I was wrong. Even when outside rec was open he worked out in the cell with no fan, so it was boiling hot, humid, and smelling like . . . well, you can imagine. He tried to be the boss. He set a schedule for when we turned lights on and off and whether we would get up for breakfast or not. When I told him that wasn't happening he postured up, then eventually let it go. Every day was a new conflict, with Omar looking for a new argument.

The last straw was when I noticed he had been stealing my coffee. We all kept our coffee in empty peanut butter jars with a plastic spoon cut in half so it would fit inside the jar. Even when I wasn't drinking it the level kept dropping.

I confronted him and he denied stealing my coffee, but I saw the look on his face.

Prison logic said I would have to hurt him or at least kick him out since he had done the violating and I had been in that cell first. I didn't care about that, I just wanted to live with someone comfortable.

I decided it was easier to move out. Paul was the on-call plumber, and I got along with him well. He lived on the other side of the pod. His cell was open, and he invited me to move in. So, I talked to the sergeant, the building lieutenant, and then the shift commander. Not one of them would move me. There had been many issues or fights between Omar and his roommates over the years, and because I was generally calm, they figured keeping me stuck with him was better than dealing with a new round of problems.

Then Paul went to the building lieutenant and told him there were two options. Either they moved me into his cell that day or every broken toilet or leaky faucet, any plumbing issue of any sort, would need a work order, and his supervisor would have to come in with tools to repair them.

Work orders were a pain. It was much easier to just call the on-call plumber or electrician and have them fix the issue. Most had spare parts or homemade tools in their cells to bring on work calls.

The lieutenant moved me that day. Odd how prison often incentivizes bribery and extortion while claiming to be about rehabilitation.

Years after living with Paul, I lived with Teddy longer than anyone else. It started by happenstance. He wanted to move to the pod I was in, and my roommate was going home so my cell would be open. We talked about it, he moved in, and we got into a comfortable routine.

Teddy and I got along because we didn't need to fill the silence. Many roommates wanted to talk all the time in the cell. Teddy and I would go days without talking, then have hours-long conversations, then go back to only speaking when we needed the cell to ourselves or asking if the other wanted hot water when we were going downstairs to get some ourselves. It was the most comfortable living situation I had in prison.

Billy was my buddy. He was sometimes manic, generally smart, often emotional, and sometimes absolutely off his rocker. He had spent years in solitary confinement for trying to escape from the SuperMax prison. It wasn't his first conspiracy to escape.

Billy was also a hustler. He was dedicated—writing to every member of the House of Delegates and Senate in Virginia. He talked about systemic change. Back then, some of his ideas about transforming the criminal justice system seemed radical to me, but they make a lot of sense now.

Long before I met or lived with any of these people, around Christmas of 2005, at mail call the officer handed me a card with a return address I didn't recognize. This was always an exciting moment. In a world that was self-contained and sterile, new life and connections were priceless.

I opened it and wasn't sure what to think. It was from someone named Mary who worked in my mother's office. She seemed nice but I got the impression she was being condescending. People are always amazed when incarcerated people can read and write beyond a fifth-grade level or find meaning in captive lives or have intelligent takes on things. I assume it's an internalized bias and expectation from the way the media represents prisons and the people in them.

I wrote Mary back and said something to that effect. I told her I really appreciated her taking the time to write and I thought it was important to have conversations about the realities in prison, as well as the capabilities of incarcerated people.

She wrote me back the following week and I responded. Then the next week she wrote back and I responded, every week for the next fourteen years.

I got to know Mary and her partner John. I heard all about the little area they lived in, the country store that was the center of all cultural things. I heard about all of the family and people she knew. Mary became a found-family mother who had taken me in as her own.

She even visited me after connecting with my step-grandfather Bill. They became fast friends, with her calling him a saint as well. They came together to see me. A lot.

Mary had no connection to me other than that my mother had asked her to write me a Christmas card. She stopped having any interaction with my mother after experiencing the rage I witnessed as a child. Yet she stayed in contact with me. She is still in contact with me—we just had lunch the other day.

There's the power of relationships. The power of someone seeing something in me and believing in me. The power of small gestures that make an absolute world of difference.

Mary and my grandfather Bill helped me become a different person. They weren't the only people from outside who did this. Kristen, Jason, Susan, Vanessa, Leslie, Elizabeth, Don, and countless others . . . I owe them so much.

Their kindness, attention, and support gave me the opportunity to become who I am.

I remember this every day, or at least I try to. I try to remember that it's easy to be angry at, for example, a driver cutting you off in the road. But it's a lot more effective to recognize that something must be going on in that driver's life that is making them be erratic or aggressive or whatever. It's easy to take a hateful comment on social media personally. But it works a lot better to ignore it—or even respond and send best wishes or be vulnerable and share a time when I was struggling. It doesn't always make a difference (in fact it rarely does). But those rare moments when it does can be magical. I've had amazing conversations with people who started out attacking me and ended up thanking me for listening. They had gotten used to yelling because they felt like no one ever listened.

Not all of these life-changing people from the outside came to visit me in prison, but when they did visit, it was magical. I started out having to wear a jumpsuit for every visit—awkward and uncomfortably institutional. Then when I was transferred to Buckingham, I was allowed to wear my blues (button-up shirt and jeans). Wearing blues felt human—almost *normal*. That normalcy is what the world should want for people in prison, so they can learn to live normal lives, and learn to succeed in the normal outside world. Otherwise, prisons are just building better prisoners.

When I first started getting contact visits—actually able to hug and sit with my visitors rather than seeing them through glass—we felt together in a totally new way. We got food from the vending machines. Family and friends brought big bags of quarters so we could eat together. My favorite vending machine invention was a pizza burger—a microwave pizza with a vending machine hamburger on top, using the pizza as the lower bun of the burger. It was delicious, and I had one every visit when I could.

Inside the walls of the prison, all I drank were water, milk, and instant coffee. But, when I first got to Buckingham, I saw YooHoo chocolate drink and V8 in the vending machines, two of my favorite drinks, and I hadn't had them in years at that point. So, I got one every visit until they got another vending machine that didn't stock them.

During a visit, we would sit and eat and drink and play cards and feel like people together.

It was one of the most profoundly impactful and helpful parts of my incarceration. In a sterile, stark, and often barren place like prison, the opportunity to hug someone and to be hugged by someone is priceless. So much of prison life was spent in a constant level of tension. Over the years my shoulders only grew more tense, and my sighs grew deeper. So, during each visit, I seized the opportunity to let my guard down among people I could trust. When Bill hugged me, or when I picked Mary up and swung her around one-armed, tension melted away. I felt seen and connected. At least for an hour or two.

Then they started to take it all away.

A new anti-drug policy had sweeping consequences for mail and visits. Now when going to the visiting room we were required to change into backward-facing brown jumpsuits. They looked like potato sacks. In a stroke of typical prison absurdity, these baggy jumpsuits made it easier for guys to smuggle drugs back inside. A guy could more easily access his rectum (also known as "prison pockets") than he could in jeans.

After the policy change, chips and sandwiches disappeared from the vending machines, leaving only drinks and candy bars. The claim was that visitors were passing drugs to incarcerated people in chip bags, and the guards had no way to detect the handoffs.

Then they started strip-searching visitors before they were allowed entry. A TSA-style body scanner was installed at the entrance to all of the prisons in Virginia. That alone should have prevented the need for strip searches but, instead, it was used to justify them. Plus, they randomly posted K9 drug dogs to sniff everyone coming in—other than the staff, that is. I heard officers admit they were never properly trained to use the body scanner, and the training standard for the K9s was inadequate.

The policy was clear: Visitors had the option to refuse to be searched, but there were consequences. Not only would they be denied the opportunity to visit that day, they would be banned indefinitely. So, mothers, children, sisters, and friends were forced to choose: endure the humiliation of a complete strip search or potentially never see their loved one again.

It happened to a number of my visitors. They even strip-searched my 84-year-old grandfather, Bill. They made him strip off his clothes in front of them, then squat and cough. They didn't find anything.

And even after that humiliation they wouldn't let him have a contact visit. They ushered me around to the outside, then to the non-contact visitation room normally reserved for people in the hole. I wasn't the only one. With this warden and more searches, there were more non-contact visits than ever before.

Bill and I sat with glass between us. There were no phones like there had been at the jail—just small holes in the metal frame that had been painted over so many times they were no longer holes. We had to yell to try to be heard under normal circumstances. With three other visitors on his side and three other incarcerated people on mine yelling back and forth we couldn't hear each other at all. It didn't help that Bill had lost much of his hearing in the army.

He sat across the glass from me with tears in his eyes. He kept mouthing apologies, as if it were somehow his fault that we were separated by glass.

Sitting across from him, I felt powerless. My chest felt empty. I cried. I was so fucking angry. I felt responsible. It definitely wasn't his fault that these policies were in place. It was my fault that he had to endure them to visit me. I hated myself so much.

On top of my self-hatred, what made me so angry was that it didn't even make sense. Ten to twenty visitors were being strip-searched every weekend, but the officers weren't finding drugs. The visitors didn't have drugs on them.

They strip-searched Elizabeth, one of my visitors, and then made her sit behind the noncontact glass, because the body scanner had detected an "irregularity in her breast area." Of course there was—she was the mother of a newborn, and her breasts were full of milk. She was strip-searched, talked to in a really ugly way, and denied contact visitation because it was one of her first trips away from her baby. Even after she removed her clothes and they physically examined her breasts—an absolute violation—they wouldn't let her have a contact visit. They strip-searched her and *then* denied her visit because she was a mother.

Policies only started to change when they strip-searched a child without parental consent.

Let's be real: They were already strip-searching children. They said children were used to smuggle drugs. What was never talked about were the collateral consequences of this "standard procedure."

One day rumors started in the prison. Then we all saw the story on the news. A woman had brought the child of an incarcerated father to see him. This person was not the child's mother. The guards told her the dog had alerted on the child—sitting when she walked by—and that if she didn't consent to a search, the child would not be able to see their father—not that day, and possibly not ever again. Afraid of the consequences if she refused, the adult gave consent, even though she had no legal right to since she wasn't the child's parent or guardian. The child was strip-searched. No drugs or contraband were found. And the child was still denied a contact visit.

The father was livid, and so was the mother. She called newspapers and TV stations, who reported it. The governor of Virginia, a pediatrician by trade, called it unacceptable and disturbing. The shift commander who had ordered the search stopped coming to work—we never found out if he was fired or allowed to retire or just left. The officer who actually conducted the search was widely reviled in the prison.

There was one quiet hero. An officer we all knew refused to do the search. She couldn't stop it from happening because she was merely a corporal. She risked her job by standing up to her commanding officer, telling him it wasn't okay and that she would not follow the order to strip that child. It may have seemed like a small gesture. But it was so fucking big. Let me tell you, after that moment, there wasn't a person in that prison who wouldn't have done absolutely anything for that officer because of that simple, small thing she did.

Sometimes connection came out of nowhere.

As time passed for me in prison, I saw more and more guys in relationships—even saw them getting married. I began to realize Craig's experience, back in the jail, wasn't a fluke. It was just two years in prison I felt the magic happen to me.

A small envelope addressed to me came in the mail one day. It was from E.

The return address had a set of parentheses: "(My married name)." One of my friends had set us up to talk. E had just been through an ugly divorce and I had been going through particularly rough times, so my friend thought we could support one another.

It was an amazing letter. She was an amazing woman. I wrote back that night. We continued to write to each other. Then we made the leap to phone calls. This was when a regular fifteen-minute phone call cost $7. It was double that for out-of-state calls (which she was). So obviously we didn't talk that much.

Then she came to visit. I remember sitting in my room, dressed to go to visit, just waiting. I was vibrating at a higher frequency. I couldn't believe this woman was driving hours through rural Virginia to come see me.

Then I saw her, and she was beautiful and she was smart and she was everything. I was smitten. After two visits she pulled away. She told me, "I have too much respect for myself to wait twenty years for someone. You're amazing but you're also in prison." That was more like what I expected. And as much as it hurt, I appreciated that response. It was grounded and honest. It was realistic. On the inside, there were plenty of times when I felt a spark and then fantasized about the future. The women on the other end did as well. We would dive deeper, dream bigger, and eventually hurt a lot more.

Pen pals, who often turn into romantic partners, were hugely popular in prison. Inside we had a lot more time and often a lot more inclination to show up emotionally than people in the world. Imagine having someone spend all their time and energy on you. Imagine getting notes and poetry and drawings every week or even every day. Imagine knowing that you are someone's absolute priority. Imagine that spanning time and even continents.

The single best pen pal letter I ever got was from North Africa. The letter was smart, funny, and self-deprecating. The woman was fascinating. I immediately wrote back and included information about the recently instituted for-profit email that could be processed much faster than international mail. For $.25–.50 (depending on how many e-stamps bought) she could send me an email. Sometimes it would go straight through to my email, and sometimes it was flagged for manual review.

With that system, I could log onto the new kiosk and check emails. If there weren't any waiting for me, I looked through my email list to see if anyone new had signed up. When a new name appeared, it was always the best feeling.

The day my North African pen pal's name appeared, it was a burst of adrenaline, dopamine, and possibility. It was electric. I immediately wrote back without waiting to see if she had emailed me. (With the monitoring, emails were processed out of order or in some bizarre haphazard way.)

We emailed back and forth so many times. Then she set up a call-forwarding number so we could talk. The very day we set up to finally talk, the FCC set new regulations about interstate calls and companies followed suit, dropping intrastate calls, too. The phone calls went from $7 to $.85. So, we talked an awful lot. Hours at a time, day after day.

She was done with school. She had been doing a double major at a university in North Africa but was planning to return to the States. I couldn't imagine her moving back home to California, because from where I was in Virginia it felt just as remote and impossible as Egypt.

Her specialty didn't really make sense in SoCal. She needed to be in DC or New York to be in the middle of her field. Through our phone calls, I learned about dozens of applications and that she had gotten an internship in DC. Like a movie, she told me that she was moving just two hours away from me.

I couldn't believe this fairy tale could be true. We had been writing and talking on the phone for months. I was excited—the most I ever remember being. I was nervous.

Finally, the day came when we met face to face. We hugged and then we kissed with the full force of a storm. Then the visit got sort of awkward. It was as if our "broken parts," which with remote communication played nicely, came out in real life. By the end of the visit, we had talked through it, though it still didn't feel totally comfortable. We had a long goodbye kiss, and I watched her as she walked away through the doors, then pushed my luck and stayed in the visiting room so, from the courtyard window, I could watch her walk out to the prison's entry building. She came again a week later. She came to see me almost every weekend for months, even after she was traumatized by getting pulled aside at security and strip-searched.

To be clear, there were problems between us, big problems. We each had trauma and little broken parts. Together, we broke those parts into even smaller pieces. We both followed a familiar pattern: trying to make the other person okay instead of taking care of ourselves. There was a personality disorder involved. It was at times profoundly ugly, and I spent many days crying my eyes out and wondering what I had done wrong.

Ours was the relationship where I felt the highest highs and the lowest lows. Sometimes it hurt so badly that I made poor choices and turned to destructive coping mechanisms. This slow spiral led me to one of the darkest moments of my life, where first I was again relying on narcotics for comfort. Then, eventually, I felt so hopeless that I saw no other way than to end my own life.

I was sitting in my cell, eyes half open, facing the wall, trying to meditate through the pain. Tears were streaming down my face. I was trembling. I felt hopeless and lost. The pain was building, growing stronger and bigger. I knew I could not face another day with this much pain.

Then, as I resigned myself to my life being over, something happened. I've only been able to describe it by borrowing from Viktor Frankl, who borrowed from the Psalms: "Pushed to the wall, I called to God; from the wide open spaces he answered."

I'm not a religious person. I meditate, I practice kindness and compassion. But what happened was a genuinely spiritual experience. I had felt so closed in, so hopeless, so lost. Then, in the midst of shaking and sobbing, I felt the space around me expand, almost infinitely. I felt not myself but a part of this vast, amazing world. I started sobbing harder but now the tears were of joy instead of sadness.

Life isn't a 1980s movie montage, though. I couldn't just speed through the healing process. I was still in a lot of pain. I still had a lot of work to do. I still had a lot of changes to make.

That was when I deepened my daily practice. I again committed myself to sitting with uncomfortable feelings. I would face all the things rather than kicking them down the road. In many ways, this moment in my cell was like the day I was arrested—the end of something terrible and the beginning of something much better. I can only see that now, in retrospect. At the time it was fucking terrifying.

August 16, 2016. I had been in prison for nearly fourteen years and I didn't know that it was the first day of the rest of my life.

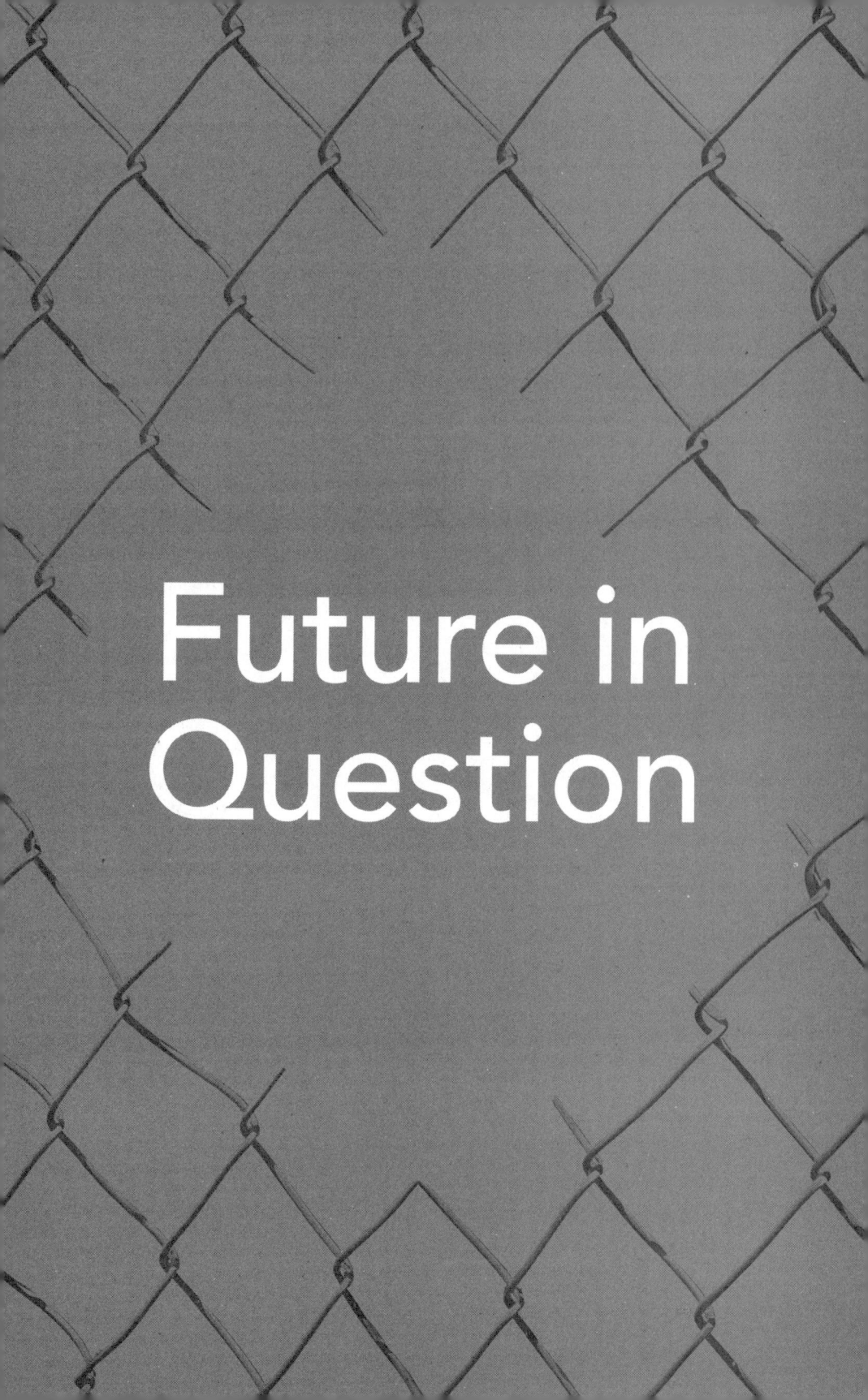

Future in Question

Chapter 19

The Tipping Point

When I was first arrested, I couldn't imagine spending days or weeks in the jail waiting for a bail hearing. When I was denied bail, I couldn't imagine spending months or years in prison. When I was sentenced to serve thirty-two years, it broke my brain. I hadn't even been alive nearly that long. So, I broke things down into shorter periods. The first month. The first year. One quarter of my sentence. Halfway.

Because of good time and considerations, I knew my earliest possible release date. I marked down the big fractions on a calendar, a practice I repeated over the years.

I was excited when I finished one quarter of the sentence. It felt like a sign that I could actually make it through. Every day was the same, but each day started to feel like I was moving toward something.

When I was coming up on the halfway point of my sentence, I thought it would be another big success.

The last night of the first half of my sentence, I marked it off the calendar. I breathed deeply. I was smiling. It would all be smooth sailing from there. I went to sleep feeling optimistic.

The next morning, I could barely get out of bed.

It was all hitting me in a new way. The harm I had done. The length of my sentence. How tired I was. I had spent more years in prison than I had spent in school. It was all I knew for the entirety of my adult life.

I didn't know if I could do it all again—the second half. Rather than feeling like I had accomplished something, I felt even more hopeless and lost.

My arrest had been important. It took me off the street and forced me to reckon with myself. It helped me clear my head and get perspective on my life. It taught me how to stand on my own two feet and work toward something. At this point, looking at the rest of my sentence I didn't feel growth happening. I just felt worn out. With every day I felt like I was coming apart more and more, like I was becoming less.

The force of habit can overcome the heaviest of emotions. I started moving but felt like a shell of myself all day. Then all week.

Slowly, I got back into my groove of making the best of things. I tutored and I exercised. Sometimes I even smiled and laughed. Behind it all, though, I felt a weight. I was getting back to life, but I worried who I would be in a year or a decade or when I finally got out.

I had seen people broken by their time in prison. Their spirits were squashed. The light in their eyes was gone. They were so institutionalized it reminded me of Brooks from *Shawshank Redemption*, who couldn't make it in the outside world when he was given the chance.

I focused on gratitude. I did for others. I did all the things that had brought me peace and meaning in the past. It worked, sort of, because I still couldn't shake the fear that prison would eventually break me.

Chapter 20

Old Law, New Law

Once I completed sixteen and a half years in prison, the high point of the sentencing guidelines in my case, I started putting together a petition for conditional pardon. I had worked in the law library for five years, but I still didn't have clear direction on how to file a meaningful petition. There were almost no guidelines, just a one-page sheet asking for particulars including a requirement to meet "extraordinary circumstances"—with no explanation of what that meant. From what I saw, guys sent off pardon petitions, then never heard anything back. The process was opaque and mysterious.

The constitution gave the executive branch the ability to substitute its judgment for that of the courts. Because of the traditional separation of powers, this was rarely used.

I had never known anyone who had gotten a pardon, so I couldn't ask what the process looked like, much less what had worked or what to avoid. I started from the beginning. I answered the questions asked on the single-sheet application put out by the secretary of the Commonwealth. I wrote draft after draft. I accepted responsibility for the things I had done. I described earning a bachelor's degree over fifteen years, becoming a journeyman electrician, helping start the peer-support mental health program, mentoring and tutoring others, and writing articles for publication. Then I explained the work I wanted to do when I got out—how I wanted to find a way to give back and help heal where I had harmed.

I gathered all the evaluations, certificates, and awards I could find. By that point I had taken every program and class that was available. I included my yearly assessment—an algorithmic evaluation of all the factors in my case as well as my answers to an in-depth questionnaire, which concluded that I was at the lowest risk for recidivism possible.

The conditional pardon was my last resort. I had long ago exhausted appeals and habeas corpus petitions. Some guys didn't need it, though; they were still parole eligible.

When I was first arrested in 2002, everyone was divided into two camps: "old law" and "new law"—those who were sentenced before 1995 (so eligible for parole) and those who were sentenced after 1995 (so not eligible).

Old law people had a chance at release regardless of the length of their sentence—even life sentences were usually parole eligible—but they lived in uncertainty. Once they reached their eligibility date—usually no more than fifteen years—they would meet with a parole investigator and have their case reviewed by the entire parole board. They could be granted parole, denied parole, or denied parole with a "three-year hit," meaning they wouldn't be considered again for three years.

They might go up for parole once and have it granted. They might go up every year for thirty or forty years and never be released. New law guys like me knew what our sentence was. If it was life, then we were never going home. If it was fifteen years, we would be going home in fifteen years or slightly less. Sometimes I was envious of the parole guys, having the possibility of earning their way home. Sometimes I was grateful to know, for sure, that I had a release date; even if it was decades in the future.

In 1994, Governor George Allen signed Virginia's Truth-in-Sentencing bill as part of a sweeping national movement to abolish parole. Anyone arrested after January 1, 1995, was, instead, sentenced under ESC, meaning that instead of parole, they would be eligible for "good time"—from 0 to 4.5 days off their sentence for every thirty served, based on good behavior and participation in treatment plans.

Ironically, I met and visited Governor Allen's office as a kid, not realizing just how dramatically his actions would one day impact my life.

In Governor Allen's office on a Cub Scout trip. I'm on the very left. The young, coyly smiling kid.

Had Governor Allen never signed that bill I would have been parole eligible and I would have had an incentive to stay out of trouble, take classes, help other people, and change my life because it would make it much more likely that I would be granted parole and released prior to the end of my sentence. Under the "new law" system I could do drugs, fight, gangbang, and do little else without a significant impact on my release date. This put judges in the position to be fortune tellers and guess, based on a few minutes of interaction, when someone will be safe to return to society. It is about punishment rather than rehabilitation.

I spent months working on the language of the pardon petition. I wrote dozens of request forms, to my counselor and the school, asking for copies of relevant documents. I reached out to people, both within the prison and outside, asking for letters of support. My mother started a wide-ranging campaign to promote my petition and created a website to inform people about my case and to request support. I didn't expect to be released. At that point, the pardon process felt like a black hole. Any grants were outliers and usually happened at the end of a governor's term, to a handful of people for PR reasons, or because someone (conveniently and of course totally unrelated to the person about to be pardoned) had donated a significant amount of money to the governor's campaign or their future campaign for a role in the federal system.

I applied because I wanted peace of mind. I wanted to know I had done everything possible so I wouldn't always wonder if things could have been different. That would mean I could let go and serve the rest of my time. Once again, it was about doing the next right thing and letting go of the result.

Over the years I had been writing essays and random musings that I shared with friends and family. Eventually, my mother started sharing everything I wrote on my Facebook page. Once I started the pardon process, I asked her to use that Facebook page to friend request everyone possible. I didn't know anything about social media, only that the more people I got to read my story, the greater chance that I would have support. I didn't know if it would help but, at the very least, I knew it couldn't hurt. Plus, it felt good to hear that dozens or even hundreds of people had reacted positively to my writings and posts. Many people interacted and contributed and supported my efforts. No one had a bigger impact than Courteney Stuart.

Courteney had accepted a Facebook friend request without realizing that I was incarcerated. Then, one day when she was scrolling, she came across one of my essays about accountability and people "trapped" in the old parole system. I had written about how the parole board is appointed by the governor, and so its tone and the percentage of grants given to old law guys are political rather than scientific. I mentioned that there were more than one thousand "old law" guys still in Virginia and they wondered if they'd ever be going home. Some of those guys did really heinous things. But most, or at least most of the guys I met over my years inside, were ready to come home. They just wanted to get a job, settle down, enjoy a cup of real coffee in the morning and time with family at night. I highlighted that Virginia was spending tens of thousands of dollars every year to keep each of them in prison without providing meaningful programs, opportunities, or a path to release. The state wasn't addressing their medical issues until they became catastrophic and enormously expensive. Courteney was the investigative reporter for a local TV station, researching a piece on the effects of the abolition of parole, and so it was a perfect fit. She contacted my mother, saying she wanted to interview me as a counterpart to the local representative who was fully in support of the abolition.

Then Courteney reached out to me. I was nervous about speaking with her because several of the TV stations had a reputation for being very "law and order," and failing to give fair or equal coverage to anyone or anything in the criminal legal system. I was worried how she would approach the issue. I asked everyone in Charlottesville—where I was from and from where she reported—and heard nothing but universally positive (even glowing) praise. They said she was an excellent journalist and insisted on giving fair coverage to all parties. I agreed to do the interview. It was by phone because the Virginia Department of Corrections (VaDOC) had banned all video recording in prisons.

At our scheduled time, I sat in the housing unit in a plastic chair next to the phone bolted to the wall, picked up the receiver, and dialed the big silver buttons. Courteney answered right away and accepted the prepaid call (she had offered to pay the collect fee but I was grateful for the opportunity and paid off my account). I immediately liked her. We talked through one twenty-minute call, then another. She told me to stay in touch.

She also interviewed my mother, asking her about the experience of a loved one powerless as they watched their child get locked away. I really think incarceration can be harder on the family members than the one incarcerated because the families feel completely powerless and only imagine the worst. In the interview my mother told Courteney that when I got arrested she thought it was over for me—I would "really turn bad in prison." I saw it on TV that night, or maybe the next. Courteney gave the details of parole, the abolition, and the good time system that replaced it. It showed her interview with the delegate. It cut to her interview with my mother. Then the program cut to a screen with my picture on one side and hers on the other, with our interview audio playing and captions on the screen.

Everyone in the prison saw it. People in prisons across the state saw it. Many in the Charlottesville community saw it.

I have never gotten so many high fives and hugs in my life. Guys in the prison said, "You didn't forget about us." Because I had talked about parole and my clemency petition, but I had also talked about the kids—fifteen or sixteen years old—as well as the adults who were sentenced for fifty, sixty or 100 years for crimes in which no one had died. I had made it about the issues rather than myself, and I got a lot of support for that.

I also got support in the wider community across Virginia. People sent friend requests. They sent letters to say hi. They wrote letters of support for my petition. One friend pulled strings to try to get someone in touch with the governor's chief of staff. Somehow, miraculously, the far-fetched idea of getting pardoned started to have wheels.

Plus, I met Courteney.

Prison is a dark void offset by a dim hue of camaraderie and bright flashes of connection. Sometimes this is genuine human interaction inside. At times it's with people far away, like two quarks somehow spinning in the same direction despite being separated by space and time.

Courteney was one of those bright flashes spinning in the same direction as me. We were miles apart, had vastly different life experiences, and had never met in person. It didn't matter.

We had only talked on the phone because of recording restrictions, but bizarrely, she had actually come inside the prison where I was, to interview (in person) another incarcerated person pursuant to her podcast and investigation into the international and arguably famous Jens Söring and his claims of innocence. As chance would have it, Jens was someone I talked with regularly.

It turns out her visit to the prison was just the tip of the iceberg. Courteney and I had been ships passing in the night for decades.

As a teenager I hung out at the outdoor downtown mall in Charlottesville. I was there with my baggy jeans, long hair, and mass of insecurity. One of the coffee shops I often sat in front of had apartments above it—apartments where Courteney and her then-husband lived. The door to the steps was right next to my favorite seat. We probably passed hundreds of times.

When I was old enough to get my license, she had moved out to the country, on the same road that I grew up on. As a young, new mother, her biggest fear was the cars that sped along recklessly, taking the curve in front of her house too fast. She was always worried that someone would hit her old minivan as she was pulling into or out of the driveway.

I was one of those dumb kids driving a 1986 Mustang GT.

There again we must have crossed paths hundreds of times over the years. We didn't realize it at first, but when we did it almost seemed like the flashback scene of a romance movie.

After the story on the abolition of parole we stayed in touch. She told me to call anytime I had a story and—surprise!—prison is full of stories of mismanagement, neglect, conflict, and other newsworthy issues.

She covered the scabies outbreaks. She covered the family members being strip-searched before visitation, then still being denied contact visits. She was especially upset about the seven-year-old girl who was strip-searched without parental consent.

I was so used to being locked away— the fences kept people out as much as they kept us in—that having a line to the outside *and* someone who cared enough to tell my story, our stories, was amazing. It was empowering to have someone willing to broadcast our voices to the world. It was transformative.

Eventually Courteney decided to invest in herself and leave the news station to focus fully on her podcast and the complex investigation that would eventually lead her to a central role in a Top 10 Netflix special. When she told me she was leaving the station, I asked if I could keep calling. I loved what Courteney did as a reporter, and I had grown to appreciate her as a person. Plus, I just really enjoyed talking with her. Then, one night I called and heard panic in the pitch and cracking of her voice. I had learned young to be hypervigilant and recognize small cues—facial expressions, body tension, inflection.

I asked what was wrong.

Courteney offered me a choice: We could maintain a professional relationship or she could talk to me personally—and she would never again be able to use me as a source for her reporting. There are a lot of reporters in the world but only one Courteney Stuart, so I jumped at the opportunity to be there for her.

She was in a panic because someone in her life was not doing well. Things had come to a head with life-threatening action and danger—sorry to be vague but that isn't my story to tell—and she was unsure of what to do. I had some experience with life-threatening danger and some of the specific issues so I listened, I shared my take, and she was able to find a little relief.

Once we broke through the professional barrier, I called more often and we quickly developed a much more complete friendship. We talked about books and life. We joked about daily stressors and realized we both had the same neurotic ADHD mindset backed by morbid humor as a coping mechanism. We started to really like each other and looked forward to each call, whether they were a few days or weeks apart. All this was happening while I was still exploring a long-distance relationship with a different woman, whom I also had not yet met in person.

Courteney and I were clearly destined to exist in each other's lives in some way, we just didn't know how. I kept in mind that no one gets to choose the outcome, so I focused on the daily steps. We kept talking and enjoying each other's over-the-phone company.

Chapter 21

Prison Highs and Lows

I had it made when I moved into the honor pod.

Reginald worked maintenance with me. In his sixties and in prison for more than half his life, he was a fount of information because he had seen and fixed pretty much everything that could break in those prisons. Plus, he had a great personality and sense of humor. One morning, he came to work with an excited smile. He told me, "Pack your bags!" At first, I thought he meant I was getting transferred to a different prison, then I realized I would be moving to the honor pod, the most coveted housing unit.

The tough guys around the prison talked badly about the honor pod, saying it was full of old guys and snitches. It was definitely full of old guys because it took so long to get into. In reality, the tough guys talked badly about it because they knew they'd never make it there. After twelve years of waiting, including a few months of being number one on the list, I finally was going to be moved into a single cell.

Unlike every other pod in the prison, which were all doubled up, there were thirty-two cells and only thirty-two people. These were still single cells as the prison had originally been designed: one bunk in a room. That meant half the number of people in the pod to compete for the shower, phone, or microwave. The solid doors were only locked during count times or at night. They created a sense of privacy rather than captivity. There was a back patio with picnic tables. Oh, and there were dogs.

The pen pal program took in abused and neglected dogs who weren't "fit" for adoption and connected them with incarcerated handlers who trained them and helped them acclimate to human contact. It was broken people helping broken dogs. It was the most healing thing I saw in all my years.

Quinn was one of those dogs. He was so well behaved and loved that the program decided to keep him full time at the prison. He was our mascot. He was my daily source of joy.

Quinn, the best dog ever, and me on the patio of the honor pod at Buckingham Correctional.

Once I was in the honor pod, I had my coffee most every morning on the back patio. Quinn came running out the door and sniffed everyone, looking for treats. He jumped up, tried to lick my face, then happy-waddled to the next person and eventually out to the grass where he did his business.

This brought me more joy than I know how to share. Early on in my time, the only dogs I saw were the security dogs at Nottaway that were used to menace us as we moved from one area to the next, or the K9 officers' dogs who pointed out so many people to be strip-searched without cause. Quinn wasn't being directed by a handler. He was free to just be a dog. I loved being around him.

This incredible, healing, wonderful program was only available to a tiny fraction of the population. There were six handler positions in a prison of nearly 1,100 people, and these positions were only open to someone living in the honor pod, which took more than a decade to get into.

That's how prison was: Here is this good thing. It's clear that it works. We are going to underutilize it, if we use it at all.

The honor pod also felt relaxing and comfortable in a way that I hadn't experienced up to that point. I had my own space. I didn't constantly worry about whether my roommate would need the cell or have to go to the bathroom. It was the first time during my incarceration that I was living in a way that felt human and dignified.

Then the whole world got tipped on its head.

The first time the Covid-19 pandemic became real to us, as opposed to something on the news, was the notice in every pod on DOC letterhead: "Visitation is suspended until further notice."

We had never not had visitation for more than a week or two. This was hard to grasp. When would it resolve? Would it ever resolve?

I had gotten a heads-up about the pandemic from my friend during a visit. We were sitting across the small table from each other, and she started describing how much Covid was going to "mess things up." But with her cocky smile, her relaxed stance taking up as much space as she could with one ankle across her other leg, I thought she was giving me a hard time. She was serious, though. Then I believed she was being alarmist. There was no way a flu in China would affect us in the United States. And especially not me in prison.

I was looking forward to my grandfather Bill visiting me soon. He normally visited every month but a perfect storm of funerals, changed plans, and complications meant I hadn't seen him for nearly three months. Finally, he was scheduled to come that weekend. Then, on Friday, the visitation suspension notice went up in the pod.

Visitation was where I was fully able to share and feel and process. Not being able to see anyone, or hug anyone—indefinitely—was scary as hell. Especially when I thought about my grandfather.

Bill had always been active. He ran and he biked, sometimes hundreds of miles. He lived, again, in the small town where he was born but had traveled and lived all over the world. He had done a dozen different things but always lived a life of service. Unfortunately, in his eighties he was starting to slow down. With visitations suspended till further notice, I was afraid I would never see him again.

First, they canceled visits. Then they canceled school and programs. They had the prison factories manufacture masks made from the lining of state-issued jackets. Then I vividly remember the rattle of carts rolling down the boulevard. We all ran to the windows and saw guys in masks, their eyes haunted, pushing carts with all of their belongings from population down to the hole, where they would be quarantined. Walking in front and behind them were nurses in full PPE. I looked at the guy next to me and recognized my own shock in his expression. The pandemic was here. They sent the prison-wide order. Each of us was locked away in our cell.

I paced a lot that first week. Back and forth in the small space. It was the first time I could do it without bothering my roommate. It was my attempt at self-soothing. Not sure it worked.

It was near total isolation. We were locked in our cells for months. Commissary was closed for most of that time and some guys who hadn't prepared started yelling out to see if they could borrow toothpaste or soups or coffee. An officer would come by and drop a Styrofoam container of food on our door three times a day. If we were lucky, every few days we would be allowed, one at a time, into the pod for a brief call or shower. Then back into our cells. During a normal lockdown people with vital jobs were searched first, then let back out to keep the institution running. Not this time. No exceptions, at least at first. Because they didn't have the incarcerated kitchen workers to cook, the institution made a mass purchase of hot dogs, junk food, and microwavable items. Staff not only had to do their normal jobs but also heat and serve thousands of hot dogs and make bag breakfasts, lunches, and dinners every single day. They had to clean and take out the trash. They were not happy.

Then the National Guard came.

Sitting in my cell, I heard the pod door open. Traffic from outside the pod had become less frequent since the pandemic started, since we didn't go in or out and the staff was busy with other tasks. It wasn't the door that caught my attention, though. It was the thunder of boots. I peered out my slot and saw someone in a military uniform leading a dozen or more people wearing hazmat suits, full helmets, and respirators marching through the door and forming inside the pod. It was like something out of a sci-fi movie set in space.

I heard the cell door at the end of the row open. Then it shut a few moments later. I heard orders given in breathy mechanical voices. One cell at a time. Then they got to my door. It opened, and I followed their directions to come out. I sat at a table, leaned my head back then felt the sting as someone shoved a stick up my nostril. They were thorough, even forceful. The insides of my nose felt scratched and almost sore. We would get the results in a few days.

Then the first guy died.

We had all known him or at least known of him. He was relatively young and healthy. It scared the crap out of us.

Then another guy died.

Then, somehow, just as we had adapted to prison, we started to adapt to our new reality.

After a few months, we were able to leave our cells for longer periods. We could use the phone regularly and hang out in the pod and eventually go out on the patio for a bit to exercise or enjoy the air. When I first got locked up, I couldn't imagine being stuck in even one building for long. Now, after months in a cell, I was beyond grateful just to be able to walk out of my cell, even if it was into a larger, locked room. That felt like freedom.

Eventually we could go out onto the big rec yard for an hour every few days. That felt like heaven. I usually hate running but being able to run around that track felt like traveling the world after being stuck in small spaces for months.

Jail and prison taught me the extremes we can adapt to. I can get used to being locked in boxes, I can cope with all sorts of stressors, and I can find ways to experience joy in even the darkest of times. Every place, no matter how barren and hopeless, offers an opportunity.

Before the pandemic, I had been going back to the SAM pod to teach Spanish and a nonviolent communication class. When they canceled school and programs they also canceled movement between pods, so there was no way to hold classes. The psych head came up with a solution and, much to my surprise, it was approved by the central office. That's why, in the middle of the day, she was able to get me from my cell and take me to the school building. We were alone. There were no officers on post, because no one had used the building in months.

We walked into one of the back classrooms. She handed me a set of markers and set up a phone on a tripod in front of the whiteboard. I then taught Spanish and nonviolent communication to the phone as she recorded a video. It was my first time being recorded like this, so I felt really strange speaking into a camera lens, but she stood behind the phone and encouraged me, made a few suggestions, and recorded several lessons in a row. I credit those initial, truly awkward moments as a big part of why I'm so comfortable in front of a camera or an audience today. These videos were recorded onto DVDs and sent to every prison in the state. (At least the Spanish lessons were; something happened with the NVC recordings and they never got sent out.) I was used to a base level of SNAFU (situation normal all fucked up) in prison, so I was disappointed about the NVC lessons, but not surprised.

Every person in a Virginia prison could now turn on their TV (if they had one) and tune in to the prison station to watch classes and presentations that normally would be held in person, including classes taught by me and other incarcerated people.

Once everyone saw my Spanish videos, I became known as the "Spanish guy." I was doing social media before I knew social media was a thing.

During Covid, all transfers to other facilities had been canceled. But with a renewed interest in safety and ventilation came the realization that the airflow in Buckingham was not adequate. Out of the 1,100 people at Buckingham, sixty-four people—the number of individuals in a pod—had to be packed up and moved so they could have an empty unit to repair, then shuffle people around and repair another unit.

I had found a relative level of comfort in the honor pod at Buckingham.

So when I heard names called to pack up for transfer, I didn't want to leave. I had been fearing a transfer for the entire thirteen years I was at Buckingham. To be fair, I should have been gone long before. Buckingham was a level 3 facility and I had scored level 2 points for years because I had stayed out of trouble and done all the right things. But moving down to a level 2, which usually had dormitories rather than cells, was a punishment. I started having literal nightmares about being locked in a dormitory, about the lack of quiet and no privacy. I tried to spin it in a positive way, but there was no part of me that felt optimistic.

Someone else in the honor pod was called and told to pack his stuff. I felt terrible for him (and also breathed a sigh of relief that it hadn't been me). I wondered why he didn't have the pull to get his transfer canceled—he had been a hearings "inmate advisor" before being a dog trainer. He had rubbed elbows with the administration.

The next day I was called to the booth. The dog trainer had, in fact, managed to get his transfer canceled, and another name had been picked. That person had a medical emergency and had to be replaced. One more name, from nearly 1,100 people.

They drew my name.

I had been lucky, but my time was up. I packed my stuff. It was amazing how much I had managed to fit into my small cell. Over the years I had accumulated more and more things. I had packed it all in the foot and wall locker, shoved it under the bed, and piled things on top of the large fluorescent light housing that I used as a shelf. Policy dictated that I was limited in what I could bring to the new prison: No more than thirteen books, a few pens and pencils, personal clothes, and the purchase limit for food, hygiene, and stamps. So, I had a giant "Buy Nothing Estate Giveaway" of all the extras and the contraband I had collected over the years. Then I carried my stuff over to the property office, packed it into boxes, and waited for the next morning when those of us being transferred would be loaded onto the bus and taken to our new home. They even told us our destination: Coffeewood. I sighed, because it was a level 2, a dormitory. Exactly what I had feared.

The night before I left was like *A Christmas Carol*, except that I was visited by ghosts of random kindness. People often think of prison as hard, violent, and tragic. It can be. But people are also sometimes kind, silly, and utterly human.

One guy carried his TV to my cell, saying, "I have some reading to do, and I don't want you to be bored." He knew my TV, as well as all my books, were packed up and stored at property. Another guy brought me burritos he had made—the good kind, wrapped in chip wrappers so they crisped up in the microwave. Someone else pulled me aside, shook my hand, and told me what a pleasure it was to know me.

Each of these things felt really good.

Chapter 22

The Power of Adaptation

Transfer day: Thursday morning at 7 AM, an officer came in the pod and said, "Come on, Crosson, they're waiting for you."

Guys were out milling around in the pod, making their coffee, reading bibles, and doing puzzles. I shook a few more hands and headed out the door. I felt heavy. When I got down to the property office, only the property officers were there so I thought I was late. I hurriedly changed into a jumpsuit, got locked into shackles and the black box that makes picking handcuffs impossible, then shambled out to the bus.

I heard a beeping before I even got on. High and loud: *beep, beep, beep.*

I stepped onto the bus. It was empty. I wasn't late after all—I was the very first person. The guard carrying my TV balanced it on my lap and told me to be careful with it (not the easiest in handcuffs and shackles chained together).

Beep, beep, beep.

I had been thinking a lot about tiny home van and bus conversions, so to distract myself, I spent time looking around, trying to imagine how I'd lay out living quarters, a bathroom, and the like.

Beep, beep, beep.

They loaded another guy.

Beep, beep, beep.

An hour and a half and sixty-two more men later, guards boarded the bus and engaged the parking brake—and finally, finally stopped the beeping. (Prison taught me how profoundly the little things can irritate and wear a person down. I vowed to notice those little things and address them, whether they affected me or not.)

There was good news. My old roommate from before the honor pod ended up in the seat in front of me. We caught up, chatting about his daughter, recent prison stories, and the woman in my life.

The bus exited the sally port and headed out into the parking lot. A flashy SUV was waiting with a pair of new jeans and Jordans on the hood. From our idling bus, we watched a guy walk through the gate wearing brown release clothes. Stink was going home. After thirty-one years he was leaving the right way, beneficiary of the spike in parole releases of "old law" guys during the pandemic. I was shackled in the back of a bus and watching someone else walk to freedom, and I felt joy. It gave me hope. I wouldn't want to see any person who was ready to go home spend another day behind those walls. Prison breaks people. Whatever someone has done, it doesn't serve any purpose to further break people who will one day come home.

With a lurch, we pulled out onto the road.

I hadn't been outside the gates of Buckingham for thirteen years. It felt like the biggest road trip of my life. Just being in a vehicle felt alien. With tiny homes still on my mind, I assessed the square footage of every van, bus, RV, and house I saw. After eighteen years in a sub-seventy-two-square-foot cell, I couldn't imagine why someone would live in some of the farmhouses and mansions we passed.

It had been a mild summer, and we couldn't see much from within the prison. On the road, I was taken with the now-changing colors on the trees. Seeing the world again—even through the small bus window—felt so different than seeing it on TV. I could hear horns and traffic noises. I could smell the fields as we passed them. Like a little kid I was gasping and gaping and smiling. Even the shackles couldn't contain my spirit during that hour-and-twenty-minute drive.

Then we saw a sign, Coffeewood Correctional Center. We had arrived. After the ride I somehow felt full of hope. Maybe this would be a positive step.

We drove down a long, winding road and came within sight of the prison. Then we pulled around and into the sally port where we saw a long line of officers and civilian staff. A welcoming committee just for us.

Sixty-four men from the culture of a level 3-4 prison arriving at a level 2 was probably the biggest event Coffeewood had ever seen. It was a shock for both sides—we were coming from cells, some single-man cells, to an institution with eighty-two-man open dormitories. We were coming from a place with more violence and bigger issues.

As soon as I saw the dormitories, I thought, *Crap*. They were open bays with row after row of double bunks, with some single bunks in the middle to allow the staff to maintain line of sight. Less than three feet between each meant we would have to squeeze by our neighbor if he was in the "cut" between bunks or to get to the locker welded to the end of our bed.

The bathroom had urinals and toilets in a line facing a line of sinks. When I sat down to use the bathroom after breakfast, the seat was always warm from the person before me and I had to be careful so my bare leg didn't touch the leg of the person sitting next to me. A hand dryer was right in front of the end toilet so, when drying my hands, I had to stand with my ass in the face of someone sitting on the toilet. When I brushed my teeth in the morning I smelled and heard the men shitting two feet behind me.

The showers were on the other side of the sinks. Five shower heads in a row with a button on the wall and no temperature control. Sometimes scalding, sometimes chilly, never private.

Oh yes, and all of this during a pandemic. From being in cells where we could stay away from groups of people to sleeping in bunks where we could reach out and touch three other people at any time—CDC guidelines indeed. An outbreak began in the dorm next door almost as soon as we arrived, like a welcoming present. It quickly blossomed and spread.

I slept a few hours at most over the first few days. After eighteen years of being told to keep my guard up until the door was locked, I no longer had a door to lock. It put me into a panic. People walked right by my bunk at all hours of the night. Conversations, arguments, and noise from TVs carried across the dorm. I couldn't sleep.

Covid restrictions meant we couldn't get rec on the big yard. Instead, we got outside on a small, partial basketball court behind the building for an hour each day. There was no school, no programs, no meetings, and once Covid spread, almost no one around. Staff was stretched so thin that head count regularly happened an hour late.

There was no structure, no reliable timeline, and no variety between the days. There were also lots of people on drugs, lots of testosterone, and a pervasive feeling of hopelessness.

I despaired.

There were times when I would have given anything for just one night back in my single cell where I could sleep comfortably and in silence.

There was never a moment of quiet. Never a moment of solitude. This place was perfect hell for an introvert like me.

Courteney emailed me. She had tried her best to get my transfer stopped but she was no longer with the news station and I'm not sure who she could have called anyway. In her email she laid out her view: "We can't control the environment or details of the story but we can control how we tell it." That struck me as profound. I saw that I was feeling sorry for myself. I wallowed in it just a little bit more, then I got back to the things that made my life full and meaningful.

I started a daily Spanish class. Then two daily classes. I wrote. I exercised. I read.

There were issues. During one of our Spanish classes, as we sat in chairs in a circle in the day room, an officer approached and told us we couldn't "congregate."

"Ma'am, just out of curiosity, why not?" I asked.

"Covid regulations."

My jaw dropped. Here we were feet apart—farther apart than we were forced to sleep—and she was telling us that we couldn't congregate because of Covid regulations?

I had put up with a lot of dumb things and a lot of dumb regulations, but this was a hill I would die on.

I paused and focused on keeping my voice steady. "Ma'am, I understand if you have to do your job. I'm bored and miserable and absolutely struggling, so I'm teaching Spanish because it helps. It helps me and it helps these guys who don't have any programs, any classes, any visits. If you need to write me a charge, go right ahead."

She looked at me. I hadn't been argumentative or combative. I had just been honest: I really was struggling, and teaching a Spanish class really was one of the few things keeping me sane.

"Well, I guess you're not hurting anyone," she said and turned to walk down the aisles where guys were packed in like sardines.

After a few weeks, I wasn't comfortable but I had adjusted to regular discomfort. The Covid outbreak was now in our dorm as well as throughout the entire prison. Except no one in the dorm was acknowledging it. Within a few days there were long lines of guys moaning and never getting out of their bunks. It looked like a hospital ward instead of a prison. I had symptoms: a headache, sinus pain, lethargy, and body aches.

I raised hell, asking the unit manager why the nurses weren't checking on us, and why no one had been tested. The unit manager gave a genuine apology, and the nurses arrived within an hour.

Most guys denied having any symptoms, despite looking like zombies as they had their temperatures and oxygen levels checked. They didn't want to have to move or have their lives disrupted but I didn't feel the same—this was my ticket out of the dorm. I described my symptoms with a few coughs for good measure.

Thirty minutes later, four of us were told to pack up. Two others and I had complained about Covid symptoms. The fourth had dangerously low oxygen levels.

Twenty minutes later I was rolling a cart with all my belongings to building 7-B. Normally operating as the hole, it had been half cleared out to accommodate a quarantine. Cable had been run to each cell, and I could keep all my stuff, including my TV. I was going to get my first good night of sleep since leaving the peace and quiet of an honor pod—and all it took was a Covid outbreak.

For a few days, I had a peaceful time in the hole. I watched TV. I ordered commissary. I read. Isolation isn't a good thing. It slowly wears on the human spirit. I've seen it break people. That said, I grew up an only child, in a rural area, and hiding with a good book felt comfortable. A lot of people struggled doing time in the hole but, even if I hadn't had the TV and commissary, I would have preferred the quiet to the madness of the dorm, at least for a while. I had long ago learned to be comfortable in the quiet. I had learned to be comfortable in the darkness. I had learned to adapt.

After a certain number of days, whoever was in charge of medical transfers decided there was no further threat of us being contagious. They packed us up, and we rolled our carts back to the dorm across the hall from where we had been. I rolled my cart to my bunk and saw a few familiar faces but mostly people I didn't know. My stomach sank.

When we were first transferred, we had all moved into the same dorm. It was all guys from Buckingham who knew each other, or at least knew of each other. We all had similar attitudes and structures. Basic things were understood.

Entering a new dorm with mostly people I didn't know meant navigating new politics, a new prison culture, and new phone lines. There were guys unofficially responsible for each phone. In some cases they worked to make sure everyone got a chance. Others made sure that they and their buddies got as much time as possible. Many people had to take "scraps"—meaning they could get on only when no one else wanted to, which was rare. Even with people running lines, I saw more fights over the phone than anything else.

I settled into my bunk and met my neighbors. The guy above me proudly talked about being a pimp. The guy next to me mentioned working for the CIA. I assumed both of them were lying. Damned if they weren't both telling the truth.

I talked to a guy who looked familiar. He had been a gang leader at

Buckingham but had left it behind and was now imam for the Muslims at Coffeewood. We had a good conversation about martial arts and life. He told the guy who ran his phone line to put me in. With this guy's blessing I was put into the line regularly and able to use the phone almost as much as I wanted. We started to make meals together. Soon there was a crew of us—a heavyset Latino cook, a DC gangster, the facility imam, and whatever the hell I was. I really liked those guys.

I also met Brownie Man, a tall bald guy who followed a Norse religion. He had a temper but was also the nicest, most thoughtful person I met. If I was ever on the phone when trays were being handed out, Brownie Man would bring mine to me or go set it on my bunk. He also brought me different samples from his new brownie recipes to taste.

I was settling in. I was learning to be okay. Then I got a job in medical.

I needed a job to get out of the dorm. Even after they changed the guidelines and we could use the big rec yard for an hour a day, I felt claustrophobic being locked inside. I applied for every job but the kitchen. Never the kitchen, never the 120-degree heat, the long hours, low pay, and thankless work. This from someone who used to love working in restaurants as a teenager.

At my interview for the medical job, the supervisor asked me about my qualifications. I was about to ask her exactly what qualifications she expected me to have to sweep, mop, and clean up bodily waste. Then I read the room and realized that this woman wouldn't see the humor in that. Apparently, I read the room correctly, because I got the job.

Every day I headed over to medical. I swept and mopped. I cleaned and organized. I flirted with the nurses. I got to use the bathroom in private. For the hours I was there, I felt almost "normal."

I was "trained" to handle biohazard waste. The training consisted of my watching a twenty-minute video produced by the Tennessee Department of Health in which the gist was "Do not touch the biohazard waste with your bare skin and don't let anyone else touch it either."

That led to call-outs when an old man lost control of his bowels in the shower or someone overdosed and puked all over their bunk, or their neighbor's bunk, or their neighbor. The worst was the night I had to clean a medical holding cell. A guy had smoked way too much "spice" or "K2"—synthetic marijuana—and probably done something else. He had vomited, shit his pants, then removed his pants and shit all over the cell, then smeared it around with his body. So, I suited up in my Tyvek suit, put on gloves and a mask, and walked into what looked like a crime zone.

The crazy thing is, I didn't mind. It meant getting out of the dorm. I was glad to do something, anything, other than just sit around trying to create structure for myself—I had been doing that for more than eighteen years. I guess I was adapting again. Then, right when I was getting into a routine, things changed.

February of 2021. I called Courteney and heard an absolute wreck of a human being on the other end. Someone close to her had been arrested. All she knew were the bullet points: "high-speed chase," "pistol," "drugs," and "punishable by up to twenty-five years." She was despondent, lost, and beyond consolation.

At that point in my life there wasn't a lot that I considered myself knowledgeable about. But grief, powerlessness, and the criminal legal system? I had them covered. So, we talked—or really, I mostly listened, gave space for her fears and feelings, and then answered her questions. I promised that I would call every morning, even if just for five minutes. We would talk or she could cry or scream or whatever she needed but I would be there to help her get through the start of each day.

That evening it got even crazier. I was walking through the day room and saw the email kiosk open—usually someone was sitting reading or typing emails with a long line of people waiting. Taking the opportunity, I logged in and saw a new email from my mother: "Call me! Your petition is being investigated. You could be home by the end of the year."

I read the words over and over again, not fully comprehending or believing, feeling hope and doubt and insecurities run through my body like electricity. Best-case scenario, I had nearly ten years left on my sentence. I had submitted my petition years before. Even with the positive response, the idea of release had always been a distant fantasy. Now it felt like a real possibility.

The next morning, I started a new routine. My watch alarm went off at

5:30 AM. I made instant coffee at the hot water spigot, walked back to my bunk for reading and meditation, stood up when the whistle blew for count, then waited for them to call, "Count clear!" so I could walk over to the phones and call Courteney.

Count usually cleared around 6:30 AM, and the phones were usually turned on when the count was cleared. That wasn't guaranteed, but since most guys went back to sleep, that morning time was the easiest to make back-to-back calls without someone asking to be next or getting upset over the phone.

Courteney and I talked for one full call—twenty minutes straight. She was crying but, even in her agony, she mentioned that my mother had called her about the potential pardon and she congratulated me, excited that I might actually get out.

The next day we talked for two full calls—forty minutes. The following day, it was three calls. At first it was mostly her crying and screaming while I listened, but before long we started to talk about other things to avoid dwelling on the worst-case scenarios. We talked about our hopes and dreams and also our pasts—what she has called a "data dump." We even laughed. We shared the habit of taking the steam out of difficult things by finding the (often dark) humor in them.

We were both in raw, emotional states, both still isolated due to the pandemic and both very open, verbal people. We were talking for an hour or more every day. We became each other's anchors. We were connecting without the opportunity to spend time together—everything had to be verbalized, which meant we had to look deeper into ourselves to really recognize what we were feeling and thinking so that we could express it. We talked for hours that first month. It was one of the most intimate and real connections I had ever experienced.

On March 3, 2021, a month after Courteney and I began our daily talks, I called and she answered. We chatted about the normal things, then she paused. She asked if we should talk about what was happening between us. I had been feeling this too, that *something* was happening. I said yes, grateful that we could talk about big things as well as small things. Even so, I wasn't ready for what she said next. She told me, plainly, "I'm in love with you. I don't know what you do with that, and I don't need you to say anything, but I need to tell you." No one had ever been that direct with me. I had developed a connection over the phone before but never like this—and no one had ever been so sure. In the middle of battling hope and despair, not knowing whether to believe in the possibility of release or steel myself for the next ten years in the most unpleasant place I had ever been, I had entered a new relationship.

Courteney and I continued our daily calls. Our connection deepened. In the middle of uncertainty over my fate and the fate of her loved one, we both had someone to laugh with. We read books together. We even came up with the idea for a podcast, which was mostly topical conversations recorded from our prison phone calls, though we did have a really cool intro song.

With pandemic restrictions continuing, there were still no in-person visits. But video visits were permitted. When I describe this now, people immediately assume it was as convenient and clear as a FaceTime call. Instead, imagine paying for 1970s-level technology that may or may not work, and a nonprofit organization having the state contract for the service and doubling the cost of the video visits to subsidize transportation for in-person visits, of which there were none during the pandemic. This disproportionately impacted the many families already struggling with poverty, and all they were trying to do was to stay connected. Courteney and I decided we should have a video date and see each other face to face for the first time. We were both excited. Right up to the moment of the call, when I told CIA Jack I was heading to the visit kiosk with the video camera, I had butterflies in my stomach.

The call was horrible. So horrible that I blocked it out of my head walking back to the dorm, then my bunk. Jack eagerly asked me how it had gone. I tried to mouth something but couldn't come up with the words. I didn't know what to say. Had it all been a mistake?

I couldn't imagine what Courteney had felt. I was scared and didn't know how to address it. But her first words on our next call were, "That was fucking awful, right?"

Laughing, she described how the camera on the visit kiosk was looking up my nose, with a bright fluorescent light directly behind my head. I described feeling a misaligned connection, how I felt uncomfortable or unsure with this person I knew so well but who I had never been able to see while I was talking to.

Then we laughed about it. We were both really good at catastrophizing, and the only way to disarm that process was to push it even further, to take our minds to even more outlandish extremes. That way anxiety turned to absurdity and we found ourselves laughing about just how insane our brains could be.

We weren't particularly hopeful that in-person visitation would return anytime soon. We often joked that we would meet in person the day I was released, when we were having sex in a cornfield next to the prison, as one does.

Even though we laughed, that didn't stop Courteney from feeling stress about her loved one, and so many other things. I wanted to do something for her, so I bought a massage package and had it sent to her. It made for a funny conversation when her parents said, "If you have to have a relationship with someone in prison, just make sure you don't send him any money!" and she had to tell them, "Actually, he pays for half the phone calls and bought me some massages . . ."

I wasn't "prison rich" as some people were. I didn't sell drugs or cell phones, though I did at one point sell apple pies. That was probably the best, most honest hustle I've ever had. I would bring as many apples as I could back from the chow hall. I also made rounds at chow asking people for their butter and cake if they weren't going to eat them. I peeled the apples with a plastic spork, then cut them into chunks. I coated the chunks in butter, then cooked them in the microwave with cinnamon and sugar packets. Originally, I couldn't get cinnamon from the kitchen, so I used fireball candies. Once the warehouse guys tasted the pies they started bringing me giant bags of cinnamon for a discount, or even for free.

I scraped the peanut butter icing out from between the wafers of cookies they sold on commissary. I then crushed all of the wafers and mixed them with the chow hall cake. I added a bit of milk and mixed it all into a shapeable "dough." I lined plastic trays from various commissary items with dough and microwaved them until they were hard, or even crispy.

I poured baked apples into the dough-filled trays then used leftover dough to make a crust on top. I baked them, usually for one to two minutes since everything but the top had already been cooked. I then mixed the icing from the cookies with peanut butter from commissary and a bit of water, then layered the new icing on top. The final touch was to put finely crushed wafers on top of the icing so you got a little crunch with each bite.

When my buddy told me his idea, before I took over my own "franchise," I thought apple pies were crazy. No one would both give up apples, cake, and butter—and then also pay for the finished product. I couldn't have been more wrong. Once we got into full operation, I kept being handed more apples, cake, and butter than I could carry back. We also never had a single apple pie left over. Some guys would even pay me ahead of time to make sure they could get one.

It was hard to run the apple pie business at Coffeewood, so I only had money because they were giving stimulus checks out like candy. At first only a few people in prison applied because we all thought it would be fraud. The ones who applied had life sentences or such long sentences that they didn't care about consequences.

Then a federal court faced a case where one of the state DOCs was blocking residents from receiving the check. The court examined the legislation and determined that there was no wording that excluded incarcerated people. So, with the stroke of a pen, almost every incarcerated person in the country was eligible to receive stimulus checks—we went from living on pennies to having more money than we knew what to do with. Conflict in the prison nearly disappeared. No one was going hungry or scrambling to make ends meet. It was a huge shift.

I made $0.45 per hour at my "skilled" job. All of a sudden, instead of making $54 per month, I had $1,200 on my books, then another $600, then another $1,400. I don't think I'd ever had that much money in my life.

My buddies and I made some great meals—from jerk chicken made with contraband orange soda, to cheesecake made with coffee creamer. I put a bunch of money on my phone account for calls and on the kiosk for emails. It was all good, but I was happiest to be able to buy the massages for Courteney. I saved the rest. I had ten years left on my sentence so it made sense to stretch things out as far as possible.

Courteney and I still had no idea what the future would look like. We were both scared and excited about all that might come.

Chapter 23

Sudden Release

Frankie and I took turns doing burpees in between bunks. Even at a fast pace, it felt slow and laborious to get down on all fours, do a pushup, jump back up, and clap my hands over my head. We kept going. I was drenched in sweat and felt that sweet burn in my lungs. Burpees are one thing I learned in prison that I'll probably do for the rest of my life. It's the one-size-fits-all exercise that keeps me strong and trim (when I do enough of them).

Working out inside meant I'd be able to skip rec and get on the phone. Even with my phone line access I wasn't guaranteed a spot at a specific time of day. So, in addition to our morning chats, I often scheduled time to call Courteney when others were out at rec. I loved lifting weights and doing my one-mile sprints, but as long as I got my sweat in, I didn't care whether it was inside or out. And some days I needed to talk to her more than I needed fresh air.

I walked up to the day room, where the phones were, and sure enough one of the guys motioned that he hadn't gotten through and asked if I wanted the phone. I slid into the chair and dialed, first my state number and pin, and then Courteney's number.

It rang. Once, then again, then again. That was when I noticed the counselor waving wildly at me through the entry area, across the glass partition in front of where I was sitting.

I knew something was strange because the counselor wasn't wearing a mask. At this point during Covid most people had grown lax, but she was always strict and wouldn't interact with anyone unless both people were wearing a mask.

This time she waved me right into her office. Being called into the office was how guys heard about losing a loved one or got terrible news from the outside. But she seemed excited so I wasn't as nervous as I would normally be.

As I walked in, I spotted her phone's receiver lying on the desk. The phone was on speaker. Once she closed the door, the counselor said to the person on the other end of the line, "I'm here with Mr. Crosson."

A disembodied voice on the phone asked, "Mr. Crosson, are you sitting down?"

"No, I, uh . . ."

"Because you're leaving Coffeewood today," the voice continued. "You've been granted a pardon."

My legs trembled, and I fell to one knee. Tears filled my eyes. I felt unsteady.

The voice over the phone continued, "Congratulations, Mr. Crosson. I don't get to deliver a lot of these messages. Now get ready, you're going to have some paperwork to fill out."

I had woken up on August 16, 2021, with zero expectation that it would be any different than any other day. I had nearly ten years left on my sentence. I followed the same routine. I made coffee. I read. I meditated. I called Courteney. I went to work. I didn't know it was, once again, the first day of the rest of my life.

After getting the news, I walked back to my bunk, in shock, wondering if this was real. I called Frankie over.

"I'm going to give you all my stuff," I told him. "If something happens I'll need it back but otherwise it's yours."

A pardon didn't feel real, so I didn't trust saying the word out loud. I was convinced there had been a mistake, or that there would be an elaborate rug pull if I started to believe.

Frankie gave me a strange look. As far as he knew, I had just been on the phone—or trying to get on the phone—and he might have thought I was going to snap or go fight someone over it.

"No, it's okay. I'll tell you later," I said.

I packed all my food and my hygiene items into a bag and handed them to him. All of those things made life inside so much easier and better. I couldn't imagine them not being important to me anymore, but I also couldn't imagine taking them with me.

I was still covered in sweat from the workout. In shock and running on muscle memory, I grabbed my towel and soap, then ran to the shower, which was empty because guys still hadn't come in from outside.

Rinsing off in the shower, I heard the booth officer's voice through the intercom: "Crosson to the booth. 41-Bottom to the booth." I knew it was echoing through the dorm, but only I knew the significance. I rushed back to my bunk and pulled on my scrubs, grabbed my ID, and headed up front. The officer slipped me a pass to the administration building through the slot and opened the door.

I only remember snippets. It was a mad dash of running around and filling out paperwork. First, I signed to accept my pardon (as if I was going to refuse the long list of conditions if it meant getting out). Then to medical to sign a release for my medical history (which, by the way, I still haven't gotten). Then they assigned two officers to me. With my signature on the paperwork, I was no longer an incarcerated person. The officers were responsible for my safety and well-being, meaning they had to escort me.

With the two officers, I walked back to the dorm to pack the few things I was taking home. I still felt shell-shocked. It still didn't seem real. When the door opened and I walked inside, nearly everyone stood and started clapping, whistling, and calling my name. I felt like a presidential candidate, shaking hands while people clapped me on the shoulders. The news that I was going home had gotten out. If everyone in the dorm believed it, maybe I could, too.

Seeing their smiles and feeling their genuine happiness for me was awesome. I expected guys to be jealous or hate me, but even those I didn't like or get along with shook my hand and wished me the best.

The officers were very clear that I had to follow policy and take all of my stuff with me when I left. But they also turned their backs when I gave my TV and remaining belongings away. I knew the life-changing feeling of getting a TV when I hadn't had one or getting a good meal for the night. In that moment, I was happy to help the guys I was leaving behind. It was the only part that seemed real.

Next, to the property room, where they issued me tan release clothes. The pants were too long and hung over the tips of my shoes before I rolled them up. The blue boat shoes felt comfortable. (I actually preferred them to the state boots.) The tan polo shirt wasn't bad but felt alien because I hadn't worn one like it in twenty years. The few personal letters and books I was taking home with me were packed into a cardboard box.

I hefted the box and walked out the door, then down the boulevard. I saw Mike, one of the guys who had become a friend but who had been at work when I got the news. Part of me wanted to run over and shake his hand or give him a hug. The other part of me was on autopilot. I waved and kept going. I couldn't connect my thoughts to my actions.

I walked past the sign that read, "No Inmates Past This Point." Out of nowhere I started shaking again. Going past that sign made it even more real.

Exiting the final sally port and leaving the secure portion of the prison was like walking through the airlock in a sci-fi movie. I was going from one world to the next.

Then I spotted my mother standing across the room. Our eyes met. There had been no visits during the entirety of the Covid pandemic. I hadn't seen my mother or been in the same room as her for a year and a half. Our relationship was complicated, but the moment wasn't. It was all good.

However, I couldn't leave yet. The officer at the front desk passed me a stack of papers to fill out, one page after the next. She handed me a debit card with the remaining balance from my prison account and warned me to get the money off as quickly as possible. I picked up my box of stuff, headed to my mother, dropped the box, and picked her up for a hug. With her feet off the ground she whispered in my ear, "Jesse, let's get the fuck out of here."

I laughed and walked outside, without handcuffs or shackles for the first time in nearly nineteen years.

The colors . . . Imagine living in a world of only a few basic hues for so long that you forget the rest of the rainbow. Then walk into an explosion of color. An explosion of smells. A light brighter than you remember. I was in shock. I was also in awe.

Exactly five years to the day since I had woken up and wanted to take my life, I was free.

Reentry

Chapter 24

Outside

The morning of my release, my mother had called Courteney and left a wild message about how I was getting out and how she was headed to pick me up. She urged Courteney to meet us at the prison. Since the initial TV interview, my mother and Courteney had stayed in contact, and as Courteney and I explored our relationship, they had grown closer.

Courteney hadn't taken the call, because she was in a meeting for a consulting project at the TV station. By the time she checked her messages and called my mother back, I was being released in thirty minutes and she was forty-five minutes away.

Walking out of the prison, my mother and I made small talk. We didn't know how to talk about the life-changing release. She drove us to the end of the long, winding prison driveway. I flashed back to the day I had arrived at Coffeewood on the transport bus. The road felt so different this time—rather than to a different version of somewhere I knew, it was leading somewhere entirely new. My mother parked in a nearby gated driveway that led to a farmer's cornfield. She had the foresight to take a photograph of me. It was my first picture out of prison, and even when I look at it now, my newness to the outside world is clear.

From the driveway to a farmer's field, next to Coffeewood
Correctional Center. My first picture free.
Courtesy of Nancy Kern

Then we waited.

We ran out of small talk and sat there in silence, listening to the corn blowing gently in the wind. Under a haze of numbness, I could feel a spark of excitement—and nervousness.

A black Volkswagen pulled up, and Courteney got out. She didn't look anything like she had in that first video visit. She was stunning. Her eyes were alive and sparkling. I felt frozen, hardly believing she was standing right in front of me.

After a pause, I walked up and gave her a long hug, then a kiss. We had gotten to know each other so well yet this was the very first time we had actually met. We looked into each other's eyes for what felt like ages. We were spellbound. We laughed, awkwardly at first, then deep belly laughs.

I turned to my mother and hesitated. Then I said, "We have something we need to go do."

She nodded and gave me a hug. Courteney and I got into her car, and we went to look for our cornfield.

Her knuckles were white as she gripped the steering wheel. We drove and drove. We didn't know our destination, just that we wanted to find a place to be alone. The corn wasn't fully grown so it wouldn't offer the cover we originally imagined. Then, in the distance, we saw a sign: Budget Inn.

I was tense and didn't feel "qualified" to talk to a motel clerk. I wasn't sure I was supposed to be free—so Courteney went into the office while I waited in the car, grinding my teeth and rubbing my thumbs together. When she came out with the key, I felt relieved. I got out of the car with a smile, picked her up and carried her up the stairs to the second level of the motel and down the outside walkway to our room. I'm not sure if it was romantic or ridiculous but we were laughing the whole time.

I was nervous. After nearly twenty years of being alone and taking care of my own needs, I didn't know how intimacy would be. I didn't want to disappoint her or somehow ruin things. I had no idea how it would go.

Things turned out fine. Thirty or forty minutes (well, maybe fifteen minutes) later, my confidence boosted by our activities, I surprised the clerk by dropping off the key. He cocked his head sideways, confused, and asked if there was a problem with the room. I laughed. "Nope. The room is fine."

We made memories in that Budget Inn. It's not the setting I would have chosen, but its absurdity was perfect. To this day, every time I pass through the small town of Orange, Virginia, on my way to Washington, DC, and see the Budget Inn sign, I smile.

Courteney was going to stay with me that night at my mother's house—a house even I had never seen because she moved after I went to prison. We met my mother at Costco to allow Courteney to run home and gather some of her things together while my mother and I shopped. I had to get the money off the prison-issued debit card fast, otherwise it would be eaten up by the fees and charges. Predatory companies bid for prison contracts that allow them to charge unconscionable fees, standing to make billions from debit cards, prison phone calls, emails, commissary, video visits, and even the operation of private prisons. They profit off the poorest individuals and families.

As my mother and I walked through the open doors at Costco, I felt my chest tighten. The warehouse ceiling was so high. There were so many people.

Everyone wearing a mask meant I couldn't read expressions or see people's entire faces. It felt alien and uncomfortable.

And I couldn't grasp *all the things*. All the things to buy. All the things to stress over. All the things to have to replace.

We made it to the clothes aisle, and I just stared at the racks and racks of options. I froze. Choice paralysis. There weren't even very many options, but *there were* options. I hadn't had to choose what to wear in nearly twenty years. I shook myself out of it somehow, and grabbed pants that I thought would fit, some socks, a package of black T-shirts, and moved on.

In the meat aisle, I gazed in awe at the row of steaks and ribs. We occasionally had chicken in prison, but I hadn't had real beef or pork in longer than I could remember.

We picked out steaks, and my mother asked, "What next?"

The pressure had been building but at this moment I cracked. My chest tightened. My breaths came in fast gasps. I was hyperventilating. This giant space and all of the people around us were closing in on me.

"I need to . . . not be here," I said, looking at the floor.

I don't remember what my mother said. I don't remember leaving. I just remember breathing again once we were in the safety and security of her car.

On the drive to my mother's home, she broke some bad news. "It's too late to cook the steaks, so we'll have to wait until tomorrow."

I looked over, stunned. I had been waiting almost two decades for a steak, and it was "too late"?

She was right, though. It was too late. It was dusk when we got to her house, tucked away in the countryside and blissfully quiet. I hadn't been there before, but right after I dropped my stuff by the front door, I found my way to her kitchen. I hadn't eaten since that morning so I tried a bowl of stew from the fridge. I lifted a spoon of it to my lips—but as soon as I caught the flavorful scent, my stomach churned. Running on adrenaline, my senses were overloaded, even in this quiet house.

Courteney made it to my mother's house an hour later. We sat around the dinner table and talked. We tried—and failed—to have "normal" conversations. I had never been at this house. Courteney and I had never been in the same room together. I hadn't seen my mother in a year and a half. We knew each other well, yet we were also strangers, getting to know each other in new ways.

When we went to bed, I had been wondering whether I would be able to sleep next to Courteney after so many years of sleeping alone. In prison, someone touching me while I slept would have been a threat and would have caused me to jump up and defend myself. Sitting there, I longed for Courteney's touch—but I wasn't sure I would be able to receive it, or if it would throw me into panic.

To my relief, lying in bed with her felt natural. The intimacy, the touches. It felt like home.

Courteney fell asleep almost immediately. I didn't.

I tossed and turned, trying to keep from waking her. There wasn't a need. I probably could have shaken the whole bed, and she would have kept snoozing. I gave it an hour. Then two.

As a kid I loved *Jesus Christ Superstar*, the Broadway musical. I can't really explain it, but it just resonated. As I lay there, I could clearly hear the lead actor singing in the Garden of Gethsemane, "Will no one stay awake with me?"

The single biggest day of my life was a big deal to my mother and Courteney too, but this was their world. They knew how to go to sleep on beds that felt way too soft. They knew how to drive cars and walk to a separate bathroom with a door that closes. It was all new to me.

Finally, I got up and walked upstairs. I opened the door to the screened porch and was met with a wave of soft noise. The sounds of nature: crickets and animals rustling in a forest that was alive.

I sat on the porch, in the dark, for a few minutes. Then an hour. Slowly my tension began to melt. My sharp anxiety softened. My breathing slowed. I started to come back into my body.

That was when it hit me. I started to cry. First a tear in my eye, then racking sobs taking over my body.

It wasn't sadness, and it wasn't joy. It was a Long Island iced tea of emotion—strong, mixed, and indistinguishable. Hearing nature around me.

Feeling my body. Knowing I could get up and walk out the screened door, that I could jump in the lake, or run to the top of the mountain. It almost felt like too much. I felt free but also like a tiger that was kept in a cage so long that even after he was moved to a larger enclosure, he paced the outline of where the cage used to be, captive in his own mind.

Then I remembered that there was ice cream.

I walked through the dark kitchen, went to the freezer, found a pint, and grabbed a spoon. I did not plan to put any ice cream back in the freezer for later.

But the spoon wouldn't dig in. I checked the ice cream in the dim light of the clock on the microwave. I figured the ice cream was too hard because the freezer was too cold. So, I stuck the container in the microwave for 5 seconds. Then 10. Then 20. It was still hard.

I turned the kitchen light on and saw the ice cream was covered with a hard chocolate shell. Some specialty brand.

So, I jabbed harder with the spoon and cracked through into a pool of half-melted ice cream. I scooped up one bite and moaned. Then another. I turned out the light and went back to sit on the dark porch. I enjoyed one bite after another with a goofy grin on my face. Uncontrollable laughter was bubbling and waiting to burst free.

I sat there. I breathed. I cried. I checked my new smartphone (they hadn't existed when I went in). The sun rose, and Courteney and my mother woke up. I greeted them from the porch, and I started my first full day free.

Chapter 25

Early Days

My first full day outside I was overwhelmed with curiosity about sights and sounds. Like a child, I stopped to look at cars and people and traffic lights. Everything was different than I remembered. I tried to make a map in my mind of all the places we went, but it was too much to take it all in. Then the day was done.

I didn't sleep, though. Not that night. Not the next. And not the night after that. I was wired from all the new stimuli. It felt like I was running on battery acid and caffeine.

When I finally did crash, I crashed hard. I was out for nearly fifteen hours straight. But, after that, I didn't sleep more than a few hours a night for the first several weeks. All day, every day, I felt this energy and tension running through my body, like I was balancing on an electric wire and vibrating constantly. It was a little bit like cocaine.

At home, I felt like an insecure eighteen-year-old kid again, living with my mother. It had been the only option. The release was so last minute that the probation office had called my mom that morning to approve her address. If she hadn't been able to offer a qualified home plan, meeting their basic requirements and subject to an inspection, I wouldn't have gotten out. Courteney and

I could move in together but that seemed crazy because despite how long we had been talking on the phone, we had only just met in person.

Navigating the world on foot or as a passenger was hard enough. I hadn't driven a vehicle in nearly two decades and I didn't know what to expect. My mother and I decided to find out. With Covid protocols still in place, I had to make an appointment at the DMV and the only one with slots open was two counties away. My mother and I loaded up into her car and began our mini–road trip to get me a license.

My mother was retired and Courteney's job was flexible. Unlike a lot of other people newly released from prison, I had my own "support team" during the first few weeks of reentry. It would have been impossible for me to go to all the places I needed to go and do all the things myself. I had to get a license, I needed to go meet my probation officer, I needed to set up a payment plan at the courthouse, and that was just the beginning. There was no bus service out near my mother's house, and a taxi or rideshare would have cost $100 or more to get into town—if I had even been able to figure them out, as rideshares didn't exist when I went to prison.

Once we arrived to get my license, we hit a snag. The DMV purged licenses and records after ten years of inactivity. So, as far as they were concerned, I had never had a license and needed to start with a learner's permit. A learner's permit wouldn't solve any of the transportation problems. So, I talked to the person at the window, then the supervisor. They tried to help but didn't see any options.

I sat on the bench and tried to figure something out. Then it hit me. I had gotten a speeding ticket when I was a kid. So, I proposed an option—if I could find a court record of the ticket, would that prove I had once had a license and allow me to renew it? The supervisor thought my idea was creative and she proved to be amazing. During her lunch break she made calls all over the department, including cashing in old favors from the central office. I felt so grateful and so "seen."

It took three more trips to the DMV that week, through a power grid failure and a statewide DMV computer outage. Then, with the help of that angel-supervisor, I walked out of the DMV with a license, one week after I had gotten out of prison.

Getting a new license wasn't nearly as terrifying as getting behind the wheel of a car for the first time in so long. My mom sat in the passenger seat, I moved to the driver's side. I sat for a second. I adjusted the seat. I adjusted the mirrors. I hesitated. I breathed. Then I put the car in drive and . . . it was like no time had passed. I pulled to the corner, entered traffic, checked my blind spot, changed lanes, and was off.

It was liberating, though not nearly as liberating as the first time I got back on a motorcycle. Courteney and I took the motorcycle training class together that year. Shortly after the class I rode a "real" bike, and not just the small training bikes in class. I had dreamed about it for years because riding a motorcycle was the opposite of being in a prison cell. I was uncaged, the wind whipping, my heart racing. I had an indelible smile on my face. Motorcycles are dangerous, having no safety features other than a brain bucket, but I always felt utterly alive in the face of that danger. It also worked well for my easily distracted brain because riding a motorcycle means intense focus and assuming that everyone on the road is trying to kill you. I had always loved motorcycles or at least the idea of motorcycles. After getting out I became a bit of a fanatic (though my view about the cost/benefit evolved as I have later experienced both great benefit and great cost).

The first days out of prison I was in survival mode. Bouncing from one appointment to the next. Trying to get things in order. Not slowing down. I was still running on adrenaline and feeling more and more depleted.

One day, I went into CVS alone. I needed to get some soap or body wash. Courteney was on a call, so she stayed in the car. When I stood before the vast array of bottles and soaps, my jaw fell slack. My mind was suddenly blank. I didn't know how to choose. I couldn't move. I just shut down. Finally, I spotted a bottle with "Men's Body Wash" in the largest print. I grabbed it. Some branding agency had earned their fee.

After a blur of a week, after I got my license, Courteney and I had a night to decompress. Friday evening was the Best of C-VILLE party. They threw a blowout event every year and Courteney's podcast *Small Town Big Crime* had been nominated for best local podcast, so she got a free invite and I was her plus one.

This was during Covid, with people still wearing masks and keeping a social distance. So, I was shocked to park outside of the large downtown venue, hear loud music, and see a massive crowd in the distance. Before we could get to the party, we were waylaid by a giant, drunken sailor.

Over six feet tall, wearing a full white sailor outfit complete with ascot, the man stepped in front of us and slurred, "*Youuu* just got out of prison!" He pointed his finger at my chest. "If anyone gives you any trouble . . . you call me. I have the best lawyers in the city . . ." Then he stumbled away. He had followed my essays and story on Facebook. I didn't yet realize how many people already knew me in some form or fashion.

That was just the beginning of the weird that night.

There were hundreds of people in the buzzing crowd, with dozens dancing in front of the stage. It was a raucous "Yacht Rock party." (I didn't even know what that meant.) The venue included a fully interactive Alice in Wonderland art exhibit. To take a break from the thunderous noise, we went inside the exhibit, where it got even weirder.

I crawled through giant mushrooms, swung on a vine swing, felt bizarre texture-covered walls, and questioned just what the hell was going on. I met a bunch of people, their names and faces blurring together as I shook hands and made conversation, overwhelmed and operating like a robot. One of those was the saint of a woman who would later give me a shot.

The next day I took my first solo trip to the state capital to help Courteney move back to Charlottesville.

Courteney was worried about me driving alone. It was my first full day with a license and my first solo trip anywhere. I was also a little worried. But it was thrilling to drive on the highway, merge into "big city" traffic. I felt like a "real" adult.

We sat inside her apartment and decided to make dinner. I suggested blackened salmon. She suggested roasted broccoli. We went shopping and came back to her brown lab Luke, who I came to love, dancing excitedly. He eventually lay between us in the kitchen as we cooked, hoping that scraps might fall and he might rescue them.

As we were eating, she said, with a laugh, "Jesse, I've never been to prison and I don't know how to make blackened salmon. Who are you?" My time as a line cook when I was a teen was paying off.

When I was inside, looking toward the future, I was scared. I operated well in prison. I was afraid those skills wouldn't transfer. I had this vision of a world with people who had it all together and were all vastly more competent and capable than I was. Thankfully, that wasn't the case.

I wanted to catch up with everyone. I wanted to take on the world. I thought I'd get a job, jump into grad school, and maybe volunteer on the side. It was an overly ambitious goal. For months I struggled to make the most basic decisions, often deferring to whatever someone, anyone, suggested. I was doing really well overall but I had periodic breakdowns where I found myself curled into a ball, overwhelmed and shaking. I didn't understand what was going on. In those moments I felt like I was barely hanging on. So many people I've talked to experienced the same after years locked up. There's even a name for it: post-incarceration syndrome.

As a kid, to cope with stress I just shut down. I had learned better coping skills in prison, but living with my mother brought back the same issues from my childhood, the same tense dynamics.

One day, I cracked. She was upstairs shrieking at her boyfriend at the top of her lungs. I began to shake. I fell to the floor. I curled into a ball on the floor. I had to get out. I couldn't be around that again.

This is when the saintly woman I had met at the Best of C-VILLE party reached out to me and offered to let me live in her accessory dwelling unit in town. It was an old stable that had been converted into a tiny house. It was small to others but felt palatial compared to the cells I had lived in for years. She wouldn't let me pay rent. She wouldn't even let me pay for the utilities. She told me to just get on my feet.

Chapter 26

Reckoning with the Past

Growing up, I thought my life was normal. We all think our lives are normal. I only knew what I saw and what I lived. Prison was the first time I was totally removed from the place I came from. Inside, I began to realize that my world hadn't been storybook perfect and that I had a lot of baggage. I started to see the ways my parents were flawed and complicated. I started to see it wasn't as simple as me just throwing my life away for no reason. It was kind of shocking to realize. Yet, I was still in a bubble. It wasn't until I got out and reentered that environment that it all came crashing home.

After a childhood of being attuned to my mother's emotions, I could tell she had mixed feelings about me packing up to move from her house into town, only a month after I got out. I had been gone for so long that she wanted me close. At the same time she wanted to see me succeed—and success would be hard to achieve living so far from town, which had everything I needed. I don't think she understood how difficult it was to come home to the same dynamics that I had struggled with before prison.

Until I was sitting in a cell, I never stopped long enough to realize how much I was a product of my environment and my experiences. I had made a lot of poor choices along the way. I saw myself as the problem. I thought I had always been broken and wrong. Going to therapy, both in prison and once I got out, I started to see more and more that I had been drowning and, like any drowning person, was not thinking about anything other than trying to keep my head above water.

One of the things I learned as a kid was to stay small and never make waves. When I made waves, had wild ideas, or wanted to do something new and different my mother found all the flaws—and all the reasons I should be afraid. Sometimes she yelled. It wasn't an angry yell, but it was a panicked one. Her anxiety was so complete that she saw everything as a danger. It was all downside and no upside. I learned that I would never be able to take a risk without disastrous consequences. That translated to me getting good grades, staying small and quiet, and being, as she always told me to be, a good boy. It also meant that I bottled things up over the years until I exploded, hurt people, destroyed my own life, and went to prison.

Inside prison, it had been easier to just focus on what was in front of me. But even then, I knew I couldn't put off dealing with my family and childhood issues.

While I was inside, after a particularly difficult emotional time, I called my mother and tried to talk about some of my experiences with her. The first time I tried, she hung up on me. The second time, too. She couldn't stand to hear my perspective, because it conflicted with her own. No one wants to feel like the villain.

The third time she agreed to listen. At one point she cut me off to tell me that wasn't how she remembered it. She said that she couldn't have acted that way, that her depression couldn't have been that bad, since it was only six months after the divorce that she met my stepfather. I remember shaking and feeling defeated. It took all the courage in my body to bring this up and she couldn't hear it. She was still trying to shape things in a way that made her feel better. I never needed her to change the past—I knew she couldn't. I didn't need her to "do" anything. I just needed her to listen and acknowledge me and my experience.

After that call, she spoke with a therapist friend, who explained that kids experience time differently. The next time we spoke on the phone, my mother acknowledged that while she remembered that period as a few months, her friend had told her that I probably experienced it as an eternity. That meant a lot to me. I was grateful that my mother had tried, but even after that conversation and especially after my release, I could feel the disconnect in the way we saw and talked about things. I wanted her to understand, and I was hurt and upset that she didn't. Part of wanting someone to understand was because I didn't fully get it either. That's the hard part about the things that shape us. I was so busy and overwhelmed when I got out that I didn't even try to have more of those conversations.

After I moved into town and found some distance from my mother, I started talking with friends about what I had experienced in my childhood. Eventually, I started mentioning it on social media. One day, years later, I talked about why I had had to leave her house, how her yelling at her boyfriend had triggered old trauma that I couldn't handle. I got a text from my mother saying it hurt her for me to say those things and asked me not to. Initially I felt bad and panicked. I had spent a lifetime trying to take care of my mother's feelings and that habit was hard to shake.

Then I felt a burn in my belly. My vision narrowed. I texted back that if she didn't want the world to know who she was and what she did, then rather than trying to silence me she should work on changing who she was and what she did. It was a watershed moment for me. I was finally, fully standing up for myself.

It was easier for me to see the ways my mother's anxiety and anger shaped me. With my father, it was more subtle. I always justified and rationalized his behavior. I looked up to him so much that I always gave him the benefit of the doubt. This was incredibly unfair to my mother. After that first, painful call home after my arrest, my father came to visit me in the little jail visitation room with a glass panel between us and phones we could talk through. He cried as he told me how he blamed himself—for the stories he had told me and for all the things he hadn't done better.

He blamed himself for normalizing the criminal life to me. He blamed himself for some of the twelve-step people he brought around. I'm not sure he ever forgave himself.

I had listened to my father describe the horrendous abuse he experienced as a kid, and I had always thought, "He broke the cycle. He didn't do to me the things that were done to him." I minimalized, rationalized, and compared, which never works. Until I could acknowledge that I actually felt abandoned and unseen (instead of how I thought I should have felt), I couldn't move forward. The question I hadn't been asking all along is, "What happened to me?" Once I began to sit with that question, I began to feel relief from a stress I had carried so long I didn't even realize it was there.

My mother held on to me too tightly, and my father walked away too easily. I can't change that. They can't change that. My work is to reparent myself, to give myself the things I needed but didn't get. I was hurt and mad at my parents and wasn't entirely sure why, but there was only so much feeling and wallowing I could do. No one else can heal those wounds or make me feel whole or enough. That is my job. And it might take a lifetime.

James, the therapist-friend I connected with in prison, sent me a poem once, "This Be the Verse" by Philip Larkin. It begins:

They fuck you up, your mum and dad.
They may not mean to, but they do.

He then later told me, "We all have our mother and our father work to do."

Chapter 27

Work and Navigating Insanity

Shortly after my release, I started working for a lawyer whom I had done research for when I was working in the prison law library. He was putting his house on the market and wanted me to help ready the property for sale. (I think he was just trying to be helpful and to teach me some carpentry skills.)

The first day, he met me outside the house with a toolbelt and started explaining how to do something. My father, truly a jack of all trades, had taught me a lot. I also worked both framing and finishing jobs in and after high school, so I had some experience. But I just nodded my head and did each project. At the end of the day, he shook his head and said, chuckling, "I'm not sure there's a lot I can teach you about carpentry."

After a few weeks the lawyer gave me a final check and told me that was it. I thanked him profusely and kept looking for other work.

I submitted applications. I figured I'd start doing electrical work since I had a journeyman's license and could get a decent salary. After a long delay, I was scheduled for an interview at the local university. Most people saw getting that job as the golden goose. Once you were in the door, the possibilities for advancement and lateral job transfers were endless, with great benefits and stipends for further education. They were desperate for journeymen who could run jobs. Yet, a few days after the interview I turned down that job and ended up working for a local small business.

It was a calculated risk. The motto I lived by in prison was that it was better to have options than plans and that every decision we make creates either more options or fewer. I knew that my life was going to be different. I didn't know how, but I knew that the strict routine and in-person nature of the university job would limit my options. So, I took the more flexible, lower paying, zero benefit, 1099 job instead.

It turned out pretty well. Although there are days when I look back and wonder if I wouldn't have been happier working that university job, living in a smaller world, and having a simpler life.

Just as things seemed to be stabilizing, I was bowled over in the most unexpected way. Not long after moving into town, I received a text from my PO saying that I had to register as a sex offender and failure to do so would be a violation.

I stared at my phone. I looked around, as if this were a prank. I had never been charged with a sex offense. I didn't understand.

I called my PO. I called a lawyer. I called someone in DOC. I called everyone I could think of. I was losing my mind. I briefly thought of running to Mexico. I couldn't imagine being on the registry.

Someone from the probation office asked me to meet them in person. That person said this was "utter bullshit," and they were really sorry. They had complained to their boss and their boss's boss but had been shut down.

I went in to see the supervisor. She was very professional and straightforward. She said she was sorry, but this was standard procedure.

"With all due respect, what the fuck do you mean this is standard procedure?"

She didn't explain the reason. She just told me I had to contact the state police and go through the process. I had to dig and dig and dig for answers.

What I've put together is this. One of my charges was abduction, because my codefendant had held the maid at gunpoint during the robbery. Ernie, Marco,

Francis, and I went to that house to break in together, and so we were all held responsible for the actions of one another. If it had been an abduction to commit a sex offense or an abduction of a child, that would require being on the sex offender and crimes against a minor registry. It was neither of those things. So, the only thing I could imagine was that somewhere during my time in DOC, some counselor had looked at the charge and marked my file as requiring registration. It was that simple. No investigation. No oversight. Just someone checking a box on a computer without understanding or caring. Ernie, who committed the abduction and who got out ten years before me, was never told that he had to register.

When I got out, my file was transferred to probation. Again, no investigation. No oversight. Probation said that I'd just have to register because that box was checked. They said that if the state police determined it wasn't warranted they would remove it.

That's a lot of technical explaining to say that I was losing my fucking mind. I was newly out of prison, under tremendous stress, unsure of how to function in the world—and now I was told that I had to be on the sex offender registry and never again live a normal life. This would have drastically limited where I could live, where I could work, even prevented me from having a smartphone, among other things. The list of requirements would have made life nearly impossible.

When the local office didn't help, I put another call in to DOC and they didn't help, at least not directly. Finally, I was able to contact someone at the parole board. This was the body that had recommended that the governor grant the conditional pardon. I pleaded for help. I told them what had happened. I told them I was losing my mind. I told them I had done everything correctly and didn't understand how this could be happening.

Once again, I didn't sleep for days. Courteney and I called around, trying to find anyone who could help. She reached out to the former head of the local probation and parole office. He was decidedly unhelpful, saying that I would probably have to register and that it would pretty much wreck my life.

Then, out of the blue, I got an email. Someone had single-handedly put a stop to it and noted that I did not, in fact, need to register. This saint of a human being had gone above and beyond because they knew it was wrong. They were angry. They could imagine the effect of this stress on a person already stretched thin. They were the hero.

No one ever mentioned it again. After not being able to sleep and nearly losing my mind it was just done and ignored, swept under the rug. I wonder how many other people were told they had to register, that it was just standard procedure. I wonder how many people were pushed over the edge.

The absurdity wasn't new. It was just more extreme.

When I was first arrested, I just accepted the world around me. It was the only way I knew to cope. For most of my time inside, I assumed prisons would always be prisons—that things were the way they were for a reason. So much of living inside was about humility and accepting powerlessness. But one particular situation was a step too far.

I had been at Nottaway for a year when I went for my annual review. This is when the counselor evaluated my behavior, work, and educational progress over the past year. Most treatment plans required us to get and maintain a job, enroll in an educational program, stay out of trouble, and take specific programs to address issues determined by our file. If we failed to do so we lost good time, which meant we had to spend more time in prison.

At this particular annual review, my counselor sat me down and started reviewing my paperwork. "You didn't take anger management," he said. "We're going to have to do something about that."

"I submitted a request. I remember . . . I just never heard anything back."

"Well, you don't get good time unless you take the class. Can you show me the request you sent?"

At first I thought he was joking, but he kept just looking at me. "I just told you, I never got anything back. I can't show you something I don't have."

"In that case, I'm going to have to bump you down to a good time earning level 2."

That meant I would lose 1.5 days per month of good time and spend at least an additional eighteen days per year in prison. It was unfair. It was crazy. I filed informal complaints, then grievances, and I wrote to central officials.

Finally, after months of paperwork, I got word back that Nottaway did not, in fact, offer an anger management class, and that it had been an error to take my good time because I didn't take a class they didn't offer.

More than once in that process I felt like giving up, but I kept hoping if I complained loudly enough someone would listen. I did not want this to happen to me or anyone else.

It got better. They assigned a counselor to teach anger management and enrolled me in the first class. Along with four or five other incarcerated people, I went through the security gate, got shaken down, and filed into the small classroom.

A few minutes later the counselor came in, stomping and sighing. She threw a stack of papers on the table and turned to face us. She looked directly at me and said, "Apparently someone felt the need to complain about the fact that we didn't have an anger management class. So now, I'm here to teach you anger management, because I don't have a real job to do or anything."

Her eyes never left me, and the other guys took turns looking from me to her, trying to figure out what was going on. She then handed out the papers and told us to read them, headed back to her desk, and filled out her own paperwork, staring daggers at me every time she took a break from writing. This was pretty much the theme of the class.

The probation fiasco was when I finally understood, at my core, that the system was capricious, insane, malicious, and often indifferent, which was almost more scary. The prison system is not about accountability. It is not about rehabilitation. It is not about repairing harm done.

What would happen if we *really* explained prison to someone who had never heard the concept? "So, we take the most traumatized, mentally ill, and addicted people in society who haven't been able to function, and we lock them away together. We warehouse them in often inhuman conditions, then subject them to ever-changing arbitrary rules and punishments. We run the institutions by hiring staff who receive little training and unclear expectations. Oh, and we're often extremely understaffed because correctional officers don't get paid well enough and their job is so stressful and often meaningless that they have some of the highest rates of turnover, substance abuse, spousal abuse, depression, and suicide of any job. Then, after some arbitrary period of time, we let the imprisoned people back into the world and we just can't seem to figure out why so many of them don't adjust and do well." They would think we were crazy.

Chapter 28

A Million Second Chances

I spent half my prison time in fantasy, especially early on. With limited options and opportunities, I had dreams of what I would one day do, or dreams of what I wished I had done differently. It took me a long time to learn to live in the moment. Which is one of the reasons I am so grateful I was introduced to meditation. It allowed me to stay present even when I was bored, even when it hurt, and even when it felt good. It allowed me to honestly assess and make the best of where I was and what I had access to. That said, I still had hopes, dreams, and fantasies.

I always told myself that when I got out, I would go to my favorite short hike near Charlottesville—Humpback Rock—and finally let my guard down. I would cry and scream and strip away the burden I had been carrying. I would let go of all of those years inside. I thought moving on would be that simple. That's not exactly how it happened.

Courteney's friend Katie told me I should make a TikTok video. She said that people would be interested in my life and my experience in prison and reentry.

I thought it sounded silly—I still saw myself as some guy who had thrown his life away. Why would anyone care? I respected her opinion, though, and I was still struggling to make my own decisions. It was easier to just do what people suggested. So, I took her advice. I downloaded TikTok on the way to my hike. I had to select a user name so I picked Second_Chancer (since Second Chancer without the underscore was taken).

Just two weeks since my release, I was still fit from prison; my face looked almost gaunt, my front tooth was discolored from a lack of dental care inside. I still felt robotic in my interactions, including this new experience of filming myself. I didn't even think about the parallels to making Spanish and NVC (nonviolent communication) videos in prison for a few months.

"I just got out of prison . . ." I said in the video, and I recounted the past weeks. I then turned my phone off and climbed back down the mountain.

At the end of the day, I called Katie and asked her, "How many views is normal for a first video?"

She checked my account and said, "Jesse, ten thousand views on an account with no followers is not normal. I told you people would be interested in your story."

My reentry had just started to veer off any course I could have imagined. I had no idea how far it would go.

Technology was radically different in 2021 than it was when I was arrested in 2002. Before prison I had a Nokia block phone. It included the "Snake" game, but I didn't even know what texting was. There was no YouTube, no Facebook, no iPhone, and you had to order pizza from a landline or they wouldn't deliver, because they were afraid that it was a prank or a scam. Inside I read magazines, watched the news, and generally tried to keep up with a rapidly evolving world. Through all of that, as well as osmosis, I managed to know a little bit about a lot of things.

TikTok surprised me, though. I thought it was an app for teenagers where they and celebrities danced and people wasted hours. There was some of that but, additionally, I found a complex community of incredibly interesting and insightful storytellers. I mostly managed to stay off the mindless side of the algorithm. I kept posting videos because people kept asking questions and engaging. It was a dopamine mine. Plus, there were still pandemic restrictions, so there wasn't a lot to do at night. The more I posted, the more my following grew, until the day when I posted about living with a serial killer and my account exploded to 500,000 followers, just five months after making that first video on the mountaintop.

I understood people's draw to the crazy stories, but I had never realized how few people knew how messed-up prison was. I made videos about all of the things that didn't make sense.

The day before my release I was considered too dangerous to be housed at a level 1 facility or a work center. Because I had violent charges, I was never allowed to go below a level 2 facility and wouldn't be allowed to work outside the gate at any institution. Then, the day I was released, I was suddenly safe enough to be out in the world with no structure, no support, and no transition.

It's a recipe for failure. On my soapbox I described a plan for everyone who is being released (as about 95 percent of the incarcerated population one day will be). I talked about how they could work their way from higher-security to lower-security institutions to work camps to work release to halfway houses. It would save the government money, it would equip people with the skills they need to succeed post-release, it would allow incarcerated people to save money and build a base in the outside world, and it would provide an incentive for good behavior. Most of all it would prevent the shock of going from a fully structured and regimented environment without many choices to complete freedom with no guides, bumpers, or directions. It would help people through the experience of reentry. Everyone would benefit from the new system because people succeeding means fewer repeat offenses and greater public safety.

I was asked how we could make sure to only let the "safe" ones out. I responded that in the early 2010s, a new state contractor updated the DOC computer system and counselors started doing a COMPAS (Correctional Offender Management Profiling for Alternative Sanctions) Assessment every year at annual review. It's a tool to determine an individual's needs for rehabilitation as well as their risk of recidivism and other factors.

Every year, from the first year I took the assessment, my COMPAS said that I was essentially at zero risk of recidivism. So, the DOC's own assessment determined that keeping me in prison was spending taxpayer money for no good reason other than punishment. Maybe that's valid. Maybe punishment gave peace of mind to the people I hurt.

But does it make sense to run a system based on punishment? Where is the balance between rehabilitation and punishment for the sake of those harmed? How many people have been sentenced to arbitrary lengths of time that have no correlation to their risk of recidivism? How many people have changed and are ready to go home but cannot? On the other hand, how many people pose a clear and present danger but will be released because their arbitrary number is up?

After I was released and after the initial probation snafu, I was put on Shadow Track. This was an app on my phone where I did my required check-ins. Once a month, I logged onto the app, which used voice or facial recognition to verify that I was actually me. I checked boxes and typed out answers to several questions—always the same questions—and I was done. That was it. I didn't see anyone. I didn't go anywhere. I wasn't tested for anything. That was the level of security needed to make sure I didn't reoffend.

The use of virtual check-ins is actually evidence-based. A National Institute of Justice study found that intensive supervision, including in-person home visits, is more effective for high-risk individuals but doesn't benefit low-risk individuals and can even have adverse effects.

So, people who the DOC says pose no threat and who probation considers such low risk they don't even see a probation officer are still serving years or decades or life in prison, often without any parity with others who have committed similar crimes. Again, this just doesn't make sense.

I spent a lot of years extremely frustrated with the system. Then I became numb to it, thinking it would always be. I lost hope. It took people who refused to accept the status quo—like Billy and Karl and Ricky—to inspire me. It was the rebels and troublemakers who made me believe that maybe, just maybe things could be different.

As videos continued to resonate with viewers, I started to analyze the crossover to understand it. Some viewers had loved ones inside. Others had been incarcerated themselves. Some were just interested in the justice system. Some were voyeurs, wanting to hear about the trauma and craziness. Others saw themselves in me, or felt they could have been me if they had been caught, despite being from dramatically different backgrounds. Veterans talked to me about the same institutionalization and the same struggles getting out of the military. Athletes talked about the same confusion they experienced when they were no longer being coached and their identity wasn't clearly defined. A larger community was forming.

TikTok even flew me out to San Francisco to speak at one of its corporate events. Someone on the team that handled my presentation wanted to emphasize a brand shift from a perception of mindless entertainment to the good and meaningful stories being shared on the platform.

One of the major tech companies had me do an ad for their continuing education and training platform to make sure that citizens returning from prison knew it was available when they were released and starting over. I spoke at universities and large conferences. I went from being locked, alone, in a cage to having all eyes on me. It was like going from living in the dark underground to living in a fishbowl in the middle of Times Square. When I first went on social media, I didn't understand how people could spend hours on it. I just checked out my friends, maybe posted something, then closed the app. Suddenly with a newfound public presence, I became trapped in the pursuit of dopamine, validation, and views.

One video would get millions of views and the next would get a few thousand. I felt like a failure, as if I was doing something wrong, and I had to try harder. So I made six videos a day, every day, for two years. It was the scattershot "quantity over quality" approach. Largely it worked.

It even, bizarrely, put me in a position to start the Second Chancer Foundation.

I worked a few different jobs after release but still didn't know what I wanted to do with my life. I knew that people would judge me about my past, and if I kept it a secret, it would feel like some shameful thing I would have to keep hiding forever. So, rather than applying to jobs where I feared I would be judged or limited due to my history, I chose to lead with my story and perspective. I applied for jobs with national nonprofits dealing with criminal legal reform. I was on the fifth round of interviews for a policy role with a huge organization.

It was my first introduction to the size and bureaucracy of some nonprofits. I was hopeful but also a little overwhelmed by the number of interviews and the amount of red tape.

Meanwhile Courteney and her partner were celebrating the release of their podcast *Small Town Big Crime*. At an event they threw, I talked to a lot of people, but only one of them changed the direction of my life. This person has requested anonymity so I won't go into details. At the time I only had a vague idea of who they were. I just knew that they were an important figure. They asked about my story, about my social media—they even took notes. Among other insightful things, they said that people didn't realize social media will shape our next generation. I left that conversation so impressed and full of having been seen and validated and acknowledged. I have since realized that the greatest commonality between the most successful people I know is the ability to fully listen and make someone feel like they are the only person in the room.

The next morning this person emailed me: Don't take that job you told me about, the person had written, and here are five reasons why. Instead, start your own 501(c)(3), do something good, pay yourself whatever they would have paid you, and I'll fund you.

Courteney and I were in the car, driving to see her parents. I asked her if this email was a joke. She smiled and said, "I told you you were special, Jesse."

This definitely wasn't what I was expecting to come out of making a TikTok video on a mountain, two weeks out of prison.

Chapter 29

Second Chancer Foundation and PrisonTok

On my third try at filling out form 1023 for the IRS to recognize our corporation as eligible for tax-exempt status I began to give up hope. I had asked Google and watched YouTube videos. Some of the questions were straightforward. Others confused me. Starting a 501(c)(3) nonprofit with no experience, less than a year out of prison, was daunting.

I didn't know how long it would all take to set up the nonprofit, but my expenses were extremely low and I had a bit of money in savings so I just set off on the adventure like it was a job, because it was.

I finally filled out the paperwork, made my best guesses, then sent it off and prepared to wait. I talked with someone who had waited seven months to hear back about their tax status. Somehow, I got a response in just over two weeks.

With tax status approved and money deposited in the bank, I had to figure out what we were going to do. Most people start with a vision then raise money. I started with money and had to determine a vision.

My first thought was something around storytelling and the power of changing culture through the Trojan horse of human stories. The person who funded us had told me that policy doesn't change until culture does, so that stories and cultural leaders have to precede policy leaders.

Yet, somehow that idea didn't have enough impact. Besides, my survivor's guilt told me to tangibly help people or that I was somehow taking advantage of things or being dishonest.

I thought about training storytellers or helping others create platforms to share stories. Again, it didn't feel impactful enough. I felt great pressure to "do" something with the incredible opportunity I had been given. (Looking back, I realize this kind of initiative would have had tremendous impact, and I am grateful to other organizations for doing it well.)

Instead, I recruited a local community activist, coordinated with existing organizations, and started teaching reentry courses through the local Equity center. Prior to starting the nonprofit, I connected with a formerly incarcerated individual who designed a reentry program alongside a professor of special education from the local university. It was a great program and it now had a platform.

We got set up, secured the space, and started our first class. We had fourteen participants. They were enthusiastic and the class went well. The following week was similar. The problem was that every week the number of participants in the class got smaller.

By the end of the curriculum, we had four people in the room. Some of the former participants were working multiple jobs or going to school (or both). Some no longer felt the heavy pressure of reentry and preferred to spend time with their girlfriends or families. Whatever the reason, they weren't coming. It became clear that many people getting out of prison had a million obligations and didn't have a lot of extra time, and that our energy and money would be more impactful elsewhere.

Around this time, someone reached out to me on social media to talk to me about the juvenile detention center in Charlottesville. We met for coffee, and I learned she worked at the center. She tearfully pleaded for help and said she couldn't lose another kid. The kids did so well in the center, but when they got out they returned to the same environment—the same home or the same neighborhood—and almost inevitably fell back into the same behavior. Too many of the kids had been shot or had shot someone else. Too many had ended up dead or locked back up.

So, we organized a visit to the center and talked to the kids. I began to advocate for their situation and needs to people and businesses in the community. I was always going to meetings and conferences and happy hours and eventually I stumbled onto the idea of a monthly leadership summit. I sought out formerly incarcerated people who were now living successful and impressive lives. I found men who ran businesses, ran nonprofits, led communities, and even held elected office. Every month we went into the center with someone to tell the kids, "I've been where you are but you haven't been where I am. Here's my number, here's my hand. When you're ready, reach out and I'll help you understand the steps to get where I am."

The kids tended to be reserved or quiet. Every now and then I would see the spark. They might bravely share a dream they had but wouldn't have felt comfortable sharing before. One kid wanted to be a flight attendant. Another wanted to work at the YMCA or Boys and Girls Club to help other kids avoid his plight. One wanted to open a lawn care business. Another wanted to get into coding and do IT security work. I hope that they left those meetings with some greater sense of hope and some greater belief that their dreams could become realities.

Never feeling like I was doing enough, I set out to provide something similar to adults. I asked all of my successful, formerly incarcerated friends what made the difference for them. I looked at my own life. In each case we had a mentor, a teacher, or a friend who helped us see the world, and especially ourselves, in a different way. So, I asked how we could connect incarcerated people with mentors.

Smart people start something small and grow it while they work out the kinks. I was not experienced enough to know this. I developed a grand plan to implement a cloud-based mentoring platform that would be available to every incarcerated person in America. We built the platform, which scans handwritten letters, processes them through ChatGPT and Google, packages related information and data, and drafts a template response and sends all of this to the email of the mentor. We designed it this way because, among other things, we wanted corporate partners. A lot of corporations have restrictions on the software that can be loaded onto their computers and company phones. The way we designed it, everything just goes to someone's email—business or personal, it doesn't matter. All of the processing is in the cloud. The mentor's response is then run back through ChatGPT, has all personal identifying information removed, is checked for flagged words or phrases and evaluated for appropriateness, and then printed out and mailed back to the individual.

We started a pilot program at one institution and had meetings with several states. We could technically provide the service without partnership, but we wanted to include state agencies. We wanted buy-in from all stakeholders. It would help us roll out more wraparound services and help with funding, because none of this was free. Our original donor provided a great seed but it felt like most of my time was in meetings either trying to create partnerships so we could expand our pool of qualified mentors or asking for money so we could continue and expand our operations.

We also looked at a dozen other side projects, always trying to see where we could help or make an impact. I was trying to do everything. It took me a long time to realize it wasn't possible. We had built this great thing, but it had so many moving pieces. Sometimes I felt hopeful and happy, other times I felt exhausted. I was proud of what we had built. I loved the process and the journey getting there. At the same time there was a dawning realization that I had built my entire existence—my work, the stories I told on social media, and my professional connections—around my experience in prison.

I wasn't the only one telling stories about prison or talking about criminal legal reform on social media. There were a few social media celebrities with blue check marks and millions of followers. Most followed me back, responded to my DMs, and even took time to talk to me on the phone.

Then a national reporter did a story about "Prison TikTokers" and we were all thrust into each other's orbit at once. We started having more conversations through text, Zoom, or phone. We had never met in person, though, so it didn't quite feel real yet.

Then, out of nowhere I got a message from a random kennel owner. I clicked on his TikTok icon and saw that his page was full of grooming and boarding tips. I got lots of DMs every day, but this one was different enough that it stuck out. In another message, he offered to pay me for a phone call. When I told him we could just talk, he told me his name was Richard and recounted the story of his life, which seemed too fantastical to be true. He then told me how he was awaiting trial for attempted murder for protecting his son. It sounded like utter bullshit.

Yet, there was something about this guy that I liked. We stayed in touch, and I started googling his case and the stories he had told me. I found out that almost everything he said was verifiable and true, if sometimes exaggerated. The case itself was insane, deserving of its own book. He really was getting a raw deal.

He was facing serious time for the attempted murder. He wanted to fight to prove his innocence. He was also worried he would get scared and take a deal if they offered him one. (Prosecutors often offer "sweetheart" deals for cases they can't win at trial because that way they still get a conviction.) Richard had reached out to me because he wanted to network. He wanted to have connections inside and to know he could make it in prison—so if they didn't drop the charges he wouldn't cave if a deal came across his desk.

He asked about the broader PrisonTok community and offered us the use of his large farmhouse in Pennsylvania. He offered to bring in a cook, buy a giant charcuterie board, and make sure we had a space to meet.

It seemed crazy but I went with it. I reached out to other Prison TikTokers with this crazy suggestion that we all get together and chat. Surprisingly, they agreed. People from as far as California, Texas, and Oregon met in this remote town in Pennsylvania. We all hoped this wasn't the beginning of a horror movie. It certainly had all the trappings of one—a mysterious host, a Civil War cannonball embedded in the wall of the house, and a collection of people who had never met and didn't really know anything about one another beyond one common experience.

Instead of a horror scene, it was an inspirational one. We came together and talked and shared and ate. Vice News did a special on the get-together. We were interviewed and shared our experiences for a national audience. We also shared things off-camera, things that were just for us.

It was a profound validation to be in a room with people who understood my experience. It was a room where we could be vulnerable. We could make morbid jokes or stark admissions and not be judged because we all understood on both levels. It was a room where friendships were born.

At that get-together I met Morgan, Keri, Marci, Comrade, Colin, Khalid, and Cass. I also met an NFL first-round draft pick who became passionate about and made a fortune in cannabis. Of course, I also met Richard, the guy who reached out to me to organize this whole thing.

No one there was just one thing. They were all successful in their after-prison journeys. I looked up to Morgan, who was running a harm reduction nonprofit and working for a national organization that preserved the written history of incarcerated people. I looked up to Keri, working for a top-five newspaper. I looked up to Marci for the TV work she was doing. I looked up to Richard because he was a survivor. He had grown up in foster care, been dealt a crap hand at life, and yet he was here, running businesses, surviving and making things happen even though he was facing another terribly unfair legal situation.

We all became friends. The PrisonTok community continued to get together a few times a year. We picked up new people and lost others. Richard and I talked regularly. I ended up going to his trial. All charges were dropped on day three, and he filed a massive lawsuit against the local police department.

In an age where social media can be a time-suck or an opportunity to isolate, I found that it can also be an opportunity to connect and build meaningful relationships and have a meaningful impact. I desperately needed that as I navigated this new and alien world.

I had built a community around my past and I loved that I could use the worst times of my life as an inspiration to help others. On the other hand, part of me wanted to break from it and do something that came from my passions, independent of my experience with incarceration. I wanted to do something that young Jesse or even seventeen-year-old Jesse would have done before getting arrested. In a weird way I had used my prison experience to build walls around my life. Would I be able to handle actual freedom?

Chapter 30

The Fairy Tale

It wasn't long after I started posting before I had my first social media video with over a million views. I didn't know what to make of it, but suddenly I was on center stage being asked about every area of my life . . . including my relationship.

I talked about Courteney in a lot of the videos because she was such a big part of my life.

The pardon investigator who was instrumental in me getting out had warned me: Don't get into a relationship. I found that funny because Courteney was absolutely my rock. She helped walk me through tough times, helped me find myself, allowed me to support her, and took me places I never imagined.

Watching my buddies get out and get into trouble—mental, emotional, and legal—from the stress of relationships, I began to understand. In the past, I hadn't made the best choices or pursued the healthiest relationships, so I realized just how lucky I was to have found Courteney.

With all of the questions I was getting, we decided that it was time to introduce her. We did a video together, talking about who we were, how we met, and how our relationship was going. That video got more than six million views. All of a sudden it wasn't just about prison or about me, it was about us.

Women in long-distance relationships asked for advice, people complained that they couldn't find a girlfriend outside while I had found one inside, plenty of commenters told us that we were terrible people, for various reasons. There were supporters too, people invested in our love story. The trolls and negative voices really stuck out, though. It took me a while to develop skin thick enough to read their comments and understand that what they said was often more about them and not me or us.

The negativity, or at least the concern, wasn't just online. The first time I met Courteney's parents was one of the most awkward experiences in human history. We drove to their house in Richmond. Courteney and I stood side by side on the sidewalk and talked to them. They stood, facing 90 degrees away from us, not looking in our direction, but answering out of the corner of their mouths. I wasn't sure what to expect, but it wasn't this. At the same time, I couldn't imagine my grown child saying, "Guess what, guys, I'm in love with a guy. He's a really good guy, I promise. Oh, he's in prison and just maybe he's getting out. Can't wait for you to meet him!"

Her friends welcomed me into the circle with open arms but quite a few had concerned questions for her behind the scenes. I appreciated that. I think she was worried it would hurt my feelings, but I was grateful they cared so much, and I understood and even shared their concern. I didn't know what was going to happen. It took nearly a year and a half, but it turned out they were right.

Among other DMs on social media, a TV producer reached out. She said my story was set for a show or a movie. Initially, she wanted to do it about me. We bounced the idea around but could never settle on anything. Then, in a flash, she realized that the story was my relationship with Courteney—a fish out of water scripted series. So, a year after I got out of prison, Courteney and I were flying to LA to stay in a house in the Hollywood Hills and have dinner with LA celebrities as we talked over the pilot episode of our series. We were living a dream.

Going to Hollywood to eat fresh fruit from a Beverly Hills market while sitting in a hot tub at a producer's mansion on the side of a mountain would have been out of the ordinary for anyone. Going there just months after getting out of prison felt unreal. It felt too good to be true and I was waiting for the rug to get pulled or the prank to be announced. Life simply didn't happen this way.

We had a good dinner and a good conversation. It was nice to talk to people in person and get a feel for them. Courteney and I both really liked the idea and the team and wanted to move forward. Once we flew back to Virginia, we worked a little bit more on the project. Then the writer's strike happened, and things started to fall apart. What stuck with us was that our story was notable. Other people had felt a connection to it and thought that it seemed commercially viable. Courteney even decided she wanted to write her own book about our story.

After the hype of a TV show faded, we got back into a daily routine of friends and shared tasks and roles. We were good together. We even made the decision to move in together and managed to buy a house.

I hated the idea of paying rent and paying someone else's mortgage, so I really pushed the issue. Courteney was less committed to buying but we both agreed it was time to try living together.

We wanted to live in town and even put in an offer on a place, but we couldn't compete with cash buyers. By luck, we connected with an extremely generous individual and our story held special meaning to him. He had purchased a home for his wayward son, hoping that it would be a place for him to start over. Unfortunately, things hadn't worked out.

After he heard more about Courteney and me, he decided that if it couldn't be a second chance for his son, it could be a second chance for us. He gave us a really good deal, and before we knew it, Courteney and I had signed on the dotted line. We were homeowners. The only concern was that the house wasn't in the city, or even the county we had originally hoped for. How would we adjust to living so far away from everything and everyone we loved?

The house itself was amazing, with plenty of room for us, a fenced backyard for Luke the dog, and a large garage where we could work out and store the motorcycles. Courteney had also gotten her own bike after we graduated from the motorcycle training class. We envisioned long rides together and great adventures. It turns out that riding motorcycles, especially over 45 mph, was not her favorite pastime.

Our neighbors on either side were welcoming and helpful. One family had opened their home to foster kids and not only met their basic needs but loved, taught, and cared for them in a deep way. I really admired what they did. I also appreciated that their boys could fix anything and would occasionally mow our lawn just for the heck of it.

We made the home as cozy as we could. We had friends over (or tried to—no one wanted to drive all the way out to our house more than once). We met with a family in the neighborhood for trivia. We threw ourselves into suburban living.

However, we were slowly growing apart without acknowledging it. Courteney worked at the radio and got off at 6 PM. I worked from home or would head back from the coworking space in time to cook us both dinner. We ate dinner together, then she went to watch TV and I played video games in my office.

I loved Courtney. The only problem was that I had no idea who I was or what I wanted. I wasn't sure I was ready to commit to anyone or anything. I felt anxiety around the idea of commitment of any sort. Someone jokingly asked me if being in a relationship made me feel like I was back in prison. I laughed it off, but the comment stuck with me.

When we first talked about our feelings, while I was still in prison, Courteney had half-jokingly insisted that I sleep with ten women before we committed. Then we talked less about how to make sure this was what we both wanted. Then I got out and we didn't talk at all about the fact that I had been locked away, so I didn't get to date, find myself, make mistakes, and end up with an idea of what I wanted. Eventually, it became too painful for her to talk about any doubts I had because she was so sure of what she wanted. So, I talked through my complicated feelings with other people. That meant some of the most vulnerable emotional conversations I was having were not with my partner.

All of the friction that existed was not from her. It was in my head. I struggled with the questions and doubts and urges to explore or figure out what I wanted. I was so worried about disappointing her or hurting her. Then she asked me something life-changing.

We were at the beach visiting Katie—the woman who suggested that I make my first video for TikTok. We decided to head down to romp around on the sand. Katie brought a fancy recording gimbal and they both had an excited, nervous energy, meeting eyes when they thought I wasn't looking.

We walked ahead of Katie, and Courteney turned to me. She took my hands and told me she loved me. She asked me to marry her. Katie was recording the whole time.

I kind of knew it was coming. We had talked about marriage. We loved each other. We were already living together. We knew it might be easier financially. In some ways it seemed inevitable—it's just what you do, right?

I felt really happy at that moment. I also felt my stomach drop, because I knew we hadn't dealt with my core issues and doubts. I said yes. I wanted to marry Courteney, or at least I wanted to want to. But deep down, I didn't know if I could.

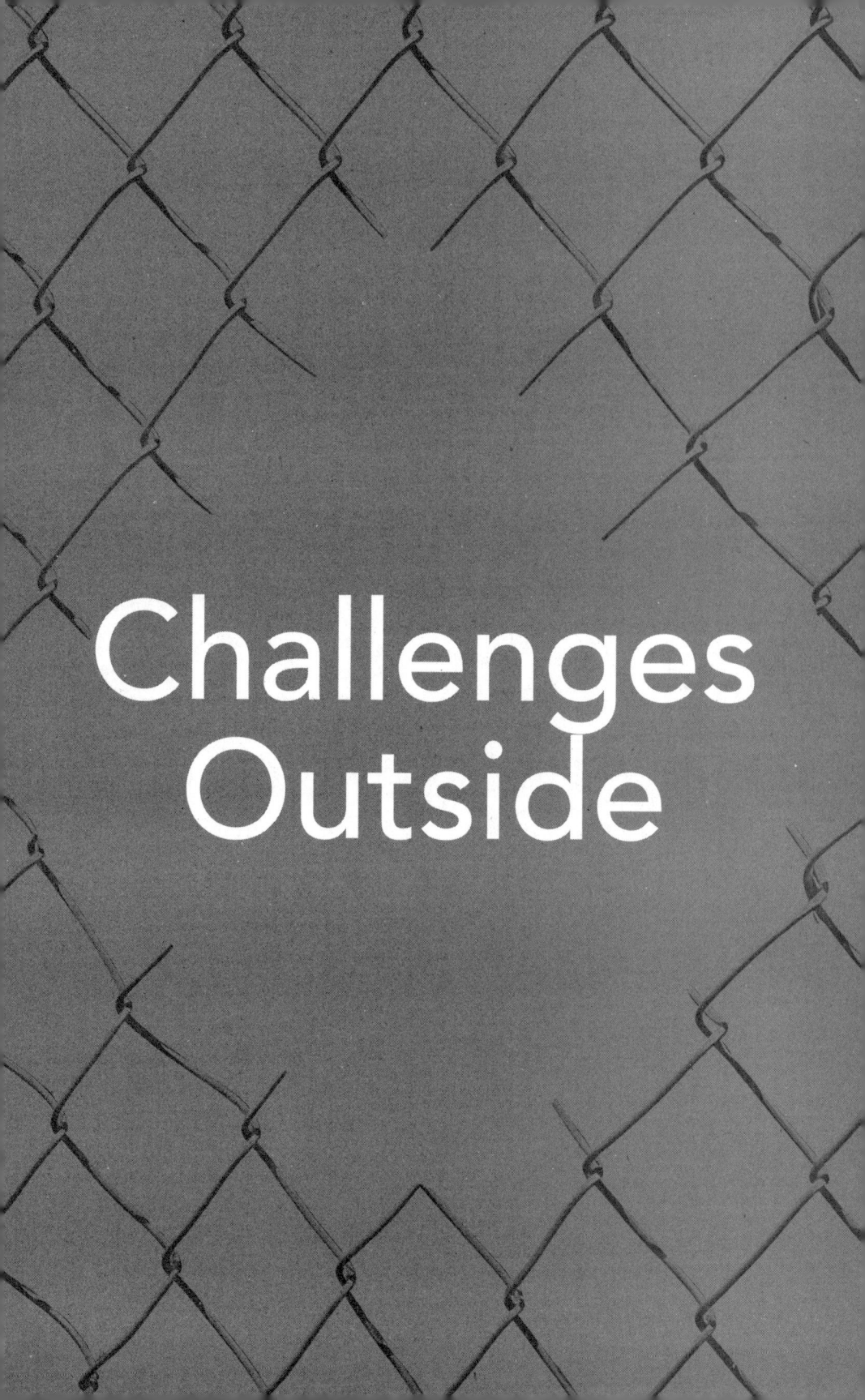

Challenges Outside

Chapter 31

Existential Crisis

A year and a half after being released, I still hadn't found my footing but I was starting to feel like things were coming together. If anything, my problem was that I had too many options in front of me. Little did I know my life was about to be shaken at its foundation.

I received sometimes dozens of messages on social media every day. One of those messages stood out. The woman had a private account (so I couldn't see anything about her), and said she was impressed by the work I was doing to help other people and to change perceptions. She said that she did the same. She also said she saw potential in me that I probably didn't realize yet.

I had no idea who this person was but I appreciated the compliment, and her messages were insightful so I continued to correspond. After a few months of regular communication, she casually mentioned talking with a world-famous individual. Finally, I asked, "Who exactly are you?" She suggested I google her.

Chandra, who I just thought of as some insightful stranger, was one of the Forbes Top 40 under 40. She had built and sold multiple tech companies and was running one now that had won awards from NASA, giving it a several-billion-dollar valuation. I was shocked. What was my life? Why had she reached out to me?

She put me in contact with her network, and I met some amazing people. Rather than just texting back and forth, she and I got onto a Zoom call, then another. It was on this second Zoom that my life changed forever.

We were discussing general things, then I remembered what one of the people she had introduced me to had recommended.

"Taylor told me to ask you to do your magic trick on me. What does that mean?" I asked.

"Ask me a question," Chandra said.

I reflected for a moment, then asked, "What do I need to do to be successful?"

She paused, then said, "Ask that another way."

"What, um, could *prevent* me from being successful?"

She looked at me, eyes piercing through the screen of my small laptop. She pursed her lips and said, "If you don't unpack your trauma, you could spin out and not move forward."

"What trauma?" I asked.

"Obviously the prison stuff, but more importantly the childhood stuff. The things that had you hiding who you were, what made you feel like your needs didn't matter, the events that led you to struggle with boundaries and self-worth."

I felt like there was a hole in my chest. I hadn't told her any of this.

As she mentioned more and more details that I had never revealed, I felt like the hole in my chest was widening. I didn't know how to process any of it. I couldn't breathe.

I saw her eyes refocus and soften. "Oh shit, you don't remember, do you?"

I was on the edge of tears, gasping for breath but trying to look composed. I felt like I was drowning and I didn't know why.

"Oh, Jesse, I'm sorry. I thought you knew."

That night I freaked out. I drove two hours through the night, completely out of my mind, flying through anger, tears, and mania. A well of emotion and memory had exploded inside of me.

The next morning, I was sitting on my friend's porch, trying to make sense of the day before and had a flash—what seemed both like a memory and a present experience. I saw and, more importantly, felt a young version of myself, locked in the closet, terrified and afraid to come out.

I nearly dropped my mug of coffee. Tears filled my eyes. I couldn't breathe.

What the fuck was happening? How had I never seen or known this part of myself?

All I knew was that this was what Chandra had been talking about.

I was so shocked by our conversation and the vivid morning experience that I started desperately seeking help. I talked to everyone I knew and respected in the area of therapy and interviewed a handful of Internal Family Systems (IFS) therapists before settling on one. She accepted me at a sliding scale, but it was still out of pocket. My life felt so on fire that I would have paid any amount of money. That was one of the most important decisions I have ever made.

Rather than talking about my feelings, she had me feel them. Rather than analyzing, she asked me if that analytical part could step back so I could speak from the place of what I was experiencing. Despite all the therapy I did in prison, I had never gotten in touch with any of this. I was so good at analyzing and dissociating and rationalizing, I had created a bypass of my emotions and my trauma. Now I was facing it head on and getting absolutely smacked around.

A lot came up around Courteney and our relationship. I could finally give voice to my fears and doubts and concerns without letting the shame I felt take the wheel. I was able to explore what I wanted and needed. It was neither fast nor simple. It was painful and confusing and sometimes accompanied by feelings of hopelessness. It still is.

It also led me to seek distance from my mother. I noticed that every time she texted or called my chest tightened and my heart started to race. One day she asked if I would come help clean her house. Usually, I would have dropped everything to help but this time I said no. I told her I would pay someone to do it but that I couldn't. We were both used to me just saying yes and coming to see her or help with whatever she needed. She pushed back, asking when I could come. And then why I couldn't. It was a calm exchange but not a pleasant one.

I knew that I couldn't fully heal until I made space to do it. I had always struggled with boundaries, so it was incredibly difficult for me to take time and space away from my mother. I thought it would be for a few days. It ended up being much longer. I felt so much shame and failure. Some people who knew us both criticized me and told me I had to "get over that stuff" and talk to my mother again. Other people reached out and shared private stories of their own struggles and attempts to distance themselves from family dynamics.

Stepping away from my mother allowed me to see my relationship with her more objectively. I began to recognize how I had long played a part in a toxic, codependent play. My mother once told me about her childhood. Her mother treated her like a doll and rather than encourage my mother and build her up, she would tear her down. No child should have to feel anything but supported and loved and empowered by their parents.

When my mother talked about her childhood, my first feeling was gratitude. I was grateful that she didn't do the same thing to me. Though, looking back, I can see the many ways in which my mother saw me as an object she had to control or shape or protect.

My mother loved me. That was never a question. The problem, as far as I can tell, is that my mother grew up without anyone ever loving her the way she needed. So, she never learned to love unconditionally; she loved as a protector and as an owner. It's terrible to consider how much harm we can do out of a place of good intention. So many parents want what's best for their kids but rather than teaching them autonomy, they just transfer their anxiety and their pain.

The unraveling continued. On Thanksgiving of 2022, Courteney and I were hosting dinner for her family and a friend. We all sat there with smiles and casual laughter, but I was dying inside. I knew this was it. I wasn't happy. We had gotten into an unsustainable, don't-talk-about-it, unhappy 1950s relationship arrangement.

We did the same thing every day. We went to bed and did it again. We weren't getting better. It was all my fault.

After Thanksgiving dinner, I was awash with emotions and couldn't hide my feelings anymore. The conversation was tearful and difficult. I told her I needed the weekend to get my head on straight. I left to go stay in town and Courteney went to stay with her family. When we talked the next day, she told me that her father mentioned that I had looked off at dinner.

After spending the weekend struggling and grappling with my feelings, I knew we needed to talk. We met in Richmond, then back at our house. It went well, until it didn't. There was so much emotion. There was so much disappointment and anger and sadness and frustration. I felt terrible. I wanted to run away and obliterate myself.

I walked out that night and didn't know if I would ever see her again.

Over the next few weeks, Courteney and I talked a little, then went radio silence, then talked again. We struggled with boundaries and emotions. We didn't know what to do with the house (neither of us wanted to live out there). We talked about whether I could visit with Luke, the chocolate lab I loved so much. Finally, we found a routine. It wasn't always the same. It wasn't always easy. We fought for it, though. I love Courteney, and she will always be an important person in my life, even if it isn't as a romantic partner.

In late November of 2022, I was alone in the free world for the first time in twenty years. I was scared. I was lonely. I was also finally doing the work I needed to become the person I wanted to be. It was another level of the reentry process. I was working to heal the things that had led me to prison in the first place. At the same time I was discovering a vice that would be as dangerous as cocaine had been.

Chapter 32

Seeking Home

I tried to continue my regular social media posts without letting on what had happened. I didn't know what Courteney would want to share. I didn't want to hurt her. I didn't want to disappoint people who had believed in our fairy tale. I didn't want to face it.

Finally, after people kept asking why they hadn't seen Courteney and if I was okay, I made a video, unsuccessfully trying to hold back tears, and said that we were not okay, that we had broken up and I didn't know what I was doing.

As soon as I posted the video, a deluge of support followed. And other things. Women messaged me, some subtle, saying they wanted to support *in any way they could*. Others were overt, offering to drive or even fly to visit me—or fly me to visit them.

Heartbroken, I also felt a bit of excitement at my newfound freedom. One woman drove hours to see me the week after Courteney and I broke up. When she arrived, I was giving a Zoom presentation in my office at the back of the house. I had left a sign on the door saying, "This is the right house. Please don't be an axe murderer."

After finishing my presentation, I walked out of my office and saw that she had come inside and was at the edge of the hall, leaning seductively against the wall. She was young and gorgeous and smiling a coy smile. I felt like I was dreaming.

In addition to new adventures, Courteney and I came to an agreement on the house. We both wanted to move back to town. For her it was easy. For me, with a criminal record, it was more complicated. When we bought the house, there had been no barriers. No one ran a background check. No one asked me for references. We brought a check for a down payment, signed some papers, and moved into the house.

As soon as I started looking for an apartment, I ran into issues. Some places had clear policies that said people with criminal records need not apply. Other places were happy to charge application fees and give no reason for a turndown. It's a common struggle for many with a criminal record.

Finally, I turned to Facebook marketplace and found a private landlord. He didn't do a background or credit check. He just asked for three references and proof of income. I had the woman who had let me stay in her accessory dwelling unit and two prosecutors write me letters of reference. I figured he would google me and see my story, so I hoped their support would make him willing to give me a chance. A year later, while doing a presentation at my landlord's church, I was surprised when he told me he was shocked because he had no idea about my story.

I traded the three-bedroom house for a small apartment in town where I could walk everywhere. In some ways I was in my late thirties, moving through personal and professional life. In other ways I was like a twenty-year-old, stumbling and finding my way through relationships, social experiences, and struggles around identity. Exploring how I wanted to live and who I wanted to build community with.

Being single, "social media famous," and fairly fit was a bizarre feeling. I remember sitting in prison and wondering if anyone would consider dating me after all I had done and been through. I asked a friend if she thought I would be able to find someone. She laughed and said, "I think you'll be just fine."

I didn't see myself as attractive. I was a ball of neurotic insecurity. I had spent most of my life in prison so I knew how be alone or surrounded by other men. I had missed intimacy, connection, and sex for so long that it felt bigger than anything else. It was all a whirlwind.

Within months someone flew me to California, took me to Lake Tahoe and Monterey, and left me with a bunch of very vivid memories. Women met me in Boston and New York. Someone flew me to Florida. Plenty of people came by the house or invited me to theirs.

It was an adventure, and I was awestruck. It wasn't long before it became unhealthy. I started turning to sex obsessively. I thought about it all the time, even when I was having it. I'd spend each night with a different woman, sometimes multiple women in the same day. I began to feel hollow. It had taken the place that cocaine once had in my life. I was dealing less with my emotions. I was masking them, throwing myself into a role that felt automatic and easy.

A woman finally noticed me dissociating during sex, basically that I was going through the motions but that I wasn't "there." She said my name, she looked me in the eyes, she put her hand on my chest and told me I was okay then held me while I cried. I didn't know what trauma this had come from. I just knew it was heavy. I am so grateful to her for paying enough attention and having the courage and the caring to stop and hold me. I had never even noticed. I wouldn't have felt like I had permission to do anything different if I had.

Over my time of exploring and indulging, I realized something: Sex is like fireworks. It's pretty and lights the night sky and makes me go ooh, but it does nothing to keep me warm at night or help me find my way home.

I had never seen healthy relationships and didn't have any idea what I was doing. I was afraid of commitment. I was afraid of being hurt and I was afraid of hurting someone else. So, I put up walls and said it was just about sex. But deep down I craved intimacy and connection more than anything. So, my words and actions didn't line up with my original boundaries. I didn't know how to separate sex and love, even if it was for a night or a weekend. I caused a lot of emotional harm.

Once I recognized the pattern, I started to seek deeper platonic connections. It was easier because I still struggled to be vulnerable and I didn't understand how intimacy, love, and sex could coexist in a healthy way.

I started to build relationships with people from practicing Brazilian jiu jitsu, from Common House—the coworking space I attended—and people I randomly met along my journey.

It wasn't easy. It still isn't easy. The central focus of my life became finding community, finding purpose, and living consistent with my values. I made a lot of mistakes. Some days were better than others.

The journey is best described by Melissa Cox, who said, "I am homesick for a place that may not exist, a place where my heart is full, my body loved and my soul understood."

I was looking for home.

Chapter 33

The World Gets a Lot Bigger

The woman who had started me on the path of looking at my childhood trauma had become a mentor and a friend. Chandra helped me move forward both professionally and personally. She also introduced me to a world I had never known existed.

I had heard about SXSW when I was in prison, and thought it was just a big film and music festival. I had no idea how many different topics were covered and just how many speakers and panels and events there were. In the hallways I walked by celebrities and elected officials and billionaires. It set my head spinning. When Chandra had suggested I submit a proposal to speak on the value of adversity, it didn't make sense to me. Courteney and I had just broken up, I didn't have a lot of money, the conference didn't pay for travel or lodging, and Austin, Texas, hotels were absurdly expensive during SXSW. I didn't feel qualified, and I wasn't sure I could afford it.

After I listed all the reasons why I couldn't do it, she said, "I've never told you to do anything. I'm telling you to do this. It will be good for you."

So I applied, with "Adversity as an Incubator"—using my story to talk about how adversity is an opportunity and how seeing it that way makes it possible to grow through hardship and challenge. I was surprised when I was accepted. Now I had to actually go. So, I figured out a way: I applied for an airline credit card that would give me enough free miles to cover the airfare. I started reaching out to people I knew in Texas and found someone willing to let me stay on their couch. Marci, one of my PrisonTok friends, met me at the airport and took me to where I was staying.

My suitcase was full of shirts that had been designed by kids at the juvenile center. They read "Together We Rise." Not only would I wear one at my talk, but I would give them out and ask if I could take people's photos with them, to show the kids in the center just how far they could reach.

At night I stayed on a couch that felt like a children's play toy rather than a thing designed for adults. Each morning, my back and neck and pretty much every joint hurt. It was free, though, and I enjoyed hanging out with Marci and her friend Jennifer, who was graciously hosting me.

The first morning I got up and headed to the convention center. Chandra and her partner were supposed to meet me the first day, but their company had all of its assets in Silicon Valley Bank. SVB, as it was known, failed just as SXSW began. They were stuck out of the country, in full crisis mode, trying to figure out what to do.

My speaking session came with a free Platinum pass, so I could get into every talk and event. But I felt stuck—like the overwhelming choice paralysis when I had first gotten out of prison. I went to a few talks, watched a few panels, and mostly felt lost, especially in the room with thousands of people as José Andrés was interviewed about the World Central Kitchen and providing food security all over the globe. I was there to present a talk, on the biggest stage I had ever been on, about adversity. Yet, I was having trouble getting through a few days at a stimulating conference. I felt like a fraud. I explored the events alone for two days, heading back each night to the tiny couch as the sun went down.

On the third day, I was wandering aimlessly around the convention center when Chandra texted that they were on their way, along with Taylor (who I had met with by Zoom) and Morgan (who I had not). Part of me still didn't believe they were real. Here was a "Fairy Godmother" character and Scott, her brilliant business partner, with Taylor, a wildly successful real estate mogul, and Morgan, the head of a giant IT company, in tow. I couldn't believe they would want anything to do with me. What was I doing here? Among an A-list crowd of CEOs, hedge fund managers, celebrities, and journalists, I felt totally out of place.

I sat in the lobby of their hotel waiting for Chandra and her entourage to appear. I was doubting myself. I wondered if this was all an elaborate prank. I even checked the front desk to see if someone had checked in under that name. I sat there some more. Doubted myself some more.

Then the elevator doors opened and Chandra and crew walked out. They were real.

Chandra had warned me that SXSW would be different when they were around. I had no idea how right she was. When I had gone to events alone, I sat in the back and filed out as soon as the talk was over. With the Chandra crew, we always grabbed seats up front. They seemed to know everyone. At one talk they yelled greetings to someone down the row. When I asked who it was, Chandra said, "Oh, that's the guy from NASA."

The real surprise was when we went to the keynote speech. Tech celebrity William "Whurley" Hurley gave an insightful talk on AI that was—big surprise—entirely written by AI, with the slides designed by AI as well. After the presentation, people rushed the stage, asking for his autograph or wanting an interview. Instead, he hopped down, gave Chandra a big hug, shook Scott's hand, and told us to meet him on the rooftop.

Before we walked to the rooftop, the tech celebrity pulled me aside and took a picture with the "Together We Rise" shirt. We stood next to the giant SXSW banner, and he held the shirt out so the graphic could be easily read. He told me the work I was doing was great and how much he appreciated it. He knew a lot of details that surprised me. He also talked with me about therapy and healing and becoming the person we're meant to be.

Whurley (William Hurley) and I at my first SXSW in 2023.

He then walked away with his team in tow. I had never met him before so I asked Chandra, "How did he know all that stuff about me?"

"Oh, he ran a background check on you." I looked at her, dumbfounded. "We ran a check on you too, if you want to know what it says." She was almost laughing.

Then I was sitting on the roof of a hotel in Austin, at a private bar, with Chandra's crew and the keynote speaker, being introduced to an international leader in computer science, a NASA CTO, and a few others. I had never felt so out of place in my life. Yet somehow, I also felt that I *could* come to know this place. Everyone was exceptional *and* authentic. That mythical cast of characters has, over time, become people I chat with and look forward to seeing at events.

A few days later, the people from the rooftop, as well as a very kind and smart VR innovator from New York City whom we had just met, helped me prepare for my presentation in the green room, a few hours before I was set to go on stage. My talk was the first time I had really dived deep into my story and figured out how to tell it, rather than relying on old explanations people had given me. It's one thing to share a short story on social media; it's another to weave the pieces together and gut check what I'm really feeling and thinking.

Before coming to Austin, I had written talking points and created a PowerPoint presentation. In the green room, they sat and listened as I practiced. They asked me to repeat it and listened again. And again. They coached me on when to pause and where to change the tone of my voice. Some of the most capable and in-demand people I had ever met were sitting in the green room, encouraging me and coaching me through my talk.

Nineteen months to the day after I got out of prison, I stood on stage at SXSW. I am proud of that talk because I told my story more honestly than I ever had before. I forced myself to really remember and feel. It was, in some ways, the first draft of this book.

It went better than I could have imagined. I wore my "Together We Rise" shirt from the juvenile center. I got some laughs, and I saw a few people crying. It was the most connected I had ever felt to the audience in front of me.

I was used to my story resonating with people who had been locked up or who had a family member locked up. That day I was really surprised by the number of incredibly successful people who shook my hand and told me they had almost been where I was and that they could relate.

I was learning that maybe, just maybe, I really had grown as a result of the adversity I had faced. I was learning there was a place for me in this much bigger world.

Chapter 34

Slow Down

I had been running nonstop since the day I got out of prison. I was accomplishing a lot. At the same time, I was constantly exhausted and felt like I was losing myself to some degree. I didn't know how to slow down, and I felt so much pressure (mostly from myself) to keep going forward.

On August 2, 2023, I was on a lunch break between meetings and grant applications and needed some air and time away from my computer screen. It was a nice summer day, so I jumped on my motorcycle and headed out to see Grahm. I had connected him to a job at a motorcycle shop on the edge of town. He had some time, so we decided to go for a ride together. It was surreal, and thrilling, to be able to ride together in the free world after so many years of talking about it as we walked the prison rec yard.

We rode down a country road where I had grown up, a long loop of beautiful views and cool curves. We weren't riding for speed, we were riding for the feeling of freedom. I loved this road because I knew it so well. The bike felt like an extension of me.

We turned off the main road and onto Watts Passage, another twisty back road that would lead us back toward the shop. Over our Bluetooth headsets, we laughed and commented on the scenery. We were in tune with the whole experience. I leaned into the first corner on this new road. Then I saw gravel strewn across the road. I yelled a warning to Grahm through the helmet intercom. I remember the slide of losing traction, then it all went black.

The next thing I remember was standing at the side of the road looking through a haze at my right pointer finger. It was bent like an S. I frowned, wondering how it had happened. With my left hand, I cracked each joint back into place, snapping my finger reasonably straight. I asked Grahm to hand me my phone so I could cancel my afternoon meetings. He was saying something to me. I couldn't understand. Then I tried to put weight on my left leg and felt like a knife was stabbing into my hips. I screamed.

While we waited for the ambulance, Grahm said he had heard me yell about gravel and then slammed on the brakes. When he rounded the corner, he saw me flying and the bike tumbling end over end. It had high sided—when the bike slides out but then the tires catch, which catapults the rider and the bike through the air.

On the ambulance ride to the hospital, I was back in work mode, texting and emailing people, avoiding my right pointer finger but telling everyone I wouldn't be able to make meetings. Then the pain in my chest and pelvis started really kicking in, and I put my phone down. I looked out the back window of the ambulance. The experience reminded me of prison transport.

Life had been busy. I was constantly in meetings, making videos, giving talks, and putting together proposals. I watched the countryside go by. It was the first time I had stopped in months. The world is just beautiful, I thought to myself.

After that brief pause, it was back to the business at hand. I contacted a friend to apologize and tell them I couldn't make it to help do maintenance on their condo after the ride. I had been going to replace a toilet before heading home for my last virtual meeting. My friend asked why I couldn't make it, and I said I was in an ambulance headed to the hospital. "Why the hell are you apologizing?" my friend yelled, exasperated. They were at the hospital soon after I arrived and stayed with me as I talked to nurses and doctors and the police when they came for the accident report.

After hours and hours of X-rays, CT scans, and probing they told me that my sacrum was fractured and my sternum was displaced. Pain from the cracked sacrum was what I had felt when I put weight on my leg after the crash. My finger still hurt like hell but there didn't seem to be anything they could do for it. I needed to stay the night for observation. My friend left and I was rolled out of the ER and into a room.

I didn't sleep much that night. The pain, the pain meds, and having to pee into a urinal jug regularly then call the nurse to empty it kept me up. I did a lot of thinking that night. It reminded me of a night in prison that I spent with an untreated dry socket in my mouth from an extracted tooth. I had been so miserable, and I had fought that misery with all my might. Finally, exhausted, I gave up. In surrender, the pain made way for space, and in that space I found clarity.

Before that night in the hospital, I had been on the verge of making some big leaps. I had been looking at moving out of state to pursue a complicated relationship that I wasn't 100 percent sure about. As I lay sleepless in the hospital, I reflected on how often I dealt with uncertainty by jumping headfirst only to regret it days or even hours later.

Around midnight, it really sank in that I was rushing, making decisions that I wasn't ready for. I was trying to do it all at once and to make myself fit into someone else's situation rather than doing the hard work to figure out what I wanted and needed. I marveled at how big the world was and that there was no deadline to meet. I had time to let things develop naturally. The accident, like prison, had been unexpected and unwelcome, but somehow it had given me a much-needed pause and perspective. In a weird way, both had saved my life.

The speed and recklessness that had defined my youth were still with me, but after prison it came out as a need to produce and move forward. For all of my growth and change and success, I still had a long way to go.

Chapter 35

Full Circle

My biggest concern after the accident wasn't physical recovery—I could dissociate from pain and always believed I would bounce right back, no matter what the situation. My worry was whether I would recover in time for two trips at the end of the month. That was how much my life had changed. From being stuck in the same cell, in the same building, on the same plot of land for nearly two decades, to flying across the country for conferences and concerts.

One involved seeing Chandra and crew as part of my role on the advisory board of Rally Innovation, a tech conference in Indianapolis. For the other, I'd been invited to "Labor Dave" weekend at the famous music venue The Gorge in Washington state. It was three nights of Dave Matthews Band shows. Those worlds couldn't be more different: one with conference rooms full of tech minds, VCs, and million-dollar grants, the other a vast outdoor expanse of people partying, enjoying tribal connection, and listening to music in a venue that looks over a picturesque river that defies the mind.

Despite my injuries, I didn't need bandages or casts, and several of the hospital staff bluntly told me that unless I was independently wealthy, I should get out of there as soon as I possibly could. So, after one night in the hospital, Courteney helped me into a wheelchair, pushed me downstairs, then loaded me into her car. The steps of my apartment complex were the most complicated to maneuver, but I figured once I made it up, I wouldn't have to come back down for a while.

I was on bed rest for a week. I used a urinal jug for days until I could make it to the bathroom on my own. Despite the pain, it gave me a challenge and something to work toward. I always performed better with some sort of challenge or task in front of me.

Morgan, my PrisonTok friend, got on a plane the next day and flew three thousand miles to take care of me. People from the Brazilian jiu jitsu gym stopped by and brought me food. Folks from the coworking space "broke me out" and took me to trivia night. I felt connected and supported. All I had to do was slow down and ask for help to realize how lucky I was.

I made progress over the next few weeks—even the nurse practitioner at my follow-up said I was healing well. So, less than a month after my accident, I put aside my crutches and got on a plane to Indianapolis. It was the opportunity to reconnect with Chandra and Scott, who I hadn't seen since SXSW. It was also the chance to reconnect with the people they had introduced me to, as well as to make new connections. Even at a distance, that group had started to feel like family in a way I had never imagined possible. At dinner one night, someone joked that Chandra and Scott were somehow both parents and siblings to all of us. Sometimes found family dynamics work like that.

It was reassuring that the magic could be re-created. My first trip to SXSW had felt new and beyond description. Part of me doubted I would ever again be able to meet extraordinary people over tacos (networking is always best done over tacos) or have thrilling conversations into the wee hours of the morning with strangers. This time I met Neal, the head of a venture firm that focused on health tech and med tech. He told me to visit him if I was ever in Seattle. So, I pushed my flight to Seattle up a day before the concert and met him for coffee. We've since become friends, and I've done work for his venture firm and their portfolio companies.

Labor Dave weekend was completely new to me. Despite growing up in Charlottesville, where the band got its start, I had never seen the Dave Matthews

Band in concert. I had certainly never flown clear across the country, then ridden three hours into the scrub desert to see any concert.

I had been invited to the concert by Shawn, who also received a conditional pardon after serving sixteen years of a thirty-year sentence for embezzlement. Shawn and I had connected shortly after my release. We lived only an hour apart, but our relationship was mostly professional. He worked as a policy strategist for a nonprofit and I was often brought in to talk or give media exposure. We hadn't done anything personal together.

After Courteney and I broke up I had committed to a year of saying yes, so when he invited me to the concert the answer was obvious, even if how I would pay for it wasn't. Somehow, I found a way. That was my new life. After so many years of being behind walls and fences, of having few choices, I was reveling in the opportunities I never could have imagined.

It started out as a wild weekend. Even before I got to Seattle, all of the connecting flights in Phoenix were delayed thanks to a massive sandstorm looming in the skies like something from the movies. I went to sleep on the terminal floor and woke up soaked from a leak in the roof that had dripped down the support beam I was sleeping next to.

We landed in Seattle at 3:30 AM. I crashed for a few hours in a run-down hotel by the airport, then got up the next morning to board a "Magic Schoolbus." The pickup spot was unmarked. Just vague directions saying next to a structure, next to a highway. A few people wandered by on their own adventures. Three people showed up, looking quizzical and we did the "Are you here for?" dance. After meeting and deciding we were all in the best spot based on vague directions given by the website, we made small talk and hoped we hadn't made a mistake about the location.

Forty-five minutes after the scheduled pickup time a very interesting, painted school bus rolled up. This was about as far from a prison transport as I could imagine. Pot smoke billowed out when the doors opened to reveal a broad-smiling bus driver, I was on my way to the Gorge with four strangers, moderately confident we would get there alive.

The Gorge is unassuming at first. It's scrubland—until it's not. As you go from the flat toward the edge of the gully where the river flows the view is stupendous in a way that I'm not even sure stupendous is the right word.

I heard later that there were 27,000 people, spread out across RVs, tents, and yurts, overlooking some of the spectacular canyon views. It was a temporary city of people, eating, drinking, singing, laughing, and having a damn good time. It felt magical.

Thanks to Shawn, we had secured a spot and an RV. There were several of us crammed inside, and I didn't know anyone other than Shawn, but I'm a talker and can get along with anyone. I made some friends that weekend that I still talk to today. I didn't know anything about the venue or the Dave scene. It was the opposite of my prison experience—all of these people together by choice, there to commune with their tribe, rather than forced to cohabitate in small spaces and find some way to get along.

The first night was mind-blowing. I was still recovering from the accident so I wasn't in the best physical shape, but I was down in front of the stage, singing along to the songs I knew. I left halfway through the encore because my body was hurting all over.

The second day we floated on tubes down to the river that created the gorge with people who had reached out through social media. I ran into someone I knew from New York. It was one serendipity after another. I napped, hard, since I had been running on minimal sleep for five days at that point. By the second night, my body was feeling much better. This was more healing than I had imagined it could be. I danced, getting in the swing of things after weeks of bed rest.

About halfway through the concert the music paused. The stage went dark, the crowd grew quiet.

I heard the bang of a hand drum and the bars of a guitar.

"Cyrus Jones, 1810 to 1913 . . ."

I heard an echo of my eighteen-year-old self hearing this song in the holding cell the day I was sentenced.

"Cyrus Jones lived forever."

My eyes filled with tears.

"Gravedigger, when you dig my grave will you make it shallow so I can feel the rain."

I started sobbing. I cried when I heard this song so many years before. This time there was no shame. This time there was no grief. I was no longer locked away. I no longer felt that my life was over.

The same words that had nearly destroyed me in that jail cell now filled me with deep joy, freedom, and hope.

I was at the most beautiful venue I have ever seen, surrounded by 27,000 people singing along. I was free. I had far more ahead of me than behind.

I was alive, and I could feel the rain.

Epilogue

"Sitting behind concrete walls for all those years, I wondered what the opposite of captivity would look like. One day, at Moon Mountain Horse Rescue and Sanctuary in Arkansas, I found out."
Courtesy of Samantha Maechler.

Things don't often work out the way we expect them to.

In the course of writing this book, I finished probation and was free and clear as an adult for the first time in my life. I gave up my lease, sold my motorcycle, packed everything into my car, and took off on a wild road trip. I worked remotely, with the intention of traveling for an indefinite period of time. I saw Tennessee, Arkansas, Oklahoma, Colorado, Utah, Nevada, California, and then came back across the country to Missouri, Indiana, Ohio, and back to Virginia for a speaking engagement. Back home my buddy who I had sold my motorcycle to suggested we go for "one last ride" before I hit the road again.

That was when things went awry. After a long day of riding, we were about five minutes from his house. I don't know what happened. I have no memory from before or immediately after. What I do know is that I'm lucky to be alive. You might think I would have learned the first time.

In a bizarre, slow-speed wreck, I managed to find a drain culvert, the only sharp object in a 100-foot span of a field. I partially severed my arm and nearly lost my life. If it hadn't been for the safety gear and fast action of my buddy clamping the artery and applying a tourniquet, I would have bled out. If it hadn't been for the fast action of the EMTs, ER doctors, and surgical team I would have lost my arm. I just happened to be near a hospital with one of the best hand and arm orthopedic surgical teams in the country.

I also suffered a traumatic brain injury. Along with memory loss and a period of unconsciousness, I was slurring and not fully making sense for weeks. I was so off that I didn't know I was off.

Back in the town I worked so hard to get away from on my road trip I was lucky to find a "care team," who showed up at the hospital the night of my accident. Someone let me rent a place to stay so I could recover. People helped me navigate the maze of medical and insurance issues.

Over two months I miraculously regained sensation and most movement in the hand and forearm that had been severed. However, I still had no use of the bicep and couldn't lift my arm at the shoulder. It turns out that I had a traction injury in my brachial plexus. Apparently cutting my arm off wasn't the most serious issue.

It was going to be a long road.

The universe was telling me, again, that it was time to slow down. I thought of what someone had told me in prison: You don't get strong from lifting weights. You get strong from resting after you lift weights. I was doing all of the running and heavy lifting, but none of the resting. Now, I had no choice.

Maybe I would remember the lesson and not need to be reminded again in some dramatic fashion.

I even started talking to my mother again. It was hard, but I had taken time to heal. It wasn't perfect. It wasn't done. I felt empowered to make it my choice rather than something I did from the pressure or obligation.

My life has been a wild ride. One friend described it as if a six-year-old had made up a mad lib of random adventures that had somehow all come true.

Who knows what the future holds? I have had the experience of being completely locked down and I have been free on the open road. Now it's time for me to find a balance, to choose the ways in which I want to trade total freedom for structure, community, and a place to call home.

Acknowledgments

This book emerged from my memories. I can't guarantee every detail or quoted word is precisely accurate. I've shared what I remember, what I felt, and my best understanding of the experiences that shaped me. This is my truth as I lived it, helped by many people whose support I gratefully acknowledge.

Thank you to the teachers who saw me when I was young. I felt like I had no place in the world, and you made me believe I did. Thank you to those who supported me, held me accountable, and encouraged me when I had lost everything and didn't feel deserving of anything.

Thank you to those who walked the long road with me, not knowing where it would end or how we would ever figure out the details.

Thank you to Governor Northam for taking the extraordinary step of giving me a second chance. Thank you to all of the people who welcomed me and showed me that, despite my greatest fears, I do belong. Thank you for welcoming me back to my small town and to the wider world.

Thank you to my therapist, who has helped me feel all the feels, heal the things I can, and find a direction forward when I feel absolutely lost.

Thank you to everyone who does the right thing whether anyone is looking or not. The little things and the memories of people's goodness bring me back every time I lose faith.

I got to meet Governor Northam at an event in Richmond just months after I was released. I gave him a Christmas card from Courteney and me and told him how much my second chance meant.

To everyone who has helped. I could not be who I am without you. I thank you. Also, rather than promising to "pay it back," I promise instead to pass it on so that you may be part of my growth as well as the story of every life I am fortunate enough to impact.

About the Author

Courtsey of Mary Eure

Jesse Crosson, widely recognized as "Second Chancer," is a criminal justice reform advocate, speaker, and founder of the Second Chancer Foundation. Born in 1984, Crosson's early life in Charlottesville, Virginia, was marked by struggles with family drama, insecurity, and substance abuse. Shortly after his eighteenth birthday in 2002, during a period of active addiction, he committed a robbery and a separate non-fatal shooting. Despite sentencing guidelines suggesting a maximum of sixteen years, he received a thirty-two-year prison sentence.

During his nineteen years of incarceration, Crosson dedicated himself to personal growth and rehabilitation. He earned a bachelor's degree in psychology from Ohio University in 2018, became a journeyman electrician, and actively mentored fellow inmates. Additionally, he contributed articles for publication and led various programs, both as an informal GED tutor and in a peer-support mental health program.

In August 2021, Virginia Governor Ralph Northam granted Crosson a conditional pardon, leading to his immediate release. Following his release, Crosson leveraged social media platforms, notably TikTok under the handle @second_chancer, to share his experiences and advocate for criminal justice reform. His candid discussions of prison life, rehabilitation, and systemic issues have garnered him over a million followers.

In 2022, Crosson established the Second Chancer Foundation, a nonprofit organization aimed at providing support and opportunities for individuals transitioning from incarceration. The foundation focuses on connecting justice-impacted individuals with mentors to facilitate successful reintegration into society. Through his foundation, social media, and public speaking engagements, Jesse Crosson continues to champion the cause of second chances and systemic reform within the criminal justice system.